Comparing
Development Patterns
in Asia

Comparing

Development Patterns

in Asia

Cal Clark
K. C. Roy

LYNNE
RIENNER
PUBLISHERS

BOULDER
LONDON

To our families
with love and thanks for
their understanding and support

Published in the United States of America in 1997 by
Lynne Rienner Publishers, Inc.
1800 30th Street, Boulder, Colorado 80301

and in the United Kingdom by
Lynne Rienner Publishers, Inc.
3 Henrietta Street, Covent Garden, London WC2E 8LU

Library of Congress Cataloging-in-Publication Data
Clark, Cal, 1945–
     Comparing development patterns in Asia / by Cal Clark and K. C.
Roy.
     p.   cm.
Includes bibliographical references and index.
ISBN 1-55587-307-3 (hc : alk. paper)
     1. South Asia—Economic policy. 2. East Asia—Economic policy.
3. Asia—Economic conditions—1945– —Regional disparities.
I. Roy, K. C. (Kartik Chandra), 1941– . II. Title.
HC430.6.C58   1996
338.95—dc20
                                                            96-34627
                                                            CIP

British Cataloguing-in-Publication Data
A Cataloguing-in-Publication record for this book
is available from the British Library.

Printed and bound in the United States of America

The paper used in this publication meets the requirements
of the American National Standard for Permanence of
Paper for Printed Library Materials Z39.48-1984.

5 4 3 2 1

CONTENTS

ILLUSTRATIONS

Tables

Figures

PREFACE

This book represents a significant intellectual journey for us. It began with the intention to combine our different disciplinary backgrounds (economics and political science) and geographic specialties (East Asia and South Asia) to rethink the standard stereotypes of the political economies of two Asian regions. In particular, neoclassical orthodoxy explained the rapid growth of East Asia and the stagnation of South Asia by the former's embrace of and the latter's disdain for the free market, both externally and internally. We believed that this was far too simplistic a picture and, consequently, might be taken to imply far from efficacious policy prescriptions in certain instances.

The research involved in this project did not change our minds on that score, but it did point the way toward a somewhat different and perhaps more sophisticated line of argument. We argue that not only neoclassical economics, but also the competing developmental state model greatly underestimates the role of societal or private actors in determining how well an economy performs. Thus, the debate over "state versus market" leaves something essential out. In short, there is a need for "bringing society back in" because both strong states and strong societies play a vital role in successful economic development and transformation.

Our research owes much to the help of other scholars with whom we have collaborated over the years, especially Steve Chan of the University of Colorado and Clement A. Tisdell of the University of Queensland. More specifically, our analysis here represents collaborative work on India with Brian S. Trinque of the Department of Economics at the University of Texas, Austin, who coauthored Chapter 5 on the political economy of India. We also wish to thank Martha Peacock of Lynne Rienner Publishers for all her help and faith in this project. Last, but certainly far from least, we express our gratitude to our long-suffering families, whose support has been crucial in our effort to transfer ideas to the printed page.

—Cal Clark
K. C. Roy

1

Dueling Development Debates

For the last three decades, the political economy of development has been marked by a series of debates between competing dichotomies: modernization versus dependency theory; neoclassical economics versus the developmental state model; and state-centric theory versus the state-in-society approach. Each debate began when a dominant theory or paradigm failed to explain important phenomena of interest to development scholars; unfortunately, over time each increasingly became an unproductive "dialogue of the deaf" between schools of thought whose fundamental assumptions and conceptualizations were so divergent that their analyses became incomparable and perhaps close to mutually incomprehensible. The first two debates have perhaps run their course, producing two almost polar-opposite conclusions. The third debate remains in a nascent stage, with some of the major issues still to be defined; although it can be stated in a dichotomous form, its prime importance is its view of national development as much more complex, contingent, and contextual than that of the other approaches.

This book seeks to evaluate the applicability and limits of these various debates by comparing the performances of Asian political economies, primarily the three major nations of the People's Republic of China (the PRC), India, and Japan and the four "Little Dragons" in East Asia (Hong Kong, Singapore, South Korea, and Taiwan). This introductory chapter begins with a brief consideration of the implications raised by the contending theories in each debate and then discusses why Asia provides an interesting and valuable context in which to analyze the political economy of development in the contemporary global system.

Modernization Theory vs. Dependency Theory: Are Modernization and Capitalism Good or Bad?

From the late 1960s through the early 1980s the field was dominated by the controversy between modernization theory and dependency theory over whether modernization and capitalism promoted or perverted development (Caporaso and Levine, 1992; Randall and Theobald, 1985). Modernization theory assumed that the Western path to industrialization was a universally valid one and recommended that the developing world simply follow this tried-and-true formula. This would involve primarily the replication of Western economic and political institutions (e.g., capitalism and democracy) and the replacement of traditional societies and cultures by "modern values" that would promote this economic and political change (Eisenstadt, 1973; Inkeles, 1983; Pye, 1966; Rostow, 1960).

Whereas the modernization approach generally advocated Westernization and capitalism, the school of developmental economics that arose within the general modernization paradigm was far from committed to simplistic doctrines of free-market capitalism in its prescriptions for promoting economic development in the Third World. Rather, developmental economists generally believed that the state had to play a leading role in economic development. This is consistent with the work of Alexander Gerschenkron (1962), who argued that the state generally had to play a much stronger role in late-developing than in early-developing countries. The "catch-up" nature of industrialization in late developers, according to Gerschenkron, required a rapid and massive accumulation of capital for infrastructure and capital-intensive industries (e.g., steel) that was simply beyond the capabilities of private entrepreneurs in nations such as Germany and Russia in the late nineteenth and early twentieth centuries, not to speak of the many extremely poor Third World nations today. Thus, many developmental economists saw the state as necessary for promoting agricultural transformation, bringing together the resources necessary for industrialization, providing protection for nascent industries, and investing in the mass education necessary to create human capital in a developing society (Hagen, 1986; Jones, 1982; Nurkse, 1953; Rostow, 1960; Singer, 1977). As Bhagwati (1993: 6–7) points out, even India's highly statist development strategy was generally well received by leading Western economists in the 1950s and early 1960s:

> The early years, through the mid-1960s, witnessed an optimistic assessment of India's potential and performance. . . . The early writings of Walt Rostow, Max Milliken, Paul Rosenstein-Rodan, and many other economists such as Wilfred Malenbaum, George Rosen, and the Oxbridge dons Ian Little and Brian Reddaway . . . were thus extremely optimistic and well-disposed towards Indian planning efforts and methods.

By the late 1960s, however, the continuing impoverishment of much of the Third World indicated that development was far less simple and automatic than the modernization school was wont to assume. Given this obvious problem in empirical validity, the emergence of a contending approach is easy to understand. In contrast to the modernization focus on factors internal to a nation or society that determine whether it will take advantage of the potentialities of capitalism, dependency theory concluded that the workings of the global capitalist economy itself were responsible for the absence of development in the Third World. According to this paradigm, capitalism generates market imperfections and market power that corporations in the industrial core can use to prevent peripheral economies from participating in the more desirable and profitable economic activities. This economic power, moreover, is buttressed by international class alliances between industrialists in the core and reactionary elites in the periphery, such as compradores and large agricultural landowners, who act as bridgeheads in furthering capitalist interests (Bornschier and Chase-Dunn, 1985; Cardoso and Faletto, 1979; Evans, 1979; Frank, 1969; Wallerstein, 1979).

The debate over whether capitalism and market mechanisms are good or bad seems to have been largely resolved, to the advantage of modernization theory (or more accurately, to the disadvantage of the dependency approach), by the events of the 1970s and 1980s. It is ironic that economic changes in the First and Second Worlds were probably more important to this debate than what occurred within the developing nations themselves. In particular, the 1980s witnessed both the collapse of state socialism, due in large part to its profound economic inefficiencies (Campbell, 1991 & 1992; Islam and Mandelbaum, 1993; Kovacs, 1994; Pei, 1994; Przeworski, 1991; Stokes, 1993), and the deteriorating economic performance of most Western welfare states, where large government bureaucracies increasingly came to be viewed as drags on economic vitality (Gourevitch, 1986; Heilman and Johnson, 1992; Nau, 1990; Peters, 1991).

Most of the Third World was especially hard hit by the world economic crisis of the 1970s and 1980s. Although the policy responses of over one hundred nations varied tremendously, several themes consistent with the assumptions of the modernization approach are easy to discern. First, many nations began to question the effectiveness of a large state role in the economy, especially as the biases and predatory nature of many governmental officials became more obvious (Bates, 1981; Evans, 1995). Second, many Third World governments seem to have taken to heart analyses that suggested that the most dynamic developing nations in the 1960s and 1970s (e.g., the East Asian Little Dragons) were those that had opened, rather than closed, their markets and benefited from exporting labor-intensive manufactures (Balassa, 1981; Linder, 1986). Finally, and far less positively, many Third World nations fell deep into debt, especially with the escalation of oil prices; this subjected them in the 1980s to increasing pressures from such international organizations as the World Bank and the International Monetary Fund (IMF) to adopt austerity and open-market programs. The change in orientations within the Third World is perhaps best symbolized by the election of Fernando Henrique Cardoso, one of the architects of dependency theory (Cardoso, 1973; Cardoso and Faletto, 1979), as president of Brazil in 1994. A primary reason for his election was the anti-inflation program that he instituted as finance minister; after taking office he tried to attract foreign capital as a driver for economic growth (Hoge, 1995).

Neoclassical Economics vs. the Developmental-State Model: Does State Intervention Pervert or Promote Development?

The winding down of the debate between dependency theory and modernization theory produced two very different theoretical reactions that in turn set off a new debate about the political economy of development. From one perspective, the widespread problems with statist economic policies in developed, socialist, *and* developing countries led logically and rapidly to a strong argument for laissez-faire or neoclassical economics. Whereas this was primarily a rejection of *dependencia,* it also broke with conventional developmental economics, which had assumed that the state would have to play a leading role in promoting industrialization for late developers.

It was evident, at least to the neoclassicists, that the economy was an autonomous and self-sustaining sector of social life. What had caused the crisis of the 1970s was that too many other politically determined objectives that undercut economic efficiency had been attached to the economy. In short, politicians of various stripes, but especially liberals and socialists, were in dire danger of killing the goose that had been laying their golden eggs. Consequently, laissez-faire economics became something of an orthodoxy in many parts of the "development community"—among economists, political leaders in the industrialized world, aid donors (e.g., the World Bank and IMF), and many reformers in the Third World. A consensus apparently arose, at least among those normally most able to shape the context within which Third World development takes place, that governments should get out of the marketplace and let the "invisible hand" of economic higgling and haggling work its magic.

Yet the simultaneous failure of state economic policy in such varying contexts in the 1970s and 1980s does not logically imply that neoclassical economics holds a panacea, nor even that government policies are always counterproductive. In fact, the fundamental assumptions of modernization theory, as well as dependencia, were challenged by the rapid growth that occurred in a few places in the Third World, most particularly East Asia. Neither of the first two paradigms assigned much analytic importance to states nor to traditional cultures and institutions. Modernization theory held that state interference and traditional institutions hindered the operation of capitalist markets, while *dependencistas* argued that the economic dynamics of capitalism created social and political institutions, so that governments and cultures are only epiphenomenal. Yet the success of "Confucian capitalism" in the 1970s and 1980s has often been attributed to its reputed strong and autonomous developmental states and to the Confucian influence on its economic and political institutions (Amsden, 1989; Haggard, 1990; Hofheinz and Calder, 1982; Johnson, 1982; Okimoto, 1989; Pye with Pye, 1985; Wade, 1990).

This led to a call for "bringing the state back in" (Evans et al., 1985) as a new scholarly tradition arose that centered on the argument that strong developmental states could promote successful industrialization projects. State power, according to this perspective, is necessary to mobilize adequate resources to overcome the high "entry barriers" that late industrializers faced and can be used as a counterweight to the great disparities in structural power emphasized by dependency theory. Another line of argument—that the conventional conceptualization of development in terms of aggregate production and growth is too narrow—also bolsters the concern with state policy. Advocates of this broader definition contend that real development involves improving the living conditions, or basic human needs, of most of the affected population (Gillies et al., 1987; Hogendorn, 1987; Moon, 1991; Morris, 1979; Roy, 1986 & 1991a). State policy almost inevitably becomes much more important when the question is how economic growth can be transformed into an improved quality of life.

The rise of statist theory thus created a second dichotomous debate over whether the state or the market is the key factor in explaining the undeniable economic growth and industrial transformation that has occurred recently in a few places in the developing world. Scholars working in this new approach argue that the state must almost inevitably play a major part in promoting industrialization in late-developing nations (Evans et al., 1985; Gerschenkron, 1962; Rosecrance, 1986) and that the "strong developmentalist states" that supposedly exist in East Asia validate this point (Alam, 1989; Amsden, 1989; Haggard, 1990; Johnson, 1982; Wade, 1990; White, 1988). In contrast, these assertions are strongly challenged by advocates of neoclassical economics, who simply apply the economic parts of modernization theory to argue that the best-performing Third World economies are those that have opened their markets to establish niches of comparative advantage in the global economy (Balassa, 1981; Friedman and Friedman, 1980; Gilder, 1984; Linder, 1986).

In at least some academic quarters, however, the debate between neoclassical economics and the developmental state seems to have been resolved largely in favor of the latter because of the state's undeniable economic role in many (probably most) rapidly growing economies. Some caveats are obviously necessary. First, neoclassical scholars remain unconvinced that state economic leadership is more than a marginal supplement to market forces even in East Asia (World Bank, 1993). More important, statists do not deny the importance of markets or accept the dependencia argument that capitalism is inherently exploitative. Rather, they see state policy as an integral part of how the game of capitalism is played in the late twentieth century, but they also conclude that policy success is conditioned by how market conforming its objectives and incentives are. In essence, the developmental state model moves beyond the unicausal assumptions of neoclassical economics with the slightly more complex equation:

$$\text{state} + \text{market} = \text{economic performance}$$

The Developmental State vs. the State-in-Society: Does the State or Society Drive Development?

Although the statists seem to be gaining the advantage in their debate with the neoclassicists of late, another, very different critique of the theory of the developmental state has appeared. The central argument is that the state per se (and in combination with the market) provides an insufficient explanation for readily observable differences in developmental outcomes. Thus, recourse is necessary to additional variables denoting state–society relations and the business environment: entrepreneurial talents, the foundation of human capital, the incentives and disincentives for various types of economic activities, and, more broadly, the sociopolitical institutional setting and the cultural environment in which a political economy operates (Chan et al., 1997; Evans, 1995; Migdal, 1988; Migdal et al., 1994).

This emerging perspective does agree with the basic statist critique of neoclassical economics—that markets do not function automatically as a rational "economic person" who responds to market signals similarly in all cultures and institutional settings. The advocates of the developmental state model argue that state policies inevitably shape market outcomes. Again, the advocates of the new approach would agree, but they would quickly add that the statist argument that neoclassical economics does not recognize the processes by which markets operate in the real world can be turned against the developmental state model as well for two compelling reasons. First, state economic policy, according to this line of reasoning, does not emerge as a rational response to an economic situation by a unified, omnicompetent political institution. Rather, different groups of officials and/or parts of the state compete over policy; in many instances, their interests and goals can only be understood by reference to their interaction or identification with nonstate actors (i.e., components of society). Second, it is extremely rare that market-conforming economic behavior is dictated by state policies alone. Private individuals and groups respond at least somewhat independently to the market signals and policy incentives that they perceive. Again, what is important to understand is how and why specific segments of society act, rather than to assume that the logic of the market or state policy will automatically produce certain economic outcomes. Just as statists argue that the neoclassical model of economic markets is too simplistic, statism is now coming under fire itself for proposing an overly simplistic model of how government policy is made and how policy interacts with market forces to influence a nation's economic and social performance (Moon and Prasad, 1994).

In the same way that statist theory added state to market as an important factor shaping developmental outcomes, this nascent approach can be viewed as a call for moving beyond the developmental state (Chan et al., 1997) by bringing society back in (Clark and Chan, 1994; Migdal, 1988) to adopt a "state-in-society perspective" (Migdal et al., 1994). Thus, according to Joel Migdal and his associates (1994: 1), the political economy of development

> [needs] to go beyond "bringing the state back in" by resituating the study of states in their social setting and thus adopting a more balanced state-in-society perspective; to disaggregate states as objects of study, both as an end in itself and as a means toward a better understanding of states and political change; to rethink the categories used to conceptualize the evolving and fluid nature of social forces in developing countries; and to be continually sensitive to the mutually transforming quality of state–society relations.

The emerging debate between the developmental state and the state-in-society schools, furthermore, departs from the first two in one crucial aspect. Both of these focused on a single dimension that was generally assumed to have broad if not universal applicability. Modernization theory and dependency theory differed over whether capitalism promoted or perverted development in most Third World countries. Similarly, neoclassicists and statists argued about whether market or state was the more important causal mechanism. The state-in-society perspective, in contrast, offers a more variegated challenge to the developmental state model. Not only does it argue that another factor—society—must be taken into consideration, but it also implies that state–society relations vary widely among developing nations, creating different contexts that are central to the success of national development projects.

Asian Development: Implications for Contending Paradigms About the Political Economy of Development

This book seeks to evaluate competing paradigms of the political economy of development by comparing the postwar developmental histories of East Asia and South Asia. These are two important international regions that began the postwar era as part of the developing world (though in one case, Japan, as a country that had been smashed back into poverty status by defeat in World War II). Despite this common beginning (with the partial exception of Japan) just over fifty years ago, the developmental records of the two regions have diverged dramatically, as demonstrated by the data presented in Table 2.2 in the next chapter. East Asia has almost joined the First World, while South Asia remains mired in poverty. This certainly provides a puzzle worth exploring in itself whose answer should throw some light on the relative importance of the contending paradigms in development studies.

At first blush, the contrasting economic fates of South and East Asia seem to provide another boost to the neoclassical paradigm. As discussed in Chapter 3, many theorists attribute "East Asian dynamism" to reliance upon market mechanisms, such as export-led growth strategies, as opposed to South Asia's inward-looking strategies and much greater reliance upon state planning in the economy. In addition, the "green revolution" in South Asia, which was based on the application of Western technology and production models, has stimulated agricultural productivity throughout the region. South Asia's growing self-sufficiency in food provides another good example of the capitalist road to development.

A closer examination of the recent economic histories of these two regions, however, demonstrates that laissez-faire economics has its limits as well as its successes. Sri Lanka has extremely good social conditions for a country at its level of development (at least before the civil war broke out), indicating the efficacy of state investment in human capital. In East Asia, neoclassical orthodoxy can be challenged on several counts. First, the state has played a major role in leading and directing the development project; second, the costs of success (e.g., pollution, social decay) are becoming increasingly apparent; and, third, these national economies are becoming increasingly vulnerable to the evolving international product cycle. Thus, a "second blush" would seemingly conclude that the developmental state model should be given pride of place.

Is there room for a third blush? If one accepts the logic of the developmental state, there may well be. After all, India created a strong centralized state committed to promoting industrialization and eradicating poverty and gross inequality; the same could probably be said with varying degrees of emphasis (e.g., Sri Lanka's stress on social development and basic human needs) for the other South Asian nations as well. To understand why these developmental states failed when apparently similar ones in East Asia had spectacular success, one needs to look beyond the state itself: The performance of a political economy is conditioned by a broad complex of state and nonstate actors and institutions (that is, its state-in-society).

Plan of the Book

Part 1, "Patterns of Development: Performance and Policy in South and East Asia," begins the book by presenting a detailed statistical profile of the nations in South and East Asia. Chapter 3 discusses the economic policies adopted by the major nations in this study, in particular how open or closed their markets have been—which should be the principal determinant of their economic success (or lack of it) according to neoclassical theory. Chapters 2 and 3 provide results that are congruent with neoclassical logic, but only at a comparatively superficial level. Gross differences can certainly be discerned between the stagnation of South Asia and the dynamism of capitalist East Asia. However, a closer inspection of the aggregate data and national economic policies reveals a much more complex situation.

Part 2, "Case Studies of Asian Political Economies," seeks to advance beyond the neoclassical stereotypes by analyzing the major factors affecting economic performance in a broad range of Asian countries. Chapter 4 presents overview conceptualizations of the political economies of Confucian capitalism in East Asia that have been so phenomenally successful in promoting rapid economic growth. Chapter 5 provides something of a counter case study by discussing the factors accounting for the much less successful record of India's ostensibly strong and autonomous developmental state. Initially, much of the analysis in Chapter 4 can be taken to support the developmental state approach because of the strong state role in almost all these economies; all of the East Asian governments, with the exception of Hong Kong, engaged in massive interventions in their economies.

Again, however, a closer look urges caution before coming to any sweeping conclusions. In particular, at least three salient points raise questions about the statist paradigm. First, the Hong Kong exception is certainly a spectacular one, proving that perhaps the most laissez-faire policy in the world does not condemn a country to subpar or even average economic growth. The leadership of a strong state is clearly not a necessary condition for rapid growth. Second, and conversely, the failure in India of a strong state that was avowedly committed to development rather than predation shows that such a developmental state is not a sufficient condition for an exceptional developmental drive. Third, the reputed East Asian development states with strong records (Japan, South Korea, Singapore, Taiwan, and Dengist China) reveal substantially different patterns of state strategy, national economic structure, and regime–society relations. Especially when the exceptions of India and Hong Kong are factored in, this diversity suggests the value of moving beyond the developmental state per se to situate the state in society when modeling national political economies.

In a variety of ways, Chapters 2 through 5 argue that the political economy of development is far more complex than either neoclassical economics or the developmental state model would have it. Part 3, "Development: More Than Market, More Than State," tries to build upon these results by considering more systematically what is left out of the neoclassical and statist paradigms. Chapter 6 presents a broader model of the state's role in development, examining both the state's strengths and its limitations in regard to promoting both economic growth and basic human needs. Finally, Chapter 7 briefly models how the broader institutional and sociocultural context has shaped the developmental trajectories of the Asian political economies. The discussion illustrates the more inclusive state-in-society approach and contends that successful development may rest upon the relatively rare conjuncture of a strong state and a strong society.

PART 1

Patterns of Development: Performance and Policy in South and East Asia

2

Profiles of Development:
Adding Subtleties to the Stereotypes

The general image of development in South Asia and capitalist East Asia is one of polar opposites. Japan and the four smaller Confucian-capitalist states (Hong Kong, Singapore, South Korea, and Taiwan) are seen as open, free-market economies that have developed extremely rapidly during the postwar period from poor underdeveloped countries (with the partial exception of Japan) to modern industrial societies. The major South Asian nations (Bangladesh, India, Nepal, Pakistan, and Sri Lanka), in very sharp contrast, have had economies dominated by the state and have remained mired in poverty. Finally, among the countries under consideration, the People's Republic of China has the most extensive intervention of the state in the economy, a system of command planning. Like South Asia, it has remained quite poor, but after 1978, when it introduced wide-ranging market reforms, China's economy has grown very rapidly, suggesting that it may have stepped upon the escalator of Confucian capitalism.

Taken together, these images are quite consistent with the neoclassical approach to development. Countries that trusted their fate to the "magic of the marketplace" got rich very quickly, while those that fell prey to the various temptations for state intervention paid the price of economic stagnation. Whether this price at least produced better social outcomes than would have occurred under raw capitalism is more of an open question. China, Sri Lanka, and perhaps India have an image of promoting social equity through various types of government policies, but the societal prosperity brought on by rapid growth in the nations following Confucian capitalism should have improved the popular standard of living as well.

However, as discussed in Chapter 1, the image of capitalist East Asia as a neoclassical laboratory is open to serious question. In fact, the dominant interpretation of East Asian dynamism now focuses on the leadership of strong and autonomous developmental states. From this perspective, rapid growth in East Asia challenges the neoclassical model by demonstrating that state intervention in the economy can produce good results. Even accepting this interpretation does not necessarily validate the developmental state model, however, because the statists are left with the problem

13

of why the developmental states in South Asia fared so poorly in comparison to their East Asian counterparts. Two lines of argument are possible. On the one hand, the capacity and policies of the state itself could be determinative. For example, a government can have more sophisticated officials or be less constrained by political pressures (a pure statist model); or market-conforming policies may work, while market-distorting policies do not (a combination of market and state explanations). On the other hand, as the state-in-society perspective argues, nonstate actors (e.g., entrepreneurs) may play vital roles in development; one or more "society" variables should therefore be added to the explanatory equation.

This chapter considers summary data on the economic and social performance of the major nations in South Asia and East Asia as a broadbrush means for testing the comparative applicability of the neoclassical, developmental state, and state-in-society approaches. The first two sections describe the basic economic parameters of population and wealth and the overall sectoral structure of these nations; the third focuses upon the context of political policies; and the fourth examines the specific economic and social performances of the countries of South and East Asia. The concluding section briefly summarizes how these empirical findings challenge some of the stereotypes in developmental theory. These data do confirm the general images sketched above. However, there are more than a few significant departures from the stereotypes, which indicates a need for a subtler understanding of the socioeconomic dynamics in these regions. In particular, these exceptions suggest that neither market nor state by itself provides a complete explanation for the current levels of economic and social development in South and East Asia.

The Basic Parameters: Population and Affluence

Probably the most fundamental characteristics of a nation are the size of its population and its economy, and its level of wealth. Tables 2.1 and 2.2 present snapshots of East Asia and South Asia in the late 1950s and early 1990s in terms of their aggregate economic and population characteristics. Table 2.1 indicates that there are both differences and similarities among the regions and countries in terms of size. China and India are continental nations with huge populations; Japan, Bangladesh, and Pakistan also have fairly large populations of just over 100 million; at the other extreme Hong Kong and Singapore are tiny city-states. In contrast to these huge variations in population and geographic size, however, all share the characteristic of dense population. Even in sparsely settled (by Asian standards) Nepal, the share of the world's population is more than three times the share of land space; this ratio is about ten to one in Japan, South Korea, and Taiwan.

Table 2.1 Population in South and East Asia

	Area (1,000 sq. km)	Percent world area	Population 1961 (millions)	Percent world pop. 1961	Population 1993 (millions)	Percent world pop. 1993	Population growth (1965–1980)	Population growth (1980–1993)
Nepal	141	0.1	9.4	0.3	20.8	0.4	2.4	2.6
Bangladesh	144	0.1	—	—	115.2	2.1	2.7	2.1
India	3,288	2.5	442.1	14.5	898.2	16.3	2.3	2.0
Pakistan	796	0.6	94.5	3.1	122.8	2.2	3.1	2.8
Sri Lanka	66	0.05	10.2	0.3	16.8	0.3	1.8	1.5
South Asia	4,435	3.4	556.2	18.2	1,174.9	21.3	2.5[a]	2.2[a]
China	9,561	7.2	694.2	22.8	1,178.4	21.4	2.2	1.4
South Korea	99	0.1	25.4	0.8	44.1	0.8	2.0	1.1
Taiwan	36	0.03	11.0	0.4	20.9	0.4	2.4	1.3
Hong Kong	1	0.001	3.2	0.1	5.8	0.1	2.0	1.1
Singapore	1	0.001	1.7	0.06	2.8	0.05	1.6	1.1
Little Dragons	137	0.2	41.3	1.4	73.6	1.3	2.0[a]	1.2[a]
Japan	378	0.3	94.4	3.1	124.5	2.3	1.2	0.5
Capitalist East Asia	515	0.4	135.7	4.5	198.1	3.6	1.8[a]	1.0[a]

Sources: Russett et al., 1964; *Taiwan Statistical Data Book*, 1995; World Bank, 1995.
Note: a. Average based on equal weighting of each country.

Table 2.2, on economic development, demonstrates that a dramatic divergence in development has occurred in terms of national wealth over the last four decades between capitalist East Asia on the one hand and South Asia and China on the other. Even as late as 1957, the developmental differences among these countries were relatively muted. China and the four South Asian nations (Bangladesh being created later by the breakup of Pakistan) were among the poorest countries in the world, with gross national products (GNPs) per capita of about $75. Yet the East Asian nations were not much better off. South Korea and Taiwan also would have had to be included among the poor nations; their GNPs per capita of about $150 put them closer to Sri Lanka (then Ceylon) than Sri Lanka was to the other South Asian nations. Hong Kong, Singapore, and even Japan were also clearly part of the developing world, with GNPs per capita that were only in the $300-to-$400 range.

In 1993, just thirty-six years later, the economic situation in Asia had changed to an almost unbelievable extent. On the one hand, the South Asian nations remained among the poorest on the planet and actually lost ground in the sense that their shares of world GNP had been cut in half (from about 3% to 1.5% for South Asia and from 4% to 2% for China). On the other hand, the East Asian capitalist countries had gotten rich, reflecting a growth rate in GNP per capita that was over three times as high as that in South Asia (6.0% to 1.7%) for 1965–1989. Japan had vaulted into second place (from forty-sixth in 1957) in the world in terms of level of affluence; Singapore, Hong Kong, and Taiwan had attained GNP per capitas that put them in the developed world in the World Bank's classification system; and South Korea was fast approaching that threshold. In terms of moving up the ladder of the world's economy, the four smaller East Asian countries seemed well qualified for their nickname of the Four Little Dragons as their share in world GNP skyrocketed sixfold, from 0.5 percent to 3 percent. Japan's advance was even more spectacular: Its share of world GNP multiplied eightfold to 18 percent, making it a leading actor in the international economy. China was a strange intermediate case. Despite spectacular growth at times, it remained relatively poor in absolute terms, with a GNP per capita only slightly higher than those in South Asia.

In Table 2.1, population growth appears to be associated with economic performance in South and East Asia. South Asia (with the notable exception of Sri Lanka) was marked by high population-growth rates averaging 2.5 percent per year during 1965–1980 and only a slightly lower 2.2 percent during 1980–1993. Consequently, South Asia's population doubled over these three decades. In contrast, both the four Little Dragons and China had slightly lower growth rates of about 2 percent in the 1960s and 1970s, and then cut them to between 1.1 percent and 1.5 percent during 1980–1993, resulting in overall population gains in the 60 percent to 70 percent range. Finally, Japan had much lower and declining population

Table 2.2 Economic Development in South and East Asia

	GNP per capita 1957 (U.S.$)	Rank of 122	Total GDP (billions of U.S.$)	Percent world GDP	GNP per capita 1993 (U.S.$)	Rank of 128	Total GDP (billions of U.S.$)	Percent world GDP	GNP per capita growth 1965–1989
Nepal	45	122	0.4	0.03	190	121	3.6	0.02	0.6
Bangladesh	—	—	—	—	220	111	24.0	0.10	0.4
India	73	101	28.6	2.48	300	109	225.4	0.97	1.8
Pakistan	70	104	6.0	0.52	430	98	46.4	0.20	2.5
Sri Lanka	129	81	1.2	0.10	600	90	9.4	0.04	3.0
South Asia	79[a]	102[a]	36.2	3.13	350[a]	106[a]	308.8	1.33	1.7[a]
China	73	101	46.3	4.01	490	96	425.6	1.84	5.7
South Korea	144	75	3.2	0.28	7,660	28	330.8	1.43	7.0
Taiwan	161	71	1.5	0.13	10,850	25	222.6	0.96	5.3
Hong Kong	272	49	0.6	0.06	18,060	19	90.0	0.39	6.3
Singapore	400	34	0.5	0.05	19,850	14	55.2	0.24	7.0
Little Dragons	244[a]	57[a]	5.8	0.52	14,110[a]	22[a]	698.6	3.02	6.4[a]
Japan	306	46	27.8	2.41	31,490	2	4,214.2	18.23	4.6
Capitalist East Asia	257[a]	55[a]	33.6	2.92	17,580[a]	18[a]	4,912.8	21.25	6.0[a]

Sources: Russett et al., 1964; *Taiwan Statistical Data Book*, 1995; World Bank, 1995.
Note: a. Average based on equal weighting of each country.

growth (1.2% and 0.5%, respectively, for these two periods) during its rapid climb to the status of an economic superpower. For Japan and the Little Dragons it is probably impossible to know whether lower population growth was the cause or the result of economic dynamism, given that industrialization and urbanization usually promote the demographic transition to lower fertility. However, the gains that accrued to China (and to a lesser extent to Sri Lanka) from controlling population growth are obvious. Although the Chinese economy lost ground in the aggregate at the same rate as the South Asian economies, it had a fairly strong record of 5.7 percent annual growth in GNP per capita between 1965 and 1989 that was actually slightly higher than Taiwan's 5.3 percent. Thus, over time the PRC should be able to provide a better standard of living for its population (although a price is paid in terms of a draconian population-control policy), while the South Asian states will have to struggle just to keep even with their burgeoning populations.

The countries under analysis followed two radically different paths during the postwar period in terms of their relative wealth and poverty. The East Asian capitalist nations experienced very rapid growth and upward mobility within the international economy, while all of South Asia and China stagnated to such an extent that they represent a good example of the poor getting poorer. The picture changes slightly when economic growth rate, rather than GNP per capita, is analyzed: China joins East Asia on the dynamic side of the regional dichotomy, reflecting the rapid growth of the 1980s. These initial summary data by themselves are therefore consistent with either the neoclassical or the statist approach—depending upon whether one categorizes the East Asian capitalist nations as open economies or developmental states. It is necessary, however, to look at the distinctive features of these economies, not just their aggregate results, to see if the stereotypical images of either argument hold.

Economic Structure and Development

Most approaches to development assume that economic development generally consists of nations undergoing a series of structural transformations from less to more desirable, profitable, and "value-added" activities. In particular, these transformations include the change from less sophisticated to more sophisticated agricultural techniques, from an agricultural to a manufacturing to perhaps a service economy, and from light to heavy to high-tech industries in postagricultural economies. This section presents data on five such structural characteristics of these economies: the share of gross domestic product (GDP) contributed by the agricultural, manufacturing, and service sectors; fertilizer consumption in terms of hundreds of grams of plant nutrient per hectare; and the percentage of manufacturing accounted for by heavy industry (i.e., machinery, transport equipment, and chemicals). Given the great disparity between the economic trajectories of the five Confucian-capitalist states as opposed to China and the nations in South Asia, one would expect to find comparable differences in economic structure because the two sets of countries would be presumed to be following different economic strategies. Such differences need to be assessed in two ways. First, the actual or absolute differences between these two sets of nations are important because one would predict that the East Asian capitalist nations should be quite distinctive. A substantial difference in economic structure between these two groups would be expected, however, simply because of the tremendous gap in affluence between them. Thus, a second type of comparison should measure the two groups against the normal conditions that exist in, respectively, rich and poor nations. This is done for the socioeconomic indicators in the subsequent tables by including the median values for both low-income (1993 GNP per capita under $700) and high-income (1993 GNP per capita over $10,000) countries.

The first surprise in our examination of the stereotypes of East Asian versus South Asian development is that the expected great dichotomy in economic structures and strategy turns out to be fairly muted. Rather than choosing radically different paths toward development, almost all these countries seem to have followed a surprisingly similar strategy of stressing "sophisticated" agriculture (as indicated by heavy fertilizer consumption), manufacturing, and, with a little more variation, heavy industry rather than light industry.

Turning to the specific data on these five indicators of economic structure in Table 2.3, all the Asian nations, with the partial exception of Nepal, displayed some commitment to economic upgrading. As would be expected, the South Asian nations and China trailed East Asia considerably in moving away from agriculturally based economies. Yet all of them were participants in the green revolution, as evidenced by extremely heavy use of fertilizer (from three to eight times the low-income-nation median for the South Asian countries and even more for the PRC). East Asia's lead in industrialization over South Asia in terms of both the size of the manufacturing sector and the importance of heavy industry within manufacturing is considerable, but probably not as great as was its movement away from an agricultural economy. Again, attempts at upgrading by the poorer countries are easy to discern. The PRC joins the East Asian capitalist states with a highly industrialized profile; Bangladesh, Pakistan, and especially India have substantial heavy industry; and India, Pakistan, and Sri Lanka have manufacturing sectors much larger than in the typical low-income country.

Many of the differences that do emerge in Table 2.3 reflect idiosyncratic policies and patterns. In terms of the development of the tertiary sector, for

Table 2.3   Indicators of Economic Structure, 1993

	Agriculture percent GNP	Fertilizer use (100 g plant nutrient per hectare)	Manufactures percent GNP	Services percent GNP	Percent of industry heavy[a]
Nepal	43	391	9	36	5
Bangladesh	30	1032	10	52	24
India	31	720	17	41	39
Pakistan	25	1015	17	50	21[b]
Sri Lanka	25	964	15	50	9
China	19	3005	38	33	39
South Korea	7	4656	29	50	40
Taiwan	4	—	31	57	—
Hong Kong	0	c	13	79	23
Singapore	0	c	28	63	63
Japan	2	3954	24	57	48
Low-income median	36	132	11	42	16
High-income median	2	2253	22	65	31

Sources: Taiwan Statistical Data Book, 1995; World Bank, 1991 & 1995.
Notes: a. Machinery and chemicals.
b. 1989.
c. Agricultural sector too small to yield meaningful results.

example, Hong Kong has by far the largest (79%) and China the lowest (33%)—resulting from the former's history as an entrepot and financial center and the latter's communist ideology. In addition, Sri Lanka, the wealthiest country in South Asia, places the least emphasis on heavy industry, along with Nepal. Despite a fairly strong state role in the economy until the late 1970s, Sri Lanka differs from most of the other East and South Asian developmental states in that it has never seriously tried to stimulate industrialization through import substitution (Bruton, 1992), which probably explains its low level of heavy industry. Finally, China's large manufacturing sector (38% of GDP) is far from being an indicator of industrial success. Rather, it reflects the Stalinist strategy of forced-draft industrialization, creating a heavy-industry sector that is now obsolete and inefficient (Cheng, 1982; Lardy, 1978; Prybyla, 1981).

The data reviewed here show that the differences between structures of the East and South Asian economies, though certainly significant, were far less stark than might have been expected. This result is surprising because the tremendous differences in economic performance revealed in the preceding section would suggest that the Confucian-capitalist nations pursued one strategy while China and the South Asian nations did something else. Yet the similarities in economic structure indicate that this is not so. Almost all of these nations display evidence of upgrading their economies toward more advanced agricultural techniques and toward industry—generally heavy industry. These attempts were successful enough to leave a similar mark on their economic structures.

Success in altering the gross nature of the economy, however, did not necessarily carry over into similar levels of economic performance. The East Asian economies were much more efficient and dynamic than the South Asian ones. Theoretically, this difference could be explained in either of two ways, although we have not yet found sufficient evidence to evaluate the alternative answers. On the one hand, the market and the state could be combined by noting the market-conforming policies of East Asia and the market-distorting ones of South Asia. In contrast, the state-in-society perspective would focus analytic attention on regional differences in the nature of society and state–society relations.

The Policy Environment

One of the central assumptions in development studies is that the level of development and the structural features of the economy discussed in the last two sections exercise important influences over a nation's economic performance and social outcomes. Although there may be some difference in emphasis and attention given to such costs of development as pollution and social inequality, almost all scholars and government officials agree that wealthier, more industrial, and more capital-rich nations are generally the best situated in the world economy.

Such consensus completely disappears, however, when attention moves to the political or policy context. Neoclassical theory argues that state intervention in the economy distorts the natural pursuit of comparative advantage and inevitably leads to national stagnation (Balassa, 1981; Friedman and Friedman, 1980; Gilder, 1984; von Mises, 1983). This perspective has been challenged by a variety of arguments: that state policy can stimulate development (Amsden, 1989; Gerschenkron, 1962; Haggard, 1990; Wade, 1990); that government policies are necessary to offset the costs of raw capitalism for basic human needs (Moon, 1991; Moon and Dixon, 1992; Roy and Clark, 1994); and that the market relations of global capitalism prevent and pervert development in the Third World by enforcing dependency upon the industrialized nations (Amin, 1974; Bornschier and Chase-Dunn, 1985; Frank, 1969). This section examines the policy context in terms of factors that might affect nations' economic and social performance. It explores whether the pronounced regional differences in efficiency that exist despite a surprising similarity in fundamental economic structures can be explained by the policy context, in particular whether governments pursued conservative laissez-faire or liberal welfare-state policies.

Neoclassical economics is especially contemptuous of "bleeding-heart liberalism" that tries to divert resources from economic production to meet the social problems of a nation. Such well-intentioned policies, advocates of the free market contend, lead to declining economic performance, which itself exacerbates economic problems. In many cases, advocates of the basic-human-needs approach to development do not contradict this logic, but only argue that the trade-offs between growth and equity are less severe than pictured by the neoclassicists and that the social ills in many developing nations are so severe that redistributive policies are a necessity. However, the argument is now beginning to be advanced that growth does not necessarily have to be bought at the expense of equity, based on case studies of individual countries such as Taiwan (Chan and Clark, 1992a; Fei et al., 1979) and sophisticated statistical analyses of the comparative economic performance of developing nations (Moon and Dixon, 1992).

Three dimensions of government liberalism are examined here. First, the size of government is measured by the ratio of the central government's budget to GNP (more-liberal governments should be larger). Second, its spending priorities are measured by the percentage of social spending (education, health, housing, and welfare) and of defense spending in the central government's budget. Finally, because liberal governments are widely perceived to be tolerant of public debt in the pursuit of economic expansion and social-welfare programs, several indicators of fiscal self-restraint are examined as well.

The data in Table 2.4 confirm the stereotype about the East Asian capitalist nations in several key respects. Japan and the four Little Dragons have fairly conservative governments in terms of size and welfare-spending priority. All are considerably smaller in terms of the budget/GNP ratio and devote substantially smaller portions of their budgets to social services than would be expected of countries at their level of affluence. (The missing data for Hong Kong and Japan almost certainly would not alter this picture.) Although missing data make the picture a little cloudier for South Asia and China, some of the expected difference from East Asian conservatism is clear enough, although the contrast is not stark. China (with its huge socialist economy) and Sri Lanka (with its fairly high budget priority for social welfare) can be considered to have fairly liberal governments; however, none of the other four countries in South Asia display any of the posited liberal characteristics. To some extent this results from idiosyncratic factors, such as the Indian–Pakistani arms race (which limits the proportion of their budgets devoted to social services) and India's powerful state governments (which limits the size of the central government). Still, these data make it hard to conclude that the conservatism of their governments per se holds the key to explaining East Asian dynamism.

Whereas conservatives are normally assumed to be promilitary (in a departure from their broader antipathy toward government), defense spending is often stimulated by idiosyncratic security threats or rivalries and thus would not necessarily be a good indicator of a nation's ideological proclivities. This is especially true in Asia, with its multiple arms races. In fact, defense spending is probably more important for its assumed economic consequences. There is a general belief that a heavy defense burden detracts from economic growth (Chan, 1985). For example, Japan's minuscule defense budget and the U.S. role of superpower have been used to explain Japan's growing economic challenge to the United States (Chan, 1993; Kennedy, 1987). The data on defense spending in Table 2.4, however, indicate that this is not the case in South and East Asia. Although high levels of defense spending in the conflictual and stagnant India and Pakistan contrast with dynamic Japan's low military budget, Singapore, South Korea, and Taiwan all have high levels of military expenditures as well. This demonstrates that a high level of military spending does not necessarily preclude rapid economic growth.

The final two columns in Table 2.4 examine possible debt problems as indicated by the government's budget balance and by total debt burden as a percentage of GNP. The data on government budget balances are quite consistent with the stereotype of greater conservatism in the East Asian capitalist nations. All the South Asian countries have fairly significant bud-

Patterns of Development

Table 2.4   Indicators of Policy Liberalism, 1993

	Central government budget percent GNP	Social welfare percent central government budget[a]	Defense percent central government budget	Budget balance percent GNP	Total debt percent GNP
Nepal	18.7	22.4	5.9	-6.3	26
Bangladesh	—	21.3[b]	11.2[a]	—	31
India	16.9	11.2	14.5	-4.8	29
Pakistan	24.0	4.3	26.8	-7.4	39
Sri Lanka	26.9	32.8	11.4	-6.4	42
China	—	2.8	16.4	—	18
South Korea	17.1	29.0	20.1	0.6	14
Taiwan	32.6	36.0	13.7	-7.8	—
Hong Kong	—	—	—	—	—
Singapore	19.7	37.4	24.5	12.6	—
Japan	18.4	—	6.2[b]	-2.6[b]	—
Low-income median	25.3	25.7	10.7	-4.8	52
High-income median	43.9	52.6	6.0	-3.8	—

Sources: Chan, 1993; *Taiwan Statistical Data Book*, 1995; World Bank, 1991 & 1995.
Notes: a. Education, health, housing, social security, and welfare.
b. 1986–1989.

get deficits, in the range of 5 percent to 7.5 percent of GNP, while only Taiwan in East Asia approaches this level. Consequently, debt is certainly not a drag on the East Asian economies. China's debt level is still low; Japan, Singapore, Hong Kong, and Taiwan have moved beyond worries about debt burdens; and South Korea's very rapid growth made its strategy of "indebted industrialization" feasible, although most other countries that chose this strategy became mired in debt (Frieden, 1981). However, greater debt burdens probably do not account for economic stagnation in South Asia because total debt as a proportion of GNP is still fairly modest in these countries.

State size and policy orientation are important not only in themselves but because governmental activities are presumed to produce important consequences for economies and societies. Conservative advocates of neoclassical economics, for instance, argue that large states tie up financial resources that could be used more productively by the private sector. Conversely, liberal supporters of an activist government argue that state programs (e.g., universal education) are necessary to develop the human capital upon which development depends. A brief comparison of East and South Asia on investment and education finds support, perhaps strangely, for both these theories.

The role of savings and investment is usually considered crucial for economic development, and in many poor nations it generates a vicious cycle. Investment is necessary to generate growth, particularly the transition from agricultural to industrial endeavors. However, many countries may simply be too poor to permit adequate savings, estimated by Hagen (1986) at about 12 percent to 15 percent of GNP, for financing such investment. Their alternatives are either to borrow money or to hope for foreign investment, but neither of these is unambiguously attractive. Debt can strangle an economy, and foreign multinational corporations (MNCs) may simply exploit the natural resources or cheap labor of the host country while contributing little to its overall development project.

There is a substantial difference between the savings and investment rates of East Asia and South Asia, as indicated by the data in Table 2.5. The East Asian nations, including China, average high savings and investment rates of, respectively, 35 percent and 30 percent. South Asia, in contrast, has a much lower savings rate, but most of these countries save in the 12 percent to 15 percent range that is considered to make development viable. These rates are actually impressive compared to the 6 percent average for all low-income countries; India, at 24 percent, stands out as a notable overachiever on savings among the poor nations. Moreover, South Asian investment rates average a quite respectable 21 percent to 25 percent, with the exception of Bangladesh's 14 percent. The higher levels of investment than savings in South Asia also indicate that a significant

Table 2.5 National Savings and Investment Rates, 1993

	Savings percent GNP	Investment percent GNP	Investment growth 1980–1993
Nepal	11	21	—
Bangladesh	8	14	1.6
India	24	24	5.7
Pakistan	12	21	5.6
Sri Lanka	16	25	2.4
China	40	41	11.1
South Korea	35	34	11.8
Taiwan	28	25	7.8
Hong Kong	31	27	5.0
Singapore	47	44	5.7
Japan	33	30	5.5
Low-income median	6	17	2.4
High-income median	23	21	2.4

Sources: Taiwan Statistical Data Book, 1995; World Bank, 1995.

amount of international capital flow must be occurring that mitigates the tremendous differences in savings rates without creating a huge debt burden (see Table 2.4). The East Asian record is clearly superlative, even (or especially) in comparison with other developed nations. However, South Asia's record is far from shoddy, considering that only Bangladesh's savings and investment rates seem really substandard. India has strong levels of savings and investment, and investment growth in India and Pakistan during 1980–1993 was quite dynamic compared to either low-income or high-income countries.

Much the same situation holds true for the education variables presented in Table 2.6, in that East Asia has a far better absolute performance but the South Asian countries appear significantly above average for low-income nations. The East Asian capitalist states and Sri Lanka now have literacy rates and high school enrollment ratios nearly twice that of Bangladesh, Nepal, India, and Pakistan, with China holding an intermediate position. For primary schools, all the countries except Bangladesh and Pakistan have come fairly close to full enrollments (some enrollment ratios exceed 100% because of the presence of children older or younger than normal in primary school). This again indicates the liberal nature of the governments in China and Sri Lanka: Both are overachievers in providing mass education to their populations, given their low levels of GNP per capita. The data on earlier school enrollment and literacy rates in Table 2.6 demonstrate that these national educational differences are not a recent phenomenon but date back to the 1950s and 1960s when (as shown in Table 2.2) the developmental differences between South and East Asia were fairly muted. These data on education show the East Asian governments to have a liberal as well as a conservative face. The conclusion lends some support to the human-capital perspective for explaining East Asia's much better economic performance.

Overall, capitalist East Asia conforms to its stereotype of the home of conservative governments and high investment rates. Although this could be taken to support the neoclassical view of East Asia as a group of small, conservative governments unleashing the forces of capitalism, the failure of the South Asian nations to display their expected profile implies otherwise. In fact, these data are probably more consistent with the statist argument that the economies in East Asia are dynamic not because their governments do not intervene in the economy, as neoclassicists would have it, but precisely because they have learned how to intervene effectively without spending large amounts of money and accruing huge bureaucracies. Furthermore, a strong commitment to mass education is one of the factors most often cited to explain East Asian dynamism (Chan, 1993; Hofheinz and Calder, 1982; Thurow, 1992; Vogel, 1979); indeed, the East Asian capitalist nations, as well as the PRC and Sri Lanka, appear quite liberal in this pol-

Table 2.6 National Educational Performance

	Literacy rate		Percent age group in primary school		Percent age group in secondary school	
	1950	1990	1965	1992	1965	1992
Nepal	5	26	20	102	5	36
Bangladesh	—	35	49	77	13	19
India	19	48	74	102	27	44
Pakistan	13	35	40	46	12	21
Sri Lanka	63	88	93	107	35	74
China	48	73	89	121	24	51
South Korea	77	96	101	105	35	90
Taiwan	54	94	99	99	—	93
Hong Kong	58	88[a]	103	105	29	74[a]
Singapore	50	96	105	107	45	69[a]
Japan	98	98	100	102	82	95[a]
Low-income median	9	48	42	76	5	23
High-income median	98	98	99	103	56	91

Sources: Taiwan Statistical Data Book, 1995; World Bank, 1991 & 1995.
Note: a. 1985–1988.

icy area. Such an emphasis on human-capital formation also turns attention away from the question of state versus market and toward the contributions of society stressed by the state-in-society approach.

Current Economic and Social Performance

The proof of the pudding is in the eating—or, in this case, how well nations are performing in the economic and social realms at present. Has the past success of East Asia carried over into short-term economic superiority? Or has South Asia's performance picked up? Have the East Asian capitalist countries paid a price in social deterioration for their rapid growth fueled by raw capitalism? Is lower growth in South Asia compensated for by a better meeting of basic human needs? In short, does there appear to be a fundamental trade-off between economic growth and social equity? It is best to begin by examining economic growth and inflation during the 1980s and then move on to social outcomes, such as the degree of income inequality and indicators of the citizens' quality of life.

The data in Table 2.7 on the recent economic performance of East Asia and South Asia are perhaps somewhat surprising. The East Asian countries (including China) had a superlative record and, in general, outperformed South Asia, consistent with the stereotype of East Asian dynamism. The stereotype of South Asian stagnation clearly missed the mark, however: All the nations on the subcontinent had stellar economic records, at least in terms of aggregate growth. The East Asian nations averaged 6 percent to 10 percent per year growth in real GNP (except wealthy Japan, at 4 percent, whose growth would be expected to be lower than others because of its high GNP per capita). In comparative terms these growth rates were much higher than the 2.6 percent median for advanced industrial economies. Growth in South Asia generally fell in the solid 4 percent to 6 percent range, which was also about twice as high as for the average nation with a similar level of development. Inflation followed the same pattern as GNP growth. Although the average inflation rate in South Asia was about twice as high as in East Asia (9.5% to 4.5%), both regions had slightly better records than comparable nations.

The data on sectoral performance in Table 2.7 are even more positive for South Asia. In agriculture, South Asia (whose agricultural growth during the 1980s and 1990s was respectable, averaging between 2% and 3.5%) actually outperformed the East Asian capitalist nations, where agriculture is becoming a lagging sector. The improving agricultural performance in South Asia is quite promising because it suggests that the past inefficiency in agriculture and the drag on economic growth that it created are finally being overcome. China had by far the best record in Asia, marking

Patterns of Development

Table 2.7 Average Annual Growth, 1980–1993 (percentage)

	GDP	Agriculture	Manufacturing	Exports	Inflation
Nepal	5.0	3.6	—	11.2[a]	8.6
Bangladesh	4.2	2.6	3.4	9.8	11.5
India	5.2	3.0	6.3	7.0	8.7
Pakistan	6.0	4.4	7.3	10.1	7.4
Sri Lanka	4.0	2.1	6.7	7.3	11.1
China	9.6	5.3	11.1	11.5	7.0
South Korea	9.1	2.0	12.3	12.3	6.3
Taiwan	7.7	2.0	6.5	7.1	4.4
Hong Kong	6.5	[b]	—	15.8	7.9
Singapore	6.9	[b]	7.2	12.7	2.5
Japan	4.0	0.6	5.6	4.2	1.5
Low-income median	2.7	2.4	3.4	2.1	11.3
High-income median	2.6	1.4	2.3	4.7	4.6

Sources: Taiwan Statistical Data Book, 1995; World Bank, 1991 & 1995.
Notes: a. 1980–1989.
b. Agricultural sector too small to yield meaningful results.

the success of the "household-responsibility system" for stimulating increased production, although by the early 1990s rapidly rising urban and industrial prices had turned the terms of trade decidedly against agriculture (Wu, 1994). In South Asia, Nepal, India, and Pakistan clearly outperformed countries with similar economic profiles.

Many analysts have focused upon East Asia's open economies in contrast to South Asia's closed ones; the former's greater success is due, according to neoclassical logic, to their subjecting their economies to the discipline of the international marketplace. The data on the growth of exports and manufacturing production during 1980–1993, however, suggest that this stereotype should now be consigned to the dustbin of history. In terms of export performance, the capitalist East Asian nations had very high export-growth rates both in actual terms and relative to other industrialized nations, in line with the neoclassical stereotype. However, the South Asian nations and China almost matched those countries in extremely rapid growth. Presumably because export markets were booming for all concerned, there was also little difference between East and South Asia in the growth of manufacturing production. China and South Korea stood out for their double-digit growth in the 13 percent to 14 percent range, but the South Asian nations of Pakistan, Sri Lanka, and India (Bangladesh being an exception) were just as vibrant as Japan, Taiwan, and Singapore, with 6 percent to 7 percent annual growth.

Whereas the overall indicators of trade performance are surprisingly similar for East Asia and South Asia, there is an important difference in their export structures; this is revealed in Table 2.8 on the proportion of exports that are manufactured products, machinery, and textiles. Industrial products are very important in the export mixes of all these countries—about 90 percent or more of the exports of the East Asian capitalist states and from 70 percent to 80 percent for China and South Asia. Although East Asia has the higher absolute values, a comparison with the normal export profiles of high-income and low-income countries indicates that South Asia and China are even greater overachievers here than are the highly lauded open economies in capitalist East Asia.

There is a major difference in the nature of these manufactured exports, however. The East Asian capitalist states are very strong in machinery, while South Asia and China are much more successful in textiles. This difference in export pattern is striking, although there are a few exceptions (Hong Kong has a South Asian profile; South Korea and Taiwan retain a significant textile industry). China and all of South Asia, therefore, have been successful in taking the first step up the international product cycle, the remarkable magnitude of which becomes apparent when their progress is compared with similar economies elsewhere in the world. Given that textiles are usually the first major industrial good to be produced as a na-

Table 2.8 Structure of Industrial Exports, 1993

	Manufactures percent exports	Machinery percent exports	Textiles percent exports
Nepal	84	0	73[a]
Bangladesh	81	0	78
India	75	7	30
Pakistan	85	0	78
Sri Lanka	73	2	52
China	81	16	31
South Korea	94	43	19
Taiwan	96	35	16
Hong Kong	93	26	39[a]
Singapore	80	55	4
Japan	97	68	2
Low-income median	25	1	3
High-income median	76	32	4

Sources: Taiwan Statistical Data Book, 1995; World Bank, 1991 & 1995.
Note: a. 1989.

tion begins to climb the international product cycle, this pattern is generally consistent with the neoclassical emphasis on comparative advantage. However, the fact that laissez-faire Hong Kong has been the least successful East Asian capitalist nation in upgrading into machinery production suggests that the neoclassical emphasis upon market forces alone is not warranted either.

There is a growing conviction that humanity does not live by GNP growth alone. Nations' social performance in meeting the basic human needs of their populations is coming under increasing scrutiny. The East Asian capitalist states have had excellent economic performance that may (or may not) have some linkage with their conservative governments. One might ask, however, whether this rapid economic growth has been purchased at the cost of stagnating or declining living standards, especially considering that these governments' comparatively small budgets and low priorities for social policies obviously limit the potential for redistributive policies. Conversely, one might speculate that South Asia's and China's more liberal (or in several cases less conservative) government policies enhanced the quality of life for their citizens at the cost of higher economic growth.

The data on income inequality in Table 2.9 provide mixed support for this political logic. In South Asia, income inequality has been reduced to levels significantly below those in the average low-income country, consistent with the political stereotype. In East Asia the picture is far muddier. Japan, Taiwan, and (more recently) South Korea have fairly low levels of income inequality, but Hong Kong and Singapore have levels of inequality that are well above those found in other rich nations; it is perhaps surprising that income inequality in China is at the norm for poor nations.

Finally, three indicators of the popular quality of life are included in Table 2.10: life expectancy, the percentage of low-weight babies, and the infant mortality rate per 1,000 live births. The data demonstrate a clear division on all these variables between the relatively good scores of the East Asian capitalist states, China, and (except for low-weight babies) Sri Lanka, and the much poorer performance of the other South Asian nations. Much of this regional difference appears to be the normal result of industrialization and development, however: The East Asian capitalist states and most of the South Asian nations do not deviate greatly from the medians of, respectively, all high-income or all low-income countries. Still, it is clear that rapid growth in East Asia has not been achieved at the cost of a diminished capacity for meeting basic human needs. China and Sri Lanka again rate as substantial overachievers on these items, thereby linking good social outcomes to liberal political regimes.

A consideration of the current economic and social performances of these Asian countries paints a decidedly mixed picture. Neoclassical

Table 2.9   Income Distribution (percent of population)

		Share of poorest 20 percent	Share of richest 20 percent	Share of richest 10 percent	Ratio richest/poorest 20 percent
Nepal	1985	9.1	39.5	25.0	4.34
	1976	4.6	59.2	46.5	12.87
Bangladesh	1989	9.5	38.6	24.6	4.06
	1973	6.9	42.2	27.4	6.12
India	1990	8.8	41.3	27.1	4.69
	1975	7.0	49.4	33.6	7.06
	1964	6.7	48.9	35.2	7.30
Pakistan	1990	8.4	39.7	25.2	4.73
	1984	7.8	45.6	31.3	5.85
Sri Lanka	1990	8.9	39.3	25.2	4.42
	1969	7.5	43.4	28.2	5.79
China	1990	6.4	41.8	24.6	6.53
South Korea	1988	7.4	42.2	27.6	5.70
	1976	5.7	45.3	27.5	7.95
Taiwan	1993	7.1	38.7	—	5.42
	1980	8.8	36.8	—	4.18
	1968	7.8	41.4	—	5.31
Hong Kong	1980	5.4	47.0	31.3	8.70
Singapore	1983	5.1	48.9	33.5	9.59
Japan	1979	8.7	37.5	22.4	4.31
	1969	7.9	41.0	27.2	5.19
Low-income median, late 1980s		6.6	44.2	29.0	6.50
High-income median, mid-1980s		5.9	39.8	23.8	6.53

Sources: Taiwan Statistical Data Book, 1995; World Bank, 1979, 1984, 1991 & 1995.

expectations about the superior economic performance of the East Asian capitalist states are clearly not met; and, more positively, the capitalist economies and conservative governments in East Asia produced economic dynamism without the normally assumed social costs of raw capitalism. Conversely, these results are also somewhat inconsistent with the developmental state model. The seeming efficacy of human-capital formation turns attention to society, not only to the developmental state; India certainly demonstrates that the existence a strong state committed to social equity, at least ideologically, does not guarantee a stellar record in meeting basic human needs.

Table 2.10 National Quality of Life Indicators, 1993

	Life expectancy	Percent low-weight babies	Infant mortality per 1,000 live births
Nepal	54	26	96
Bangladesh	56	34	106
India	61	30[a]	80
Pakistan	62	30	88
Sri Lanka	72	22	17
China	69	6	30
South Korea	71	9[a]	11
Taiwan	75	—	5[a]
Hong Kong	79	4[a]	7
Singapore	75	7	6
Japan	80	6	4
Low-income median	52	12	93
High-income median	77	6	8

Sources: Taiwan Statistical Data Book, 1991 & 1995; World Bank, 1991 & 1995.
Note: a. 1989.

The Development Profiles of South Asia and East Asia: Adding Complexity to Neoclassical and Statist Stereotypes

The economic profiles of South and East Asia presented in this chapter have countervailing implications for the competing neoclassical and developmental state theories. At first glance, the Asian nations can be divided into two groups of rapidly developing (capitalist East Asia) and seemingly underdeveloped (South Asia and China) nations whose comparative success exactly mirrors the neoclassical division between market-driven and statist economies. In addition, capitalist East Asian nations also conform to neoclassical stereotypes of the nature of a desirable state. Their governments are small in size and devote a low percentage of their budgets to social welfare compared with other high-income nations. Coincidentally or not, the East Asian nations (including the far from neoclassical PRC) have a much stronger record than those of South Asia on savings and, to a lesser extent, investment, which are generally seen as prerequisites for a successful economy.

However, a closer examination of these political economies indicates that several qualifications are in order. First, China has experienced extremely rapid growth over the past fifteen years, despite its communist government and large state sector of the economy. Whereas Chinese economic dynamism was undoubtedly stimulated by Deng Xiaoping's marketization reforms, the country's performance should still be fairly shoddy according to neoclassical norms. Similarly, South Asia now appears to have established itself on the first rung of the ladder leading to development that has been called the international product cycle. Although the more developed East Asian countries seem far better off today, South Asia may begin to challenge them in labor-intensive production, such as textiles, based upon their huge supply of unemployed and underemployed workers (see Chan and Clark, 1992b, for broader data showing that South Asia seemingly upgraded its position in the international division of labor during the 1980s).

More broadly, the expected regional differences in economic strategy and structure between the more and less successful economies did not emerge. In fact, all (with the exception of Nepal) evidently engaged in various types of sectoral targeting to promote industrialization, though the effectiveness of these policies varied greatly. Furthermore, the fulfillment of basic human needs does not have to come at the expense of economic dynamism, as neoclassicists are wont to assume. The experience of the East Asian capitalist states even implies something of the reverse. Their construction of human capital early in their developmental histories probably spurred economic growth and transformation by creating the work force necessary for industrialization. Thus, rather than diverting resources from productive employment, as neoclassicists would have it, government programs that develop human capital may well be a key element in determining which developing countries can climb the international product cycle. These results also belie the neoclassical assumption that diverting resources to basic human needs will create huge, unwieldy bureaucracies.

Taken together, these findings do not really challenge the fundamental neoclassical assumption that development should occur along market-driven lines. However, they do indicate that far more than laissez-faire economics has been at work in Asian industrialization. This does not necessarily constitute an endorsement of the competing developmental state approach, however. For example, the prevailing conceptualization of the East Asian capitalist countries as developmental states, rather than practitioners of laissez-faire economics, might be considered as implying acceptance of the statist paradigm, given the economic success of that region. Yet it is also abundantly clear that more than simple statism differentiates the South and East Asian patterns of development. First, the evidently similar targeting of sectoral transformation in the two regions produced much higher performance in East Asia than in the subcontinent, indicating that more than state policy per se was involved. Second, the normal assumption that government size translates into greater state capacity certainly does not hold; in fact, the smaller East Asian developmental states appear to be much more effective than the larger South Asian ones. This anomaly calls for a more detailed examination of the linkage between state action and economic performance. Finally, the apparent efficacy of the East Asian programs for human-capital development turns analytic attention toward the nonstate actors emphasized by the state-in-society perspective.

3

The Economic Policies of
South and East Asia: More Than a
Neoclassical or Statist Differentiation

In the profiles of development in Chapter 2, the impressive performance of
the East Asian countries contrasted with the rather poor aggregate performance of the South Asian nations, despite their surprising similarity in
many aspects of both economic and human development. The conventional
wisdom attributes these marked differences in developmental outcomes to
the economic policies followed by nations in these two regions. In particular, most of the nations in East Asia are seen as opening their markets and
pursuing generally laissez-faire policies, while the South Asian states have
directed development and pursued self-reliant strategies of growth. In
short, this conventional perspective validates neoclassical theory: Reliance
on the free market produces optimum outcomes; state intervention creates
economic distortions and inefficiencies. Even the statist regimes have accepted this conclusion! During the 1980s and early 1990s, the South Asian
countries and China all implemented significant market reforms with generally good results.

A closer look at the economic policies of these nations belies the
stereotype, however. First, pure laissez-faire is hard to find, with the possible exception of Hong Kong. Japan, Korea, Singapore, and Taiwan, in
contrast, have all been marked by massive state intervention in the economy. In China's case, furthermore, Deng Xiaoping's reforms produced
spectacular growth, creating an ironic counterpoint to what might be expected of capitalist and communist economic relations. Second, market reforms have not inevitably been successful. For example, economic liberalization in Sri Lanka in the late 1970s had little impact on that country's
economic performance. Economic policies cannot be neatly divided into
efficient laissez-faire ones and inefficient statist perversions of the market.

This chapter explores the economic policies of South and East Asia
more inductively and does not make the assumption that state and market
are necessarily antithetical. The first section provides a theoretical
overview of the principal dimensions of economic policy relating to development. Based on this framework, the second section compares the East
and South Asian patterns of development policy; the third fleshes out the

39

analysis by presenting several case studies that illustrate these patterns. Although the neoclassical praise of markets is well earned, its claim that East Asian dynamism can be explained entirely by laissez-faire policies flies in the face of historical experience.

Economic Policies and Development: The Basic Dimensions

The neoclassical approach makes a sharp distinction between the free operation of markets and governmental meddling in them, but reality is almost certainly more muddled. In particular, state policy inevitably structures markets in the sense that it creates "economic institutions" (North, 1990) that channel economic activities toward certain directions and away from others. National economic policies can be conceptualized not simply as either market oriented or state oriented, but as potentially varying among four dimensions:

1. Whether a nation pursues an import-substitution (IS) or export-promotion (EP) approach to industrialization;
2. Whether state economic policies are market conforming or market distorting;
3. Whether entrepreneurship or bureaucratic leadership is seen as more important for promoting development;
4. Whether agriculture is viewed simply as a source of exploitable surplus to finance industrialization or whether the rural areas are deemed a vital component of economic and human development.

National economic policies are packages made up of these four elements. Some packages appear much more effective than others, but the differences among them go far beyond the simple dichotomy of state and market.

Import-Substitution vs. Export-Performance Policies

The difference between IS and EP is a fundamental one. Import substitution is a strategy for industrialization in which previously imported goods are walled off to permit the development of domestic manufacturing capacity for them. In contrast, export promotion ties industrial expansion to the ability of a nation to sell its products on the world market. These divergent strategies are often taken as synonymous with, respectively, statist and laissez-faire economic policies because the former requires massive state intervention whereas the latter can only succeed if an economy is competitive on the open international market. In either case, the adoption by a developing nation of a particular industrialization strategy immediately establishes a strong set of linkages among trade, exchange rates, and pricing policies that, in turn, channel the subsequent pattern of development.

Anne Krueger (1978) aptly summarizes the salient features of the IS and EP strategies. Import substitution encourages domestic production by imposing either tariffs or quantitative restrictions (even total prohibition sometimes) on imports of a specific commodity. Higher prices and limited foreign competition thus allow inefficient domestic producers to overcome the entry barriers to the industry. In theory, the domestic producers who are created by this "infant-industry" protection will become increasingly efficient as they benefit from experience and eventually reap economies of scale as their production capacities expand.

In practice, however, import substitution can act as a narcotic that undermines an economy's efficiency and competitiveness by generating substantial incentives for a misallocation of resources. Capital and other resources that otherwise would have been employed in the more efficient export sector in an open economy are diverted to less efficient import-competing industries. Furthermore, the higher cost of imported inputs makes the country's export products uncompetitive in the world market, which often leads to balance-of-payments difficulties. Similarly, the overvaluation of the domestic currency, which is often used as one of the mechanisms for limiting imports, increases the costs of importing the capital goods vital for industrialization and tends to exacerbate the trade deficit. The need to reduce the balance-of-payments deficit, in turn, necessitates the imposition of additional quantitative restrictions, which further increases the bias toward import substitution. Thus, import substitution often produces a vicious cycle of increasing government intervention in the economy (which is often accompanied by massive corruption), misallocation of resources, and increasingly inefficient economic performance.

Conversely, the export-promotion strategy contains strong incentives to create and maintain an internationally open market economy. Because tariffs cannot induce production for the international market, a production/export subsidy or a realistic exchange rate is required. However, the feasibility of most subsidies is limited. They impose a drain on the government's resources, tend to enlarge the budget deficit, and are likely to stimulate economic retaliation from trading partners. Hence, there is a strong incentive for the government not to use subsidies but to maintain a realistic exchange rate that will provide a sufficient incentive to export for competitive industries. Furthermore, an EP strategy requires that the export sector be able to obtain imported factor inputs at world prices, which forces the government to lower tariff barriers and remove other trade restrictions on any goods that flow, either directly or indirectly, into the export sector. Thus, the successful implementation of a genuine EP strategy would almost certainly require an open and liberal trade regime.

The popularity of these strategies in the Third World has varied over time. In the 1960s and 1970s, import substitution and self-reliant development were very widely adopted based on the theories of Raul Prebisch (1971), Fernando Henrique Cardoso (Cardoso and Faletto, 1979), and Ragnar Nurkse (1959) that the market mechanisms of global trading would lock developing countries into "underdevelopment" at the bottom of the industrial order. By the 1980s, however, the experience of such newly industrializing countries (NICs) as Taiwan and South Korea in generating export-based growth and transformation led such prominent economists as Anne Krueger (1978) and Jagdish Bhagwati (Bhagwati, 1978; Bhagwati and Sririvasan, 1975) to champion the adoption of the outward-looking export-oriented strategy for growth and development by developing countries.

The empirical evidence on the relative efficacy of the EP and IS strategies is not totally conclusive. On the one hand, numerous studies have suggested that import substitution distorts an economy and retards growth, whereas the adoption of an export-promotion strategy results in significantly faster GNP growth (Balassa, 1981; Bhagwati, 1978; Krueger, 1978; Little et al., 1970; Syrquin and Chenery, 1989; World Bank, 1983). On the other hand, critics have argued with some cogency that these findings were based on relatively limited samples of countries and/or that they do not control for critical determinants of economic performance (Aghazadeh and Evans, 1988; Evans, 1990; Milner, 1990). Thus, a decisive choice between these two development strategies remains somewhat problematic.

Market-Conforming vs. Market-Distorting Policies

To some extent, the debate over import-substitution versus export-promotion strategy is implicitly rooted in the conventional theory of comparative advantage. According to this view, a nation should specialize economically in its abundant resources; its factor endowments are composed of fairly permanent elements such as land, labor, and capital (Rogowski, 1989). An open economy, therefore, will use international trade to stimulate the most efficient use of resources. This static approach to comparative advantage, however, suggests a stable international division of labor.

From this perspective, the gross inefficiencies that accompany import substitution are justified because it is the only possible path to industrialization and development. However, the theory of the international product cycle (Gilpin, 1987; Vernon, 1966; Wells, 1972) suggests a more dynamic possibility. The most sophisticated and advanced products are made—usually with high degrees of capital, technology, and/or skill intensity—in the richest and most technologically advanced nations. However, as an industry matures and production becomes highly standardized and labor-intensive, the product cycle works to diffuse its production to areas with low labor costs.

Both neoclassical economics and statist theory are consistent with this description of development and competition in the contemporary world economy, but the two sides draw radically different policy implications from it (see Table 3.1). The neoclassicists argue that private businesspeople can accumulate capital most efficiently and will respond to market signals and discipline out of sheer self-interest. In contrast, states will use political power to extract "rents" from economic enterprises and to avoid responding to unwanted market signals. Thus, minimizing government interference in internal and international markets promotes global efficiency and allows all economies to benefit by specializing in their comparative advantage.

Statist theory, in contrast, argues that the international economy is so hierarchically segmented that there is little real opportunity for development in the Third World barring intervention by a very strong actor, usually the state. The private sector in most developing countries cannot generate adequate savings and investment by itself; even if it could, it would be very difficult for most infant industries in the Third World (or the developed world, for that matter) to be internationally competitive. Moreover, each movement up the product cycle threatens the vested interests of existing social classes and interest groups. Thus, harking back to Alexander Gerschenkron's (1962) arguments about industrialization in late developers, a strong developmental state is necessary to (1) mobilize resources, (2) distort prices (rather then "getting them right") to encourage new economic activities, (3) prevent dominant groups and classes from extracting rents and holding back change, and (4) bargain with and control external economic forces (Amsden, 1989; Evans et al., 1985, Wade, 1990).

This argument leads us to a second fundamental question in national economic policies: whether state policy turns out to be market distorting, as the neoclassicists depict it, or market conforming, as championed by the statists. The latter assume that with the diffusion of industrialization, comparative advantage has become somewhat arbitrary in the sense that it can be created and destroyed by state policy (Gilpin, 1987). Comparative advantage may therefore be much more dynamic than is implied by its conventional linkage with fairly permanent factor endowments such as land, labor, and capital. Thus, both primarily laissez-faire (Porter, 1990) and more statist (Thurow, 1992) theorists are now focusing upon a nation's competitive advantage, which can change fairly rapidly in response to strategic business and government decisions.

Of course, neither neoclassical nor statist scholars will be right all the time. Sometimes states will enact policies aimed at promoting popular

Table 3.1   Contrasting Implications Drawn from Product-Cycle Theory

Neoclassicists	Statists
Market signals when to move into new industries higher up product cycle	Market power freezes global division of labor
State intervention perverts market economy	State can exercise countervailing power to break barriers to development

State activities
  Extract rents from productive firms
  Bow to political pressure from
    business to permit monopoly rents
	State activities
	  Protect "infant industries"
	  Get prices wrong to stimulate
	    "sunrise industries"
	  Prevent dominant groups from holding back
	    economic change
	  Bargain with foreign states and MNCs

Dangers
  Exploited by use of others' market power
  Creates static global economic hierarchy
	Dangers
	  State becomes predatory
	  Policy mistakes produce worse outcomes
	    than markets

welfare (e.g., Sri Lanka in the 1950s and 1960s) or elite rents (e.g., India or the "crony capitalism" of the Marcos regime in the Philippines) rather than economic efficiency; sometimes states will lead their economies on rapid trajectories of growth and structural transformation (e.g., Japan, Singapore, and South Korea); and sometimes states will guess wrong and end up with market-distorting policies rather than the market-conforming ones that were intended (e.g., Taiwan's attempt to promote the automobile industry). Conversely, in a few places (e.g., Hong Kong), laissez-faire economics may be almost as it is laid out in the textbooks, but this does not guarantee that economic liberalization will always produce good economic results (e.g., Sri Lanka in the 1980s).

Entrepreneurship vs. Bureaucratic Leadership

A third dimension of economic policy concerns whether to place primary reliance upon entrepreneurship or upon bureaucratic leadership. At first this might sound like simply another name for the state–market dichotomy. However, it extends beyond a differentiation between the public and private sectors. The state can provide economic leadership through either market incentives or bureaucratic commands; governments themselves may operate either bureaucratically or entrepreneurially, and so—perhaps surprisingly—may private businesses; and government–business relations may be principally driven by either economic or political factors and considerations.

Neoclassical economists typically think of state policies as interventions in the natural activities of economic markets (von Mises, 1983). However, not much thought should be required before the basic assumption of "institutional economics" (North, 1990) becomes apparent: Government policies (systems of property rights, commercial law, etc.) inevitably structure markets. Furthermore, the leading state role in monetary and exchange-rate policy is almost universally accepted, as is (with perhaps a bit more controversy) the state's role in macroeconomic management (i.e., the use of fiscal and monetary policy to promote growth and smooth out the business cycle).

The question, then, is not really whether state policy will affect the economy, but how a government goes about using its policy tools to achieve its goals. On the one hand, the state may rely on market regulation by providing policy incentives that private entrepreneurs may follow or not at their own choice and risk. Most monetary policy falls under this rubric of "entrepreneurship" (i.e., lowering interest rates to stimulate consumption and business expansion). However, more targeted intervention in the economy, including "getting the prices wrong" in some instances, can qualify as well. For example, manipulating exchange rates or providing generalized subsidies or remissions of import duties for the export sector provides market incentives for the structural transformation of economic activities. More indirectly, policies of funding mass education create the human capital that is necessary if domestic businesspeople and workers are to take advantage of such incentives. In short, while the state structures the market to provide incentives for certain economic activities, development primarily depends upon the performance and entrepreneurship of myriad individuals in the private sector. This also suggests that governments may not always act in a bureaucratic manner: At the policymaking level, government offices can be small and entrepreneurial if economic policies are simple and designed to provide market incentives.

Conversely, the state may rely upon bureaucratic leadership in the sense that government officials make basic decisions about the allocation of resources, the production of goods, and the distribution of rewards and incomes. The most extreme example of this is command economies, in which planners set the production levels and input supplies of all major products. Even many capitalist economies in Europe and the Third World provide a large role for state corporations, which almost inevitably use political power to reap economic advantage. However, bureaucratic leadership can exist in much less tightly regulated economies as well. For example, extensive regulatory and licensing requirements may result in the establishment and day-to-day operations of factories becoming dependent upon individual negotiations between government officials and private businesspeople; subsidies and tax incentives may be directed at individual firms rather than offered generally to entrepreneurs considering entering an industry; and state influence or control over the financial system can make the credit extended to particular industries or firms a matter of political decision.

The key factor in determining whether a development strategy relies more on bureaucratic leadership or on entrepreneurship rests in the nature of government–business relations. In particular, are they "arms-length" relations, in which the government does not make decisions about who shall produce what? Or are they formed by personal connections, so that entrepreneurs have to lobby government in order to carry on their normal business activities? The latter case presents a real danger that "political entrepreneurship"—the ability to use links with powerful officials—will become more important than "economic entrepreneurship"—competition through economic efficiency. Private business is not necessarily entrepreneurial in outlook, but it may rely upon political contacts or other types of market imperfections to reap monopoly rents rather than to pursue economic efficiency. In such cases the private sector would appear far more bureaucratic than entrepreneurial. Thus, just as neoclassicists argue, there is probably a strong (though not inevitable) tendency for bureaucratic leadership to spawn political corruption and economic retrogression.

Agricultural Development vs. Agricultural Disdain

If it is recognized that governments inevitably influence markets and market incentives, the question arises of how individual sectors are viewed and treated in the development processes. Here, the role of agriculture may be more critical than is commonly recognized. Traditionally, development has been equated with industrialization. Thus, there is a tendency for a wide variety of economists, from neoclassicists to Marxists, to regard agriculture as a residual sector that is simply the source of capital, both physical and human, for industrialization. From this perspective, agriculture provides surplus resources that must be exploited for the industrialization drive.

The basic-human-needs approach to development, however, assumes that human capital is the key to successful development; this implies that rural society needs to be treated with tender loving care rather than simply exploited and discarded. At the beginning of industrialization, the bulk of any society is tied to the land, and agricultural productivity is usually fairly low. If rural resources are to finance industrialization, agricultural productivity must be increased. Human-capital investments are necessary as well if rural society is to spawn a new entrepreneurial class and illiterate peasants are to be transformed into even semiskilled workers. This imposes constraints on the means that are used to "squeeze" the agricultural sector and/or improve productivity. Draconian exploitation, from this perspective, becomes counterproductive because it stultifies rather than creates human capital.

Development strategies can thus be categorized by their basic approach toward agriculture. Does economic policy strongly favor the industrial sector and assume that development is essentially an urban phenomenon? Or is there an attempt to foster agricultural development and the transformation of rural society for its own sake on the assumption that the seeds of agricultural development will produce the fruits of industrial development? Either approach to agricultural development is possible under both bureaucratic-leadership and market-driven economies, because it is easy to manipulate the relative prices and terms of trade between the rural and urban sectors (Bates, 1981).

The distinction between agricultural development and agricultural disdain crosscuts economic theories. Advocates of the free market would be disturbed at the implications of the basic-human-needs approach for agricultural development, which subordinates current property relationships to the need for agricultural and land reform. Yet the jump to radical industrialization plans equally violates the logic of laissez-faire economics by imposing industrial transformation by government fiat to at least some degree. Conversely, the basic-human-needs approach views state intervention as probably necessary to promote agricultural transformation but sees the key factor as the creation of human capital—which implies an entrepreneurial rather than a bureaucratic approach to development.

South and East Asian Policy Patterns

The four dimensions of economic policy can be combined in numerous ways. Yet for the nations of South and East Asia there appear to be two general patterns, with a few minor variations within each country, as shown in Table 3.2. East Asia and Dengist China have followed one pattern, which appears associated with rapid growth and a fairly good record on meeting basic human needs. South Asia and Maoist China selected the other pattern, which is associated with considerably poorer economic performance and a mixed record on meeting basic human needs.

These two policy packages are quite divergent concerning the import-substitution versus export-promotion, as well as the market-conforming versus market-distorting, dimensions of strategy. South Asia and Maoist China opted for market-distorting import substitution, whereas East Asia and Dengist China ultimately took the opposite road of trying to promote development through export promotion based on conforming to (and competing on) international markets. Yet the packages are not really polar

Table 3.2   South vs. East Asia "Packages" of Economic Policies

	South Asia/Maoist China	East Asia/Dengist China
IS/EP	IS	First IS, then EP
Market conforming/distorting	Distorting	Conforming
Entrepreneurship/ bureaucratic leadership	Bureaucratic leadership	Range from pure entrepreneurship (Hong Kong) to strong bureaucratic leadership (South Korea, Singapore)
Agricultural development/disdain	South Asia: Agriculture ignored until green revolution China: Collectivization probably hurt peasants Sri Lanka/China: Significant social investments	Except city-states: Land reform, extension activities, and mass education stimulate agricultural development Ultimately, agriculture becomes declining sector

opposites; the difference between them should not be considered a strict dichotomy between statist South Asia and laissez-faire East Asia (with China switching from the former to the latter pattern in about 1980). Except for Hong Kong, all the East Asian capitalist states experienced significant periods of import substitution and were subject to a considerable number of state economic-policy initiatives.

At the beginning of the postwar era, both China and the nations in South Asia quite consciously shut themselves off from the dynamics of world markets. Despite their very different ideological stances, the governments in South Asia and in China believed this to be necessary for promoting balanced development. A common experience of imperialism made them sensitive to the dangers that untrammeled world markets and powerful multinational corporations posed to the economic aspirations of the developing world. These governments also believed that planning could promote both rapid industrialization and improvements in social conditions, whereas the natural operation of the market would have little positive effect upon their deplorable domestic conditions. Given these assumptions, the radical distortion of the market and import substitution logically appeared the best, and perhaps the only, way of achieving industrialization.

The initial situation and economic policies in all the East Asian capitalist states under their own rule (Hong Kong's laissez-faire policy was implemented by the British colonial administration) were not very different from the market-distorting import substitution of China and South Asia. Japan, Singapore, South Korea, and Taiwan all committed themselves to rapid industrialization and implemented trade restrictions to promote import substitution. East Asian import substitution was characterized by light, labor-intensive manufacturing, unlike the emphasis on heavy industry in India and China. Still, this was more a difference of degree than of kind; Japan quite consciously supported its iron and steel industry despite its comparative advantage in light industry. What separates the East Asian nations from South Asia and Maoist China, however, is that they dramatically switched strategies after a decade or so of import substitution. They opened their markets to varying extents and began to grow rapidly through export booms.

The experience of capitalist East Asia suggests that a strict dichotomy between IS and EP strategies is not warranted. Those countries used protection and import substitution to permit the establishment of industrial firms. When they became going concerns that could compete on international markets (or in Singapore's case, when its attempted union with Malaysia failed and its projected domestic market disappeared), state economic policy was reversed and EP became the dominant strategy. Infant-industry protection may be necessary to allow indigenous businesses to get started in the developing world; for example, industrial development in even the laissez-faire United States took off behind protectionist walls in the late nineteenth and early twentieth centuries (Goldstein, 1993; Lake, 1988). However, such import substitution can be market conforming if the new industries are forced to become internationally competitive as they were in East Asia, rather than allowed to atrophy behind protectionist walls, as occurred in South Asia and China.

The other two dimensions produce a less clear-cut differentiation. For each, one of the groups of countries is relatively uniform, but the other group is quite variegated, suggesting that different paths to development are possible. For the dimension of entrepreneurship versus bureaucratic leadership, South Asia and Maoist China put their faith in bureaucratism and a state-guided economy. This is certainly consistent with the neoclassical vision of how political economies work (or more often do not work). However, a brief reprise of the EP "miracles" in East Asia just as certainly establishes that reliance upon bureaucratic leadership does not necessarily lead to market distortions and poor economic performance. Only Hong Kong represents a full reliance upon entrepreneurship. Strong state leadership, perhaps rivaling that in South Asia, has marked the developmental histories of Singapore and South Korea. Japan has also had a strong developmental state led by the Ministry of International Trade and Industry (MITI), but its relationships with big business have been more balanced and consensual than in the other two statist political economies. Finally, bureaucratic states and highly entrepreneurial sectors coexist somewhat uneasily in Taiwan and Dengist China.

In agricultural policy, the answer to the question of what works and what does not is clear: Agricultural development leads to later growth. In Japan, South Korea, and Taiwan (agriculture is not relevant for the city-states of Hong Kong and Singapore), land reform coupled with strong agricultural extension programs and mass education created a system of small-holder agriculture that proved highly productive and able to provide substantial resources for industrialization. Under Deng Xiaoping's reforms in China, the responsibility system created a comparable type of family-based agriculture that immediately exhibited a strong surge in productivity (Harding, 1987). Ultimately, agriculture in all these countries (including the China of the 1990s) became a troubled "declining sector." But its strong performance earlier provided the necessary resources for industrialization.

In contrast, the different types of agricultural disdain practiced in South Asia and Maoist China cripple a developing economy. The nations in the subcontinent generally ignored agriculture for several decades; in China, Mao's collectivization of agriculture, ostensibly carried out to transform rural society for the better, actually led to breakdowns in production and a stagnating (if not declining) standard of living for the peasantry. However, when some of these countries relented in their disdain, the picture became less bleak. The agricultural reforms of the responsibility system in the PRC were spectacularly successful from the late 1970s through the late 1980s (Harding, 1987). The green revolution in South Asia improved overall agricultural performance considerably (see the data in Chapter 2), although it also created some undesirable social side effects by marginalizing poor and landless peasants (Roy, 1994). In addition, the social investments that China and Sri Lanka made account for their good records on meeting basic human needs, as noted in Chapter 2. Thus, at least for the nations of South and East Asia, investment in agricultural reform and development works; disdain for agriculture does not.

A consideration of how South and East Asia differ in terms of their economic policies shows that each had a fairly consistent policy package. South Asia and Maoist China relied upon bureaucratic leadership that tried to promote industrialization by distorting markets (most particularly, walling off manufactured imports) and short-changing agriculture. As the neoclassicists would predict, this led to fairly poor economic performance. The East Asian capitalist nations and Dengist China did ultimately succeed at a market-conforming EP strategy; however, their export competitiveness did not rest upon laissez-faire. Rather, all had initial periods of import substitution; all except Hong Kong exhibited considerable levels of bureaucratic leadership; and the successful agricultural reforms in East Asia generally required massive amounts of state intervention and violation of property rights. The basic question facing development strategy is not so much the choice between state and market but the more subtle and sophisticated task of blending market and state effectively.

Regional Policy Case Studies: India vs. Taiwan

The previous section presented a broad-brush comparison of two packages of economic policies typical, respectively, of South Asia and of capitalist East Asia. This section attempts to provide a somewhat more detailed and nuanced description of these two policy packages through case studies of India and Taiwan. The former represents a good example of the South Asian approach and the problems it created. The latter is a good example of East Asian dynamism. However, it also demonstrates that the East Asian development model is more contingent and even problematic than is generally recognized, and that neither neoclassicism nor statism provides an adequate depiction of what happened on that "beautiful island."

India

Reflecting its leadership's ideological and anticolonial outlook, India made a strong commitment to use bureaucratic leadership for promoting rapid industrialization through import substitution (in particular, ending the hegemony over the economy exercised by British firms). There have been some liberalization reforms, beginning in the mid-1960s, but many features of the state-led economy remain. As noted in the preceding discussion of import substitution, there was good reason to think that this was a viable strategy when it was initiated. Yet the economic history of the last four decades generally conforms to the neoclassical critique that statism brings economic distortion, political corruption, and far from optimum growth. In short, India was quite successful at expelling the East India Company, but unfortunately this did not prevent the Indian political economy from succumbing to the "British disease."

The Indian development strategy targeted industrial development, with heavy industry being accorded priority; the role of agriculture was downgraded; the share of the public sector in the total investment was continuously raised; and a comprehensive quantitative-restriction regime embracing industrial licensing and trade and exchange controls was implemented. The resulting industrial-planning process worked within a framework of detailed physical targets that made little reference to the concept of costs and benefits. The industrial-licensing system played a key, perhaps the most important, role in the entire development strategy because any entrepreneur obtaining a license to set up a new industry would virtually be guaranteed licenses to import capital goods and raw materials and the required foreign-exchange allocations. Unfortunately, the licensing mechanism was ill designed and concerned with excessive details. Consequently, it contributed to significant delays and usually did not apply any economic criteria in choosing among alternative projects even within the targeted capacities.

Import and foreign-exchange controls also accompanied industrial licensing after the beginning of planned development in 1951 but were implemented more vigorously following the foreign-exchange crisis that engulfed the Indian economy in 1956. However, the system failed to preserve precious foreign exchange, which was one of its prime objectives. Although the direct importing of nonessential consumer goods was greatly reduced, the domestic production of these and other consumer goods required increased foreign-exchange allocations to support other types of imports necessary for their manufacture. The allocative efficiency of the import-control system, which worked on incomplete and unsystematic information without any economic criteria, was also further eroded by the corruption that inevitably arose from the large premiums on imports that the control system generated. Many bogus firms grew only to obtain import licenses and then to sell those at high premiums for making a handsome profit. The control system further added to economic inefficiency and production costs by forcing businesspeople to spend a considerable amount of time in dealing with the bureaucratic apparatus, thereby drawing entrepreneurial talent away from production (Bhagwati and Desai, 1970).

If the IS strategy had been combined with a constructive policy to encourage exports, some of these abuses could have been mitigated during the first fifteen years of Indian planning (1951–1966). However, very little incentive was provided to the export sector during this period. Balusubramanyam and Basu (1990) argue that the primary reason for the neglect of exports and the opportunity to transform domestic savings into investments through foreign trade during the 1950s and early 1960s was the policymakers' allegiance to a very narrow interpretation of the notion of self-reliance that emphasized the need for producing everything that India was capable of producing in principle instead of producing only those goods in which India had comparative advantage. This neglect of the export sector was also due to a great extent to the IS strategy, which created a lucrative domestic market sheltered from competition.

After 1966 (the end of the Third Five-Year Plan) the hold of the IS regime over this economy began to weaken (Balusubramanyam and Basu, 1990). The first step taken in this direction was the devaluation by 10 percent of the rupee to provide it with a realistic rate of exchange. Along with this the industrial-licensing procedure was liberalized, import controls were relaxed, and the export sector was provided with subsidies that included cash subsidies (15% to 20% of FOB), import-replenishment licenses (15% to 30% of FOB), domestic material in international prices (5% to 15% of FOB), drawbacks and rebates (10% to 20% of FOB), and preferential licensing (10% to 20% of FOB).

However, these schemes were just as complicated and bureaucratically administered as the earlier fiscal measures and import-entitlement schemes were. Moreover, their efficiency did not appear to be very high (Lal, 1979). For example, Bagchi's (1981) study of export subsidies reveals that the expenditure incurred for such subsidies amounted to nearly 12 to 13 percent of the value added of the export industries between 1973–1974 and 1977–1978. Consequently, if the value of such other concessions and facilities as import replenishment, concessional railway freight, concessional bank finance, supply of raw materials at subsidized prices, and grants-in-aid extended to exporters are added to the subsidy amount, the total cost of the export-promotion effort would appear very high in relation to the net gain accruing to the country.

In the early 1980s, the Indian economy experienced the emergence of serious payment imbalances, primarily reflecting the sharp increases in oil prices and the precipitous decline in commodity prices. Problems were further compounded by inefficiencies in key economic sectors, infrastructural and industrial bottlenecks, cost–price distortions arising from infrequent adjustment of both administered prices and the exchange rate in the face of domestic inflation, and adverse weather conditions that disrupted agricultural production and interfered with power generation (Agherli et al.,

1987). On the other hand, rising government expenditures propelled by increasing social and development needs created a larger budget deficit, which in turn led to excessive monetary expansion and higher inflationary pressure.

These economic problems stimulated a set of liberalization measures designed to raise domestic savings and investment and to improve the efficiency of production and resource allocation by correcting cost–price distortions, further relaxing industrial regulations, and liberalizing trade policies. In fiscal policy, the government moved to combat the huge budget deficit with measures designed to increase revenues and restrain expenditures. The key factor in these reforms was the alleviation of cost–price distortions, because this improves resource allocation and stimulates production. On the whole in the 1980s, significant progress was made in this area by raising incentives to agriculture, reducing subsidies, and improving the financial position of public enterprises. In 1991, further reforms were implemented. The rupee was devalued about 20 percent, and a substantial dismantling of industrial trade and exchange controls occurred. However, the neglect of agriculture and agrobased industries continues; bureaucratic control over the economy has not dissipated; and strong opposition remains to the measures introducing greater competition and reducing state control over the economy.

Taiwan

In the early 1950s, Taiwan, like India, was a poor, agricultural society. Its initial economic policies differed somewhat but not completely from the Indian model. It actively pursued industrialization through import substitution; the resulting economy, although not planned to the extent of India's, was clearly bureaucratically led and was dominated by state corporations, which accounted for over half of industrial output. In the realm of agricultural policy, however, Taiwan took exactly the opposite strategy of India, putting all its eggs in the basket of agricultural development rather than treating the primary sector with disdain.

Perhaps the most momentous change in Taiwan's early postwar economy came from the radical land reform of the 1950s, which was supplemented by sizeable investments in agriculture and by a large-scale agricultural extension program to stimulate innovation in farming. The result was a sustained increase in agricultural production averaging 5 percent a year in the 1950s and 4.5 perent a year in the 1960s. Agricultural growth, in turn, created enough surplus to help finance the initial spurt of industrialization. While agriculture was serving as a major source of capital for the rest of the economy, increased production was sufficient to support a rising standard of living among farmers. Moreover, the deconcentration of landholdings produced substantial increases in income equality (Ho, 1978; Lee, 1971; Yang, 1970).

In the industrial realm, Taiwan in the early 1950s made a conscious effort to promote import substitution for light industrial products by imposing tariffs and manipulating the exchange rate of the New Taiwan (NT) dollar. This strategy proved quite successful, at least in the short run. Real industrial growth, though quite cyclical, averaged over 10 percent per year during the 1950s; the ratio of imports to total production in the targeted manufactured goods fell drastically; and Taiwan expanded its industrial base from food processing to other light industries (Galenson, 1979; Lin, 1973). However, by the late 1950s, the initial surge of import substitution began to subside as the domestic market became saturated with locally produced goods and as rising imports of capital goods and industrial raw materials increased the trade deficit. As the 1950s ended, therefore, Taiwan clearly faced a threat to its continued economic development, forcing a choice among economic strategies.

It was at this point that Taiwan's economic strategy radically departed from India's by moving in just a few years to an EP strategy. This choice was far from uncontroversial or obvious. Still, a coalition of indigenous technocrats and U.S. advisers convinced Chiang Kai-shek of the necessity for radical reform; a comprehensive set of measures liberalizing the economy was rapidly implemented to encourage exports and investment (Haggard, 1990; Li, 1988; Wade, 1990). This new economic strategy proved to be phenomenally successful, probably far more so than even its ardent advocates had anticipated. Real GNP growth accelerated to a very high average of 11 percent annually during 1963–1973. Furthermore, this rapid growth resulted from a fundamental industrial transformation of the island's economy. For example, between 1958 and 1973, manufacturing's share of net domestic product more than doubled from 16 percent to 36 percent, while that of agriculture suffered a corresponding decline from 31 percent to 14 percent (Galenson, 1979; Haggard, 1990; Ho, 1978; Lin, 1973).

The export-led nature of this economic growth and structural transformation was very clear. Exports surged by an average of 15 percent per year even in inflation-adjusted terms for most of the 1960s, and then skyrocketed by 30 percent annually for 1969–1973. Consequently, their share in GDP almost quadrupled, from 11 percent in 1962 to 42 percent in 1973, indicating that the economy had become extremely export oriented. Taiwan's export mix became overwhelmingly industrial in composition (industrial goods rising from 14% to 85% of total exports between 1958 and 1973), proving that its manufactured products were internationally competitive. Most of these exports went to developed countries, with the U.S. market being by far the largest (rising from 6% in 1958 to 37% of Taiwan's total exports in 1973). The export surge also caused a dramatic change in the country's balance of trade as the large deficits of the late 1950s and early 1960s were turned into surpluses by the early 1970s (Clark, 1989; Galenson, 1979).

The nature of Taiwan's industry changed fundamentally as well, in several important ways. First, the country began to produce a wider range of products that became increasingly sophisticated over time as the leading domestic-production and export sectors advanced from food processing to textiles to electronics assembly and chemicals (Galenson, 1979; Gold, 1986; Ho, 1978). Second, Taiwan's industrial structure has been marked by a much greater role for small and medium family-based enterprises than elsewhere in Asia. It spawned complex subcontracting relationships among small entrepreneurs, reflecting what has recently been called "guerrilla capitalism." This structure of production allowed businesspeople to respond very quickly to market demand, and reduced problems of excess capacity, thus promoting internal competitiveness and external flexibility. The strong role of small business, in addition, helped promote the geographic dispersion of industry in Taiwan; this in turn facilitated socioeconomic equality by enabling underemployed agricultural workers to seek part-time factory work (Greenhalgh, 1988; Kuo, 1995; Lam, 1992; Silin, 1976).

Taiwan's experience also indicates that India's fears of foreign capital may have been exaggerated. Multinational corporations are generally credited with a key role in stimulating Taiwan's export drive, unlike the experience of many other developing nations, where foreign capital simply displaces domestic businesspeople. This resulted from the regime's explicit attempts to harness MNCs to the island's developmental objectives. Thus, the government channeled foreign investment into export industries in which domestic businesses could not compete (most especially electronics), integrated MNCs into the overall economy with domestic-content legislation, and maintained state monopolies in those heavy industries usually dominated by foreigners (Gold, 1986; Haggard and Cheng, 1987; Schive, 1990; Simon, 1992).

This dramatic economic expansion was brought to a sudden halt by the oil crises of 1973–1974 and 1979–1980. Yet Taiwan was able avoid economic devastation; the U.S. recovery in the early 1980s set off a new period of sustained and rapid growth, which required further basic economic transformation because Taiwan was gradually pricing itself out of the low-cost labor niche in the international division of labor. In a structural sense, these emerging industries were diverse. For example, steel was based on a state corporation; petrochemicals involved a complex "triple alliance" among state enterprises, MNCs, and domestic private businesses; and much of the high-tech industry was centered on relatively small, innovative firms.

This restructuring of Taiwan's economy possesses both advantages and dangers. On the one hand, it represents industrial upgrading and a positive response to international competition from other developing countries. Rapid growth also created a large, well-educated middle class that is now making a major contribution to the island's continued economic vitality. On the other hand, ongoing economic transformation threatens the position of small enterprises, which have contributed so much to the island's economic flexibility and success in the past. Moreover, as indicated in Table 2.9, the decline in labor-intensive manufacturing has produced some backsliding in Taiwan's excellent record on income inequality (Chan and Clark, 1992a; Chu, 1989 & 1992; Gold, 1986; Ranis, 1992; Wade, 1990; Wang, 1992; Wu, 1985).

Taiwan's economic miracle, therefore, clearly represents a very successful case of market-conforming export promotion. It is just as clearly not a case of the neoclassical economics conventionally associated with such EP strategies. Rather, the state intervened massively in the economy to promote several vital structural transformations: land reform, import-substitution light industrialization, and the export promotion of an increasingly sophisticated array of light-industry and high-tech goods. Although the state made these strategic decisions about the economy, however, the process was far more contingent and decentralized than advocates of the strong developmental state in Taiwan and East Asia are wont to recognize. First, Taiwan's switch to export promotion represented the outcome of messy and muddled political infighting as much as the imposition of a grand vision. Second, the island's export boom owed far more to the independent sector of small businesses than to direct actions by the state. Finally, the success of Taiwan's EP strategy was almost certainly somewhat fortuitous, because the government opened up the country's economy at precisely the time that the world economy was expanding rapidly and many basic industries in the United States and, to a lesser extent, Japan were being forced offshore because of high labor costs.

Economic Dynamism and Economic Policy

This chapter has compared the economic policies of South and East Asia to explore whether policy differences can explain the much greater economic success of the latter. An examination of South Asia alone provides a picture quite consistent with neoclassical theory. South Asia was marked by a bureaucratic control of the economy that by explicit design followed a strategy that distorted market signals, including turning the terms of trade against the agricultural sector, in order to stimulate import-substitution industrialization. Superficially, East Asia may be seen as simply following the opposite policy track through the market-conforming EP strategy prescribed by laissez-faire economics. Thus, the importance of markets is undeniable.

However, far more was at work in East Asia than simply getting the prices right. Our analysis shows that all the East Asian countries laid the groundwork for economic development in reforming agriculture and developing labor-intensive small and light manufacturing industries, which the South Asian countries failed to do. Some of this simply represented market-conforming policies. For a long time, for example, the East Asian countries kept the scarcity value of capital at a level higher than that of labor, which facilitated the growth of labor-intensive manufacturing and agriculture and the absorption of surplus labor. However, agricultural reform included gross violation of property rights almost everywhere (Dengist China is an exception here); and light industry almost certainly could not have emerged without a decade or so of import substitution, which was not very different from South Asian policies at the same time. Furthermore, the state has continued to exercise substantial bureaucratic leadership in most East Asian economies without producing the dire effects predicted by neoclassical theory.

Yet the developmental state model also suffers from being both too restrictive and too undiscriminating. The statists argue that governmentally imposed strategies and policies form the key to development, but the Taiwan and India case studies challenge this assumption in very different ways. In Taiwan, the important role of small-business entrepreneurship indicates that although state policy created a favorable business environment, the key actors came from the private sector—that is, focusing on official national policy is too restrictive because it does not tell us the entire story. Conversely, the failure of India's development policies demonstrates that simply having a strong developmental state does not guarantee success—that is, focusing on official policy is too undiscriminating because sometimes state schemes work and sometimes they do not. The India case is consistent with a market-and-state model because, at least theoretically, it can be argued that policy failure resulted from the government's selecting a market-distorting rather than a market-conforming strategy (Bhagwati, 1993). The Taiwan case, however, clearly points to the need for a state-in-society perspective, which raises the question of whether such a broader model might illuminate the political economy of India as well.

PART 2

Case Studies of
Asian Political Economies

4

Confucian Capitalism: The Synergism of Market, State, and Society

East Asia has been the site of the most dynamic economies in the world during the postwar period. As demonstrated by the data in Chapter 2, the economic records of these six nations is superlative: high growth, low inflation, high savings and investment rates, a large manufacturing sector, and strong export performance relative to comparable countries. The data on the political variables demonstrate these to be fairly conservative states: relatively small governments with low budget deficits and less than average spending on social welfare and education. This is exactly what neoclassical economists would predict: Small government means better economic performance because small governments create less of an unproductive drag on the economy than do large governments. Moreover, these putatively conservative policies evidently did not incur the social costs that most liberals believe are brought by raw capitalism; the Confucian-capitalist countries have average to very good ratings on a wide variety of indicators concerning population growth, income distribution, education, and health. In short, if one simply looks at statistical data, East Asia might appear a neoclassical nirvana!

However, the interpretation of East Asia as a neoclassical success story is based on the assumption that laissez-faire economies dominate the region; in fact, massive state interventions are found in almost all of these economies. The currently dominant interpretation of the East Asian economic miracles attributes them to the leadership of strong and autonomous developmental states that have created, to use Robert Wade's (1990) felicitous phrase, "governed markets." But Chapters 2 and 3 showed that the developmental state model is just as open to criticism for leaving out critical explanatory factors as is the neoclassical approach. For example, the theory of guerrilla capitalism that has been used to explain Taiwan's export success depicts that economy as highly flexible and competitive precisely because it is ungoverned and perhaps ungovernable.

Beyond the aggregate data a much different picture emerges. Confucian capitalism is associated with a seemingly cohesive set of cultural values, economic strategies, social structures, and political institutions. Economic

61

strategy has generally emphasized expanding exports and finding niches of comparative advantage in the global economy, rather than using protectionism to pursue import substitution or the reliance upon internal markets. In terms of sectoral phasing, most of the countries have moved upward along the international product cycle from light to heavy to high-technology industries over fairly brief time spans, indicating that their comparative advantages are far from static. Finally, this economic success has rested upon corporate and business strategies of flexible production, rather than the dominant emphasis upon "Fordism" or mass production in the West.

The East Asian societies have been marked by comparatively equal distributions of income and opportunities for upward mobility, strong proclivities for entrepreneurship, and a heavy emphasis on education that promotes the creation of human capital. Politically, the state has taken a leading role in structuring the economy and targeting leading sectors (Hong Kong excepted); most of the countries have been marked by a high level of political stability that is remarkable in the developing world; and authoritarian governments of varying hues and rationales have predominated. (Political life in even democratic Japan was dominated by one continuously ruling party, the LDP, until 1993.) These economic, social, and political characteristics, in addition, are undergirded by the region's Confucian culture, whose values promote respect for authority, merit-based mobility, family entrepreneurship, and, in Japan, "groupist" dynamics that seem perfectly suited for large-scale corporations and bureaucracies (Chan, 1993; Chu, 1989; Cumings, 1984; Deyo, 1987; Gereffi and Wyman, 1990; Haggard, 1990; Hofheinz and Calder, 1982; Kuznets, 1988; Pye with Pye, 1985; Wade, 1990).

This brief overview of the East Asian development model suggests that the neoclassical and developmental state paradigms possess both important insights and distinct limitations in explicating East Asian dynamism. From the neoclassical perspective, rapid growth in East Asia depended for the most part on attaining and maintaining competitiveness on international markets; entrepreneurship in the form of rapid response to market signals has played a key role in keeping East Asia at the cutting edge of the competitiveness race. Yet there is far more to the story. State policies have made a key contribution, too—which would appear to belie neoclassical assumptions. Such a positive role for the state, however, does not necessarily imply that the developmental state model should be accepted uncritically. The East Asian experience demonstrates the importance of human-capital development, business strategies and practices, and the nature of state–society relations—all of which turn attention to the emerging state-in-society perspective.

More theoretically, the economic and political institutions that seem to explain the East Asian economic miracle are embedded within a broader cultural and social framework; their contribution to economic growth is much more contextually determined and contingent than either the neo-classical or the statist model assumes. Despite the familiar terms *Confucian capitalism* and the *East Asian development model,* substantial variations exist in the development strategies and trajectories of these nations. This is not inconsistent with the neoclassical prescription to follow comparative advantage or the statist prescription for governed markets, but the overviews of the various East Asian political economies that follow make a strong case for interpreting East Asian dynamism as a synergism of market, state, *and* society.

Initially, the Cold War division of East Asia created two groups of nations, each following radically different economic paths. China, North Korea, and (to a much lesser extent) North Vietnam implemented orthodox Stalinist policies of forced-draft industrialization; Japan, Hong Kong, Taiwan, South Korea, and Singapore followed the capitalist road. At the aggregate level this resulted in a neoclassical parable of tortoise and hare. The communist countries' industrialization resulted in short-term rapid growth but long-term inefficiency, bureaucratization, and decay. Consequently, they sprinted ahead like the proverbial hare, but then collapsed by the side of the road as the capitalist tortoises chugged past. Ultimately, China in the 1980s and Vietnam in the 1990s became turtles by adopting radical marketization reforms that allowed them to join the world of East Asian dynamism. To add a third small animal to the fable, the command economies were penalized for trying to "leap-frog" up the international product cycle into advanced industries in which they had no comparative advantage. Their inefficient heavy industries could only operate if they were shielded from international competition—which in turn removed any incentive for becoming more efficient. The moral would seem clear: Little frogs should stay in small ponds.

In regard to the five capitalist countries, however, this neat parable breaks down. Only Hong Kong followed anything close to a laissez-faire path; and, in the end, this strategy seemed to produce declining dynamism. In contrast, Japan, South Korea, and Singapore proved extremely adept at leap-frog. Far from becoming bumbling bunnies, they turned into mutant ninja turtles who proved highly adept at fighting in the wars of international economic competition. Thus, these East Asian nations learned to play capitalism in a different way; and the numbers on the economic scoreboard show that they play it quite competitively, neoclassical naysaying notwithstanding.

Communist Roaders: A Neat Neoclassical Fable

The Communist regimes that took power in China, North Korea, and North Vietnam in the late 1940s and early 1950s were committed to rapid industrial development to eradicate underdevelopment. In their view, the colonial and neocolonial domination of these countries had kept them dependent, primarily agricultural, and quite poor. Rapid industrialization would make these countries powerful once again and would create the resources to raise the standard of living and establish a much more equitable society.

Both China and North Korea implemented orthodox Stalinist development strategies of forced-draft industrialization centered on heavy industry such as steel, state ownership of the means of production, and full-scale planning in a command economy (An, 1989; Cheng, 1982; Kim, 1992; Lardy, 1978; Prybyla, 1981). As in the Soviet Union and Eastern Europe, this strategy proved effective in the early resource-mobilization era when state power could concentrate resources in a limited number of high-priority projects. The resulting explosion of industrial and managerial positions provided broad avenues for upward social mobility that were open to most of the population, in part because of substantial regime investments in education. Once the industrial base was laid, however, the economy became increasingly inefficient, both because it is probably impossible to plan a sophisticated industrial economy and because the administrative elite resisted necessary reforms that would make them obsolete (Clark and Bahry, 1983).

This sequence played out somewhat differently in China and North Korea. In communist Korea, primitive socialist accumulation seemed (information about North Korea being sparse) to go quite well. By the mid-1960s the North and South Korean economies were considered to be somewhat on a par—both operating fairly well to promote rapid growth. In fact, North Korea's industrial push commenced earlier, and through the late 1960s it had a significantly higher GNP per capita (see the data in Table 4.1).

From this high point, however, North Korea entered a period of gradual but steepening economic decline as its industries became increasingly inefficient and obsolete but remained protected by the "ossified thinking" (to use a Soviet phrase) of the all-powerful Kim Il-sung (An, 1989; Kim, 1992). The tremendous difference between the export dynamism of South Korea and North Korea's trade-adverse autarchy is especially evident in Table 4.1; the value of the South's exports skyrocketed from twice that of the North's in 1970 to a fifteenfold advantage in 1980. Thus, by the early 1990s the Korean peninsula had witnessed a stark contrast between the communist developmental state in the North, which had failed, and the capitalist developmental state in South Korea, which had succeeded despite its regime being "reinvented" several times. Still, North Korea's socialism did appear to have some significant payoffs in terms of promoting social equity, because it still scores approximately the same as the much richer South on many social indicators (Kim, 1992, in addition to the data

Table 4.1 Comparison of Economic Development in North and South Korea

	1953	1960	1970	1980	1988
GNP per capita					
North Korea	$55	$208	$312	$1,000	$1,260
South Korea	$56	$60	$264	$1,553	$3,850
Agriculture percent GNP					
North Korea	42%	24%	20%	25%[a]	—
South Korea	46%	37%	28%	16%[a]	—
Industrial percent GNP					
North Korea	31%	57%	65%	70%[a]	—
South Korea	10%	16%	23%	31%[a]	—
Exports[b]					
North Korea	—	—	$0.4	$1.1	$1.4[c]
South Korea	—	—	$0.8	$15.1	$30.2[c]
Infant mortality per 1,000 live births					
North Korea	—	63[d]	—	—	27[c]
South Korea	—	63[d]	—	—	27[c]
Doctors per 100 people					
North Korea	—	—	—	24[a]	—
South Korea	—	—	—	6[a]	—
Income inequality[e]					
North Korea	—	—	—	—	3.8
South Korea	—	—	—	—	7.2

Source: Kim, 1992: 67, 75, 81, 90 & 95.
Notes: a. 1982.
b. Billions of U.S. dollars.
c. 1985.
d. 1965.
e. Ratio of the income of the richest fifth of the population to that of the poorest fifth.

in Table 4.1). South Korea, in turn, was an overachiever in social development compared with other nations at equivalent levels of development.

Development in China has followed a pattern that is far less smooth. In some ways, the Maoist period (1949–1976) can be considered one of orthodox communism. However, Mao Zedong's penchant for leading revolutions against his own bureaucracy created several sustained periods of upheaval and chaos that were the antithesis of a planned and bureaucratic command economy. When the Communists took power in 1949, they implemented a strikingly dualistic policy toward social groups of "eradication or conciliation." Groups that were seen as enemies, most importantly former officials of the Kuomintang (KMT) regime and rural landlords, were mercilessly persecuted and often summarily executed. (Estimates of how many were killed run into the millions.) In surprising contrast, however, the Chinese Communist Party (CCP) appealed to most other groups—peasants, industrial workers, intellectuals, small businesspeople, and even the "national bourgeoisie"—to help in the reconstruction of a new, strong

Chinese economy and polity. Because of their alliance with the Soviet Union, the Chinese Communists decided to construct a political economy of orthodox Stalinism: a rapid drive to create a heavy-industry base; the transformation of agriculture first by land reform and soon thereafter by collectivization; a state-operated economy based on command planning; and political control exercised through the CCP (Cheng, 1982; Eckstein, 1977; Lardy, 1978; Prybyla, 1981; Schurmann, 1966).

These new institutions did not operate in a social vacuum. Rather, they helped the regime consolidate its power through the creation of what Andrew Walder (1986) has called "communist neotraditionalism." The employment structure of China is not merely a market relationship in which work is traded for pay. Industrial firms provide access to housing, insurance, and preferential market sources, in addition to lifetime employment that, until recently, often could be passed on from one generation to another—the so-called iron rice bowl. The system was also based on patron–client networks, instead of impersonal relations, which linked the individual into the much broader economic and political systems through their enterprise superiors (Pye, 1988). In the countryside, the clientelistic links were even stronger because rural cadres were directly integrated into the extensive networks, often kinship based, that were at the center of village life (Oi, 1989).

Initially, therefore, the political economy of the PRC might be considered fairly successful. State socialism concentrated resources for a major industrialization push that extended the iron rice bowl to a sizable number of workers; many peasants evidently benefited from the new agricultural system; the state provided education and highly subsidized basic amenities (e.g., housing and food); and many people were linked into the new communist economy and polity through clientelistic relationships similar to those that dominated traditional Confucian society. In fact, many Chinese look back to the mid-1950s as the best of times. China's record in the 1980s as an extreme overachiever on most of the social indicators that were presented in Chapter 2 indicates that the Maoist period laid a strong foundation of human capital. This undoubtedly made a major contribution to the impressive growth of the Dengist period.

Given the growing rigidity and inefficiency in other state-socialist countries, China's long-term stability can certainly be doubted. However, the system was attacked before it could really begin to ossify, by Mao Zedong's drive to achieve "permanent revolution" and radicalize Chinese society. Whether Maoism derived more from the power struggles among CCP elite factions, or from Mao's personal psychoses, or from his representing the anti-Confucian, mystical, and rebellious Chinese populist culture (White, 1989) is highly arguable and probably immaterial for our purposes. What is important is that Mao's initiatives—the anti-Rightist campaign, the Great Leap Forward, and the Cultural Revolution—attacked almost every social constituency that the state-socialist political economy had created. CCP technocrats were dragged out; peasants saw their social environment destroyed by the Great Leap Forward; intellectuals and the national bourgeoisie were persecuted; and even the proletariat saw its iron rice bowl threatened by economic chaos. The result was the near destruction of Chinese society and a bewildered and alienated population.

> Chinese who came through the cataclysms of the past thirty years seemed to me like survivors. They were chastened and cynical and numb. When I asked friends how they had coped with their personal tragedies, they often answered, *"Ma-mu-le"* (I was numbed). "Surviving" is a word they frequently used. It reminded me of a passage [from the wall poster of Li Yizhe]. "We are survivors," the three men had written. "We were once bitten by the tiger but it failed to grind us small enough to swallow. Its claws left scars on our faces, so we are not handsome." They spoke for the many Chinese I met who had all been clawed by the tiger [Butterfield, 1982: 19–20].

The moral of this fable appears consistent with the neoclassical view of the world. Nations try to fool Mother Nature, in the form of the comparative advantage engendered by the normal operation of the international product cycle, at their peril. Political intervention and protection may allow industries and economic institutions to be established, but if these are not "natural" they will almost assuredly fail. In fact, their political nature means that they will seek more political protection to cover up their inefficiency, in a process analogous to increasing dependence on crack cocaine. But Mother Nature will win out in the end. Ultimately, crack heads, racing rabbits, and leaping frogs keel over from heart attacks, leaving the world to their more virtuous competitors.

Hong Kong and (Perhaps) Taiwan: Turtles Can Sprint

The contrast between the communist command economies and Hong Kong could not be greater. The British colony is generally perceived (with more than a little but not total justification) to represent an almost purely neoclassical vision of a laissez-faire economy because the British colonial administration traditionally refrained from active economic intervention until quite recently, when issues of Hong Kong's impending integration into the PRC became paramount (Rabushka, 1979). Even where the state intervenes in the economy in a manner not usually countenanced by neoclassicists, the result appears to help private business. Contrary to the popular view of a minimalist state, Hong Kong's government has always underwritten a large public-housing sector. However, this investment is usually viewed not as an unproductive social expenditure but as an indirect subsidy to business, which can pay lower wages because of the artificially low housing costs in the colony (Schiffer, 1991).

A case, although a much more debatable one, might also be made that Taiwan provides another example of primarily market-driven development. As described in the case study in Chapter 3, after the initial massive interventions of the land reform and import substitution, the state's primary role in Taiwan's economic development since the 1950s has been to provide macroeconomic incentives for the subsequent structural transformations and to marshal resources for industrial upgrading into heavy and high-tech industries. This might be considered a market-conforming approach to state economic leadership, which even advocates of neoclassical policy now see as marking East Asia's successful development (Roumasset and Barr, 1992; World Bank, 1993), although such an interpretation has been challenged from a variety of perspectives (Chan and Clark, 1992a; Chu, 1989; Gold, 1986; Haggard, 1990; Wade, 1990; Winckler and Greenhalgh, 1988).

Hong Kong's developmental trajectory represents a series of market adjustments that first stimulated and then depressed manufacturing "on the rock." The 1949 communist victory in China both forced Hong Kong to reorient its entrepot economy and provided the human capital for export-oriented light industrialization. The entrepreneurial talent came in the form of refugee textile manufacturers from Shanghai who combined their knowledge of the industry with the marketing power of British trading companies (or *hong*). Refugees from China also provided Hong Kong's primary comparative advantage for light industry: its abundant and skilled but very cheap labor force. Thus, labor-intensive light industry has formed the most dynamic core of the city-state's rapid growth for most of the postwar period.

The next upgrading of Hong Kong's economy involved foreign corporations, both directly and indirectly. In the late 1950s, U.S. retailers (e.g., Sears, Penney, and Ward) came to Hong Kong when the relevant Western patents expired; they helped to start a local electronics industry by showing domestic firms how to assemble final products from components made elsewhere, particularly in Japan. This in turn stimulated U.S. producers to move their production to places such as Hong Kong in order to meet competitive pricing. Over time, Hong Kong's manufacturers (both domestic and foreign) moved into more sophisticated production, but industry in Hong Kong remained essentially labor-intensive because of the large pool of workers that continued to be augmented by Chinese immigrants (Krause, 1988; Rabushka, 1979; Wong, 1988).

The backbone of Hong Kong's dynamic export economy has been a multitude of small and medium enterprises (SMEs), many of them family owned and operated. As in Taiwan (where SMEs produced about two-thirds of total exports during the 1980s), these small firms pursue highly entrepreneurial strategies that have been termed guerrilla capitalism. Guerrilla capitalism is characterized by extreme flexibility in rapidly filling even small orders, attention to quality and design, audacious bidding, participation in complex networks of subcontracting, and only partial observation at best of government regulations and international laws, such as those regarding intellectual-property rights. The SMEs have also demonstrated a remarkable capacity to innovate and to upgrade their operations. Guerrilla capitalism took off in the textile and shoe industries in the 1960s and moved into low-tech electronics assembly in the 1970s; some firms were able to upgrade into more sophisticated high-tech production in the 1980s.

An important reason for the flexibility of these small firms is the extensive use of subcontracting networks among ostensible competitors, facilitated by the prevailing pattern of ownership in which many firms in a particular industry own each other's shares. Subcontracting enhances the efficiency of the market in two ways. First, it allows the winning contractor to make above-normal profits, through knowledge of the local industry, by subcontracting to firms that have surplus capacity that they will sell at marginal rather than full cost. Second, it keeps other firms in business and allows them to become more efficient through experience. This process explains how a layer of small firms can circumvent the limitations that would normally be placed on them by undercapitalization and the inability to handle large orders.

Guerrilla capitalism also explains how a substantial amount of technology was transferred from foreign MNCs to domestic firms in such fields as electronics in which local businesspeople had no initial expertise. Most MNCs hired a significant number of indigenous administrators because of cost considerations. These local managers soon realized that, in fact, the MNC operations were not highly sophisticated. Managers who worked in assembly operations quickly saw that there was little that was beyond their own capability to set up with fairly small amounts of capital. Naturally, many of them jumped at the opportunity and left their MNC employers to establish assembly operations on their own. Sometimes this was done entirely independently, sometimes in collaboration with a few colleagues, and sometimes with the support of large local conglomerates who wished to enter a new business. These new entrants then competed for subcontracts for subassembly from other firms. Over time, these relatively unsophisticated manufacturers learned to build more and more complex assemblies, created or purchased designs, and ultimately began to manufacture full assemblies for simple consumer electronics such as radios. Gradually their expertise improved enough for them to build tape recorders, stereos, and other more sophisticated electronic consumer goods

(Greenhalgh, 1984 & 1988; Lam, 1990b & 1992; Lam and Clark, 1994; Lam and Lee, 1992; Wong, 1986 & 1988).

An important testimony to the competitiveness of Hong Kong's small firms is the surprisingly minor role of foreign capital in Hong Kong's overall economy, despite what would appear to be an extremely attractive business environment in a booming economy for almost the entire postwar era. The policy of laissez-faire has been applied to MNCs as well as to the domestic economy. Hong Kong's government does not as a matter of policy treat local and foreign investors by different standards; and it has not sought to erect entry or exit barriers that discriminate against foreign businesses. Yet in the late 1980s MNCs accounted for only 12 percent of Hong Kong's exports; most of Hong Kong's trade is now handled by small import-export firms rather than the large (and foreign) British hong. Ultimately, however, Hong Kong's basic assembly operations began to be priced out of international competition in the late 1970s as growing prosperity brought higher wages. In the 1980s many Hong Kong entrepreneurs saved their businesses by moving production to the newly opened PRC, where more than half of Hong Kong's manufactures are now actually made.

The experiences of Hong Kong and, to a lesser extent, Taiwan can be seen as validating neoclassical arguments that playing by the rules of the free market leads to sustained economic development. Moreover, the rapidity of their growth trajectories suggests that tortoises can move almost as quickly as hares. Yet even these two cases do not lend unalloyed credence to laissez-faire economics. For Hong Kong, market forces ultimately threatened deindustrialization and economic decline, although it is unclear whether these adjustment problems would have emerged in the absence of the disruptions caused by the colony's retrocession to the PRC. More positively, even the hypercompetitiveness of the SMEs in Hong Kong and Taiwan do not really represent laissez-faire, for two reasons. In microeconomic terms, the strong relationships among these firms clearly violates the neoclassical assumption of arms-length transactions among separate and competing firms. More broadly, the emergence of guerrilla capitalism in East Asia (as opposed to South Asia or Latin America) is normally assumed to reflect special social and cultural factors that are considered extraneous and irrelevant by neoclassicalism.

On a more macrotheoretical level, rapid development in Taiwan can only be explained by a state-in-society perspective that examines the interaction of variables within market, state, and society. Land reform and import substitution in Taiwan appear to have been prerequisite for the subsequent, more market-driven stages of development. The former spurred agricultural productivity, creating the capital resources for industrialization; the latter allowed Taiwan to develop the light industries that became the basis for the export boom. This implies that (at least for some stages of development) industrial policy may be vital for stimulating economic growth and structural transformation. Taiwan's development history provides a more fundamental challenge to neoclassical economics, however, because it shows that economic, social, and political change are deeply intertwined. The economic institutions that made Taiwan competitive at its various stages of industrialization were created by intricate "path dependencies" upon previous policies and outcomes (Teece, 1990). "Institutional economics" (North, 1990), therefore, would appear far more appropriate for conceptualizing the Taiwan development model than would its neoclassical alternative.

The relationships among the interacting political, economic, and social changes in Taiwan are sketched in Figure 4.1. The initial commitment of an authoritarian regime of "Mainlanders" (i.e., those who evacuated to Taiwan with Chiang Kai-shek) to promote development led to policies that were to transform the political economy of Taiwan radically, far beyond the intentions or desires of the regime. These policies included the land reform (which itself was probably motivated in part by a desire to destroy the economic base of a potential "Islander" counterelite of landlords) and the co-optation of technocrats into the top levels of government. When the technocrats opened the economy in the early 1960s, economic change interacted with the potential for Confucian entrepreneurialism to promote export-led growth based on low-tech "flexible production," which in turn created a new counterelite in the form of the Islander business community, and a surprising degree of socioeconomic equality. An educated, middle-class society then emerged that provided the human capital for Taiwan's climb up the international product cycle and pressured the regime toward democratization. However, in a more democratic but corrupt polity the power of businesspeople can distort the economy because the government has less autonomy from dominant social interests. This is especially true at present, when Taiwan is facing a new imperative for structural adjustment to maintain its comparative advantage in the global economy (Chan and Clark, 1992a, present this model in detail).

Japan: Breaking the Western Economists' Rules

Japan represents the polar opposite of Hong Kong along several important dimensions. It is a large nation (in population if not in area) rather than a small city-state. Consequently, it can rely on internal markets for industrial products in a manner that is simply not possible for tiny Hong Kong. In contrast to laissez-faire Hong Kong, Japan is generally viewed as possessing a highly interventionist developmental state. Its industrial structure is

Figure 4.1 Interacting Dynamics Among Social, Political, and Economic Change in Taiwan

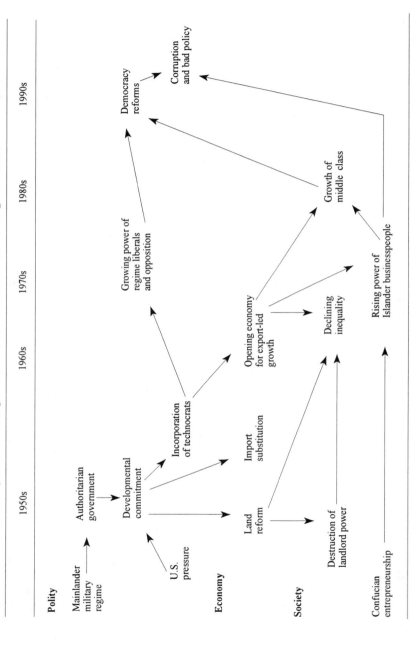

also much different in that it is dominated by large conglomerates, or *keiretsu,* as opposed to the guerrilla capitalists of the city-state. Finally, Japan has a democratic government that must be more responsive to the public than does a colonial administration. Given these great differences, one would expect that the dynamics of Japan's rapid growth would depart markedly from those exhibited by Hong Kong; and, indeed, this seems to be the case. In contrast to the neoclassical path of the city-state, Japan consciously rejected the models and advice of Western economics. A leading MITI official's reflections on the "Japanese miracle" make this point nicely (Prestowitz, 1988: 128):

> We did the opposite of what American economists said. We violated all the normal concepts.

Yet Japan was similar to Hong Kong and Taiwan in the early 1950s in its basic economic conditions. Unlike Hong Kong and Taiwan, it had been an industrial power before World War II, but wartime destruction resulted in a poor country with not much functioning industry but with a potentially educated and very cheap work force. This suggests a comparative advantage in labor-intensive light industry. Indeed, as in Hong Kong and Taiwan, such light industries as textiles played a crucial role in Japan's postwar industrial recovery and dominated its early exports. However, the Japanese government was not content to let international comparative advantage limit it to what was perceived as a tortoise-like climb up the international product cycle. Rather, it decided to play leap-frog. The results turned out to be decidedly different from those in China and North Korea, as Nester (1991: 79) neatly summarizes:

> Japan is [now] the world's leading producer of steel, machine-tools, and automobiles. By the early 1950s, Tokyo had targeted all three for development as strategic industries, and over the next four decades nurtured them with a range of subsidies, cartels, technology incentives, cheap loans, import barriers, and export incentives. None of these industries would have survived had they been exposed to free-market forces— American and European producers held a comparative advantage in all three industries up through the mid-1960s and would have wiped out their struggling Japanese rivals. However, the success of these industrial policies varied widely, with those targeting steel and automobiles being remarkable successes while those promoting the machine-tool industry had a more limited effect—machine-tools is one of Japan's few industries whose success depended as much upon entrepreneurship as cartels, government handouts, and import barriers.

Japan's attempt to play leap-frog did not fulfill the prophecies of neoclassical economics by producing the inefficient factories manifested by

Mao's China and Kim Il-sung's Korea. Instead, within three decades at least a few Western scholars were hailing *Japan as Number One* (Vogel, 1979), suggesting the emergence of an extremely competitive economy (which might fancifully be described as a mutant ninja turtle ready, willing, and able to shoot past any hare in sight).

One reason for Japan's success, as indicated by Nester's preceding summary, has been the assistance that the state has rendered to specific industries and firms in myriad forms of subsidized finance, Research and Development (R&D) support, market cartelization, protection against imports, and extremely hard-nosed trade bargaining. The government, moreover, has targeted specific industries and even firms for such support, positioning the nation to move into increasingly sophisticated and higher-value-added production, reflecting what Richard Samuels (1994) terms "technonationalism" in an interactive merging of commercial and military development. In particular, Japan's initial import-substitution policies, which were adopted with U.S. approval to revive the economy in the 1950s, have continued, even as the nation has benefited from booming exports over the past three decades. Controls on foreign capital were quite stringent up through the early 1980s (e.g., licensing of technology to Japanese firms was made a condition for doing business there); although formal trade barriers were cut, many informal nontariff barriers (NTBs) have remained. Japan has clearly benefited from a developmental state (Johnson, 1982; Prestowitz, 1988).

But the fact that Japan had a government committed to rapid industrialization cannot explain why it leap-frogged so successfully while China and North Korea failed so miserably. After all, they subsidized their industries and walled them off from foreign competition to a far greater extent. A telling comparison with the free-market United States is probably even more relevant for challenging the neoclassical claim that protection and subsidy stimulate inefficiency and monopoly rents. When Japan protected and pushed its semiconductor industry in the mid-1970s, it responded by rapidly catching up with and surpassing the United States'; when the U.S. automobile industry got protection in the form of a voluntary export restraint (VER) from Japan in the early 1980s, it paid its executives large bonuses and awaited the major thumping that it received a few years later (Keller, 1989; Prestowitz, 1988).

To say that the Japanese state pursued a market-conforming strategy is nearly tautological because it begs the question of why industrial policy did not produce the market distortions to which it could easily give rise. Rather than focusing upon just the state, therefore, attention needs to be directed to other aspects of the economy. Indeed, the nature of Japanese firms and the industrial and market structure of Japan provide a convincing explanation for why Japanese corporations did not simply extract rents from state assistance. For example, Bennett Harrison (1994: 151) concludes:

While there can no longer be any question that modern Japanese economic development has been promoted by an activist government, the innovative production networks of that country are best understood as substantially private in nature.

Japanese management practices are given considerable credit for the strong performance of its enterprises. One important characteristic is the concentration upon the quality of products and the continuous upgrading of process technology in a system of total quality management, or TQM, and flexible production—both of which contrast greatly with the traditional Western "mass-production ethic" of winning markets through low-cost, medium-quality goods. The ability of Japanese firms to pursue TQM and flexible production (which, ironically, were brought to Japan by the U.S. engineer Edwards Deming during the Occupation) rests upon a paternalistic management system that builds strong bonds of employee loyalty through such practices as lifetime employment (which is confined to approximately one-third of the work force in large corporations) and "quality circles," which involve workers in key production decisions. In addition, because of the strong company–worker ties, Japanese corporations invest far more than do U.S. firms in the training that their well-educated workers need to be flexible without the fear that they will leave for better jobs (Hofheinz and Calder, 1982; Okimoto, 1989; Prestowitz, 1988; Reischauer, 1988). Table 4.2, for example, shows that Japan has become a high-wage economy, unlike the Little Dragons, whose wage levels relative to GNP per capita are generally much lower than Japan's. Japan's comparative advantage is now a high-quality work force making high-quality products.

Japanese firms operate within an economy that is structured quite distinctively; the nature of its firms and markets explains why its business strategies have been so competitive. Unlike the economies of Hong Kong and Taiwan, in which small firms form the dynamic core, Japan's economy is organized around six huge "intermarket" keiretsu. These conglomerates include firms in major industries (electronics, chemicals, construction, machinery), a large bank, and one of Japan's famous foreign-trading companies, which own stock in each other and give each other preference in doing

Table 4.2   Average Annual Industrial Wages, 1987

Japan	$22,458
Taiwan	$5,290
Singapore	$5,087
South Korea	$4,224
Hong Kong	$3,460
Malaysia	$1,560

Source: Kang, 1989: 51.

business. In addition, there are "supply keiretsu" in industries involving multiple stages of production, such as electronics and automobiles. Corporations such as Toyota, Sony, and NEC organize huge numbers of suppliers in long-term "relational" contracting. In 1980, for example, Toyota had 168 first-tier subcontractors, 4,700 second-tier subcontractors, and 31,600 third-tier subcontractors. The parent firm diffuses technology and quality-control techniques to its suppliers, creating a reciprocal relationship. The parent is guaranteed high-quality components, and the assured sales permit the suppliers to invest in retooling and technological upgrading. To make the keiretsus even more encompassing, most of the supply keiretsus are associated with an intermarket one. Tables 4.3 and 4.4 depict this conglomerate organization. Table 4.3 presents the major members of the Sumitomo intermarket group, which includes NEC, and Table 4.4 lists some of the major companies in NEC's supply network (Gerlach, 1992; Harrison, 1994; Hofheinz and Calder, 1982; Okimoto, 1989; Womack et al., 1990).

The nature of the keiretsu system explains several features of firm behavior that contribute to international competitiveness. First, the internal market is extremely competitive. Major corporations with huge resources behind them fight for almost every market segment, keeping the pressure up for continuous improvement in quality and cost, that is, for flexible production rather than mass production. Accordingly, corporate strategy focuses upon market share rather than on short-term profits. Japan's corporations are able to take a more long-term or strategic perspective, furthermore, because of the nature of corporate financing. Unlike the equity-based financing in the United States, Japan's corporate finance is much more debt-based—which is where the keiretsu banks come to play a key role. While U.S. executives must look to how the quarterly "bottom line" will play on the stock markets, keiretsu banks form a "deep-pockets" partner for other conglomerate members. Moreover, capital is significantly cheaper in Japan than in the United States, providing another incentive for high levels of investment (Gerlach, 1992; Hofheinz and Calder, 1982; Okimoto, 1989; Prestowitz, 1988; Zysman, 1983).

This industrial and financial system enhances Japan's international competitiveness in several ways. When new products are being developed, such as semiconductors were in the 1970s, keiretsu partners form an assured market that greatly reduces the risk of investing heavily in the new technology. There is little chance of hostile takeover, so the danger of the "casino capitalism" that rocked Wall Street in the 1980s is minimized. At least until the late 1980s the incentive system drove corporations toward production rather than speculation. The fierce domestic competition naturally pushes Japan's corporations into export markets, where they hold an advantage because of their corporate strategies and lower concern with short-term profits; where this slips over into predatory dumping remains uncertain (Prestowitz, 1988; Tyson, 1992).

Table 4.3   The Sumitomo Business Conglomerate

Banking Sumitomo Bank **Trading** Sumitomo Corporation **Metals** Sumitomo Metal Industries Sumitomo Electric Industries Sumitomo Metal Mining Sumitomo Light Metal Industries **Electrical and Electronics** NEC Corporation **Machinery** Sumitomo Heavy Industries **Cement and Glass** Sumitomo Cement Nippon Sheet Glass	**Chemicals** Sumitomo Chemical Sumitomo Bakelite **Construction** Sumitomo Construction **Finance and Insurance** Sumitomo Trust and Banking Sumitomo Marine and Fire Insurance Sumitomo Life Insurance **Real Estate and Warehousing** Sumitomo Realty and Development Sumitomo Warehouse **Mining and Forestry** Sumitomo Coal Mining Sumitomo Forestry

Source: Harrison, 1994: 152.

Table 4.4   The NEC Supply Keiretsu

Telecommunications
Nippon Avionics
Nitsuko
Japan Aviation Electronics
    Industry, Ltd.
Meisei Electric
Nico Electronics
Anritsu Electric
Toyo Communications
    Equipment
NEC Yonezawa
 	
Information Processing
NEC-Toshiba Information
    Systems
NEC Data Machine
NEC Lingual Processing
    Systems
 	
Consumer Electronics
Shin Nihon Denki
	Power Electrical Machinery
	Meidensha Electric
	    Manufacturing
	Nippon Electric Industry
	
	Parts and Components
	Ando Electric
	NEC Anelva
	Kaijo Electric
	NEC Sanei Instruments
	Tohoku Metal Industries
	Tama Electric Industries
	Nippon Electric Glass
	Shinko Shoji
	Ryosan Co.
	Tohoku Kako
	
	Other
	NEC Systems Integration
	    and Construction, Ltd.
	NEC Lease

Source: Harrison, 1994: 154

At least until the late 1980s this economic system also dovetailed well with the organization of the polity, creating a highly effective political economy. Industrial policy was set by consensus between business leaders and permanent technocrats in Japan's leading ministries (such as MITI; the Ministry of Post and Communications, or MPT; and the Ministry of

Finance, or MOF). Because these relationships were reciprocal and consensual, the technocrats were able to keep corporate Japan honest, and the business community was able to keep government officials from making egregious errors of judgment. Such benign industrial or strategic trade policy was possible, furthermore, because it was generally isolated from the hurly-burly of Japan's electoral politics (Calder, 1988; Johnson, 1982; Okimoto, 1989; Prestowitz, 1988; Samuels, 1987).

Technocrats and their big-business allies were able to rule because of the strategy used by the Liberal Democratic Party (LDP) to maintain power throughout almost the entire postwar period. Despite its name, the LDP is a conservative, probusiness party; however, it retained power by periodically reaching out to new constituencies with what appeared to be liberal policies of assistance in what Kent Calder (1988) has insightfully called a pattern of "crisis and compensation." That is, economic (or political) crisis would erode the electoral base of the LDP, which would respond by extending benefits to a new constituency; this was viewed by business as an acceptable cost for maintaining political stability. This is the classic model of patronage politics that is usually considered antithetical to promoting economic efficiency. In Japan, however, an ingenious system evolved in which the patronage politics and the artificially high prices or rents that it generated were limited to sectors not involved in international trade (e.g., agriculture, construction, domestic retailing), while technocratic control over major export industries based on business–bureaucracy consultative ties was preserved (Calder, 1988; Okimoto, 1989).

Japan, in sum, has been in the forefront of a revolution in network production and flexible production that is reorienting the way the world does business, away from the microeconomic competition championed by neoclassical economics (Harrison, 1994; Piore and Sabel, 1984; Reich, 1991). In addition, it was an important case in Jeffrey Hart's (1992) comparative study that led him to conclude that political economies in which some type of cooperation occurred among business, government, and labor were more effective than in nations in which one is predominant. Japan, therefore, appears representative of what is probably the most telling criticism of neoclassical economics—that it does not understand how the game of capitalism is played in the real world.

Japan's political economy also indicates the limitations of the statist approach, which is ironic because it is often taken as the epitome of a successful developmental state, for good or for ill (Fallows, 1994; Johnson, 1982; Prestowitz, 1988; Vogel, 1979). First, the power of the state to direct the economy declined from the 1950s and 1960s, when state leadership was quite pronounced, to the 1980s and early 1990s, when business relations with the major ministries had become much more collaborative and consensual (Moon and Prasad, 1994; Okimoto, 1989; Samuels, 1987). Second, the political pattern of crisis and compensation is clearly the result of a recursive set of state–society relations in which influences from society alter the nature of the state, thereby changing future policy patterns and leadership. Thus, Japan's rapid growth and competitive success reflected a state-in-society rather than a strong and autonomous developmental state.

Japan's recent economic difficulties must also be explained by a complex interaction among market, state, and society set off, ironically, by the past successes of the Japanese political economy. A wide range of Japanese industries had become highly competitive by the early 1980s by using infant-industry protection, both direct and more informal, to get started and then applying Japanese management strategies, such as TQM and capturing market share, to outpace their foreign rivals (Prestowitz, 1988; Tyson, 1992). The combination of rapid export growth and continued import restrictions, which both the benefiting industries and sponsoring ministries were loath to surrender, created huge and continuing trade surpluses. The result was a tremendous accumulation of financial assets that created a "bubble economy" by the late 1980s; this, much like the Wall Street frenzy a few years earlier, provided innumerable incentives for corporate speculation and asset acquisition. When the bubble burst, the tremendous loss of assets for the financial system seriously eroded the ability of Japanese companies to continue the high investment rates necessary to stay competitive in leading technology- and capital-intensive industries. Obviously, the bursting of the Japanese bubble had many economic antecedents, both domestic and foreign. A primary reason for the catastrophe of the early 1990s, however, very probably lay in the failure to act decisively to threats—first economic (the bubble) and then political (voter rejection of the LDP for the first time in the postwar period) (Noble, 1994). This inaction, in turn, seemingly resulted from the "institutional sclerosis" of the political economy that had been created over the previous decades. In particular, both the state (politicians and bureaucrats) and business had developed so many vested interests that they became paralyzed in the face of crisis.

South Korea and Singapore: Statist Leap-Frog Is a Multidimensional Game

Surely, no one could label the political economies of Singapore or South Korea as examples of laissez-faire capitalism. The state has been extremely intrusive in both, probably to a greater extent than in Japan. Yet both have experienced extremely rapid growth trajectories based on exporting increasingly sophisticated industrial products. Thus, they stand in strong contradiction to neoclassical nostrums about the effects of government intervention in the economy. They also indicate that there are more than a few roads to Confucian capitalism: Their strategies and resulting economic structures diverged radically, suggesting that comparative advantage is far more manipulable and arbitrary than neoclassicists are wont to believe.

South Korea followed a strategy that was quite similar to Taiwan's and Hong Kong's until the 1970s. In the 1950s it used protectionism to encourage import substitution in light industry, similar to Taiwan; in the mid-1960s (a couple of years later than Taiwan) it engaged in a major transformation to exporting its labor-intensive manufactures. As the 1970s opened, Hong Kong, South Korea, and Taiwan had fairly similar export-based economies, with the major difference being Hong Kong's lack of government intervention and protection to jump start the cycle of import substitution for light industry.

In the 1970s, however, South Korea and Taiwan decided to transform themselves from tortoises to hares by engaging in "secondary import substitution"—that is, the state-sponsored development of the heavy, chemical, and high-tech industries (Gereffi, 1990)—while Hong Kong continued its laissez-faire policies. The data in Chapter 2 demonstrated that both were successful in leap-frogging into bigger ponds. However, South Korea was able to change its industrial structure more radically (i.e., leap faster and farther) than Taiwan for two reasons. First, South Korea's domestic market is much larger than those of the other Little Dragons, so that it can pursue industrial deepening, with an emphasis on the heavy and chemical industries, to a much greater extent than can the smaller East Asian nations, where internal demand is much more limited. Second, the powers of the state were much stronger, so that it could forge new industries much more quickly.

The rapidity with which South Korea became internationally competitive in these industries is almost breathtaking. Between 1971 and 1984, heavy industry's share of total industrial production rose by a half, from 40 percent to 62 percent. What is much more impressive, though, is the tremendous transformation of South Korea's export mix. In 1971, heavy industrial products constituted just 13 percent of all industrial exports, demonstrating that the heavy industries were primarily import-substitution ones. In 1984, in astonishing contrast, they formed 60 percent of industrial exports, almost exactly the same as their proportion of industrial output (Amsden 1989; Chu, 1989; Haggard and Moon, 1983 & 1990; Jones and Sakong, 1980; Kang, 1989).

To promote rapid industrialization the government resorted to a battery of policy instruments, including the allocation of financial credit, production subsidies, tariff protection, export quotas, and tax rebates to influence entrepreneurial incentives. The financial system was probably by far the most important and distinctive policy instrument in the state arsenal. South Korea has had extreme governmental control of its financial system, including the large amounts of funds borrowed abroad. This has allowed the government to funnel these funds to enterprises selected as "national champions" in a specific industry and to enforce performance standards by threatening to withdraw credit if production, export, or quality goals are not met (Amsden, 1989; Fields, 1995; Wade, 1985; Woo, 1991).

Such a strategy of financial control can only work, however, when there is a relatively limited number of economic players; this is the case in South Korea, where large business groups (*chaebol*) are even more dominant than the keiretsu in Japan. Table 4.5 contrasts the extremes in industrial concentration in South Korea and Taiwan. In the 1980s, for example, the top five South Korean chaebol accounted for just over half of GNP—five times the share of Taiwan's top five business groups—and a similar ratio existed for the ten largest companies in the two nations (63% to 14%). The heavy-industrialization campaign was the major factor stimulating this concentration of national champions. In just the decade between 1974 and 1984, for example, the sales of the top five chaebol skyrocketed almost fivefold, from 12 percent to 52 percent of GNP. Until the early 1980s, the state essentially dictated to the business community, even the large chaebol. However, the success of the state-led national-development project ironically made the chaebol so rich and powerful that the balance of power began to tip in their direction (Amsden, 1989; Hahm and Plein, 1995; Kang, 1989; Moon, 1988 & 1990; Shin, 1991).

The heavy-industry program is also quite useful for testing the neoclassical and developmental state models in the Korean context. South Korea instituted this program as a reaction to the same pressures on its labor-intensive exports that Taiwan and Hong Kong faced in the early

Table 4.5   Indicators of Industrial Concentration

	Taiwan	South Korea
5 largest business groups percent GNP, 1983	10.3	52.4
50[a] largest business groups percent GNP, 1983	31.7	93.8
10 largest companies percent GDP, 1987	14.3	63.5

Sources: Fields, 1995: 6; Hong, 1992: 63.
Note: a. Largest 96 for Taiwan.

1970s. Because the state's links with and control over private industry were much tighter in South Korea than in Taiwan (and most certainly than in Hong Kong), South Korea was able to take a much more aggressive strategy that ultimately proved far more successful in upgrading into such heavy industries as automobiles, steel, and petrochemicals (Amsden, 1989; Chu, 1991; Mardon, 1990; Mardon and Paik, 1992; Wade, 1990). The ability to defy the short-term logic of the market by launching such a "big push" is consistent with the statist critique of neoclassicalism, but more than a developmental state was in operation within South Korea's political economy. First, most of these heavy industries were in private hands. Thus, their ultimate success rested on the efficacy of the chaebol, not the developmental state. For example, the upgrading in semiconductors primarily was the result of private initiative in an area that state policymakers relatively ignored (Hong, 1992). Second, although the heavy-industry strategy ultimately succeeded, it did so only after a decade of economic imbalances that caused considerable criticism and political upheavals that significantly altered the nature of the regime (Haggard and Moon, 1990; Hahm and Plein, 1995; Moon, 1988 & 1990). Thus, even this victory of a developmental state points toward the value of a state-in-society perspective.

South Korea also stands out for its statist practice of placing stringent limits on direct investment by foreign MNCs. However, these restrictions on foreign capital were not aimed at simple exclusion. Rather, the regime acted to channel MNCs into a few high-priority sectors and to regulate them to maximize their contribution to development of South Korean national champions. According to this strategy, foreign investment in an industry would first be solicited but would only be allowed in the form of joint ventures with domestic firms. Once the domestic partner learned the business and the technology and was strong enough to carry on operations on its own, the MNC would be forced to divest itself (under the terms of the original contract), thereby leaving a new industry in local hands (Amsden, 1989; Haggard and Moon 1983 & 1990; Mardon, 1990; Mardon and Paik, 1992).

South Korea's utilization of foreign capital in its developmental strategy is well illustrated by its efforts to create a petroleum-refining industry, first through joint ventures and then by promoting divestitures. This process started in the early 1960s when the government convinced Gulf Oil to enter into a joint venture (about which Gulf was none too enthusiastic) with the Korean Oil Company by offering it a lucrative package, including a guaranteed profit of 15 percent, a monopoly for providing crude oil, and various tax concessions. As the demand for refined petroleum escalated, the regime negotiated similar joint ventures with Caltex, Union Oil, and the National Iran Oil Company between 1965 and 1976, each with a corporate member of a different chaebol. By the late 1970s the South

Korean partners had gained the know-how, technical sophistication, and financial resources to take over these projects; the government provided subsidized credit for most of them to buy out their foreign partners when international instability (e.g., the Iranian Revolution and the second oil shock) made this possible. As Mardon and Paik (1992: 158–159) conclude:

> Today, South Korea refines 100 percent of its domestic oil requirements, . . . hauls the bulk of it on its own ships, and holds total financial and operational control. . . . All these refining operations are owned by large and diversified domestic corporations. The capital earned and the technical knowledge gained . . . are applied to the expansion of these firms in other sectors. Such policies and actions led to the establishment of Korean-owned and Korean-controlled production in a wide range of heavy and chemical industry sectors.

Like South Korea, Singapore has an authoritarian state that exercised strong leadership over the economy and was able to play leap-frog quite successfully in the global economy. Its explicit industrialization strategy was almost the polar opposite, however. While South Korea built national champions and excluded MNCs, Singapore staked its fate on surrendering dominance of its economy to the multinationals, albeit on its own terms. Furthermore, state leadership in Singapore has depended upon two factors different from the South Korean situation, one geographic and one idiosyncratic. Because of the small size of the city-state, exercising command and control over public officials is much easier than in larger countries; and Singapore has benefited from a strong and effective leader in the person of Lee Kuan Yew.

Although Singapore's economy is in many ways the polar opposite of Hong Kong's, the derivation of its general strategy was similar to the Hong Kong case in the sense that it came from a "big bang" in the external environment. Initially, Singapore (like Japan and the Little Dragons) planned to follow a path of import-substitution light industrialization after independence primarily aimed at markets in the much less developed Malayan states. However, when Singapore's union with Malaysia proved abortive, this strategy became unworkable. Thus, the regime switched gears radically and began to create an export-based economy by recruiting foreign MNCs to bring their internationally competitive industries to the island, and by using state corporations to develop or maintain shipbuilding and, in joint ventures with MNCs, petrochemicals. In addition to these heavy industries, the electronics industry became a leader in the initial export drive.

Multinational corporations consequently play a far larger role in Singapore than anywhere else in East Asia and come close to dominating the Singaporean economy. MNC production, for instance, constitutes about 70 percent of Singapore's exports (compared with 10% to 15% for laissez-faire Hong Kong); foreign capital dominates such leading sectors as electronics and petrochemicals. Table 4.6 provides a summary overview of foreign capital's dominating role in the Singaporean economy. MNCs have provided most of the investment in manufacturing and a sizable share of total investment as well. Compared to local firms, foreign manufacturers are larger, more capital intense, more export oriented, and more profitable (but surprisingly equal in wage levels and productivity). The overall impact of MNCs on the Singaporean economy is greater than in any other Asian nation.

Because of the MNCs, Singapore started significantly higher up the international product cycle than did the other Little Dragons. Nevertheless, the Lee government felt the need to adopt a specific program for industrial upgrading in 1979 called the Second Industrial Revolution. This included an emphasis on high-tech production, a state commitment to increased education and training and to several huge infrastructure projects, and a "corrective wage policy" that tried to force wage increases of 50 percent over a three-year period. The program was successful in attracting substantial new investment in the computer, chemicals, and petroleum industries. However, it fell short of many of the more ambitious goals for more sophisticated production and was supplemented by an increased emphasis on services, especially banking, in the late 1980s.

The institutional basis for Singapore's strong state resides in several specific programs the regime has used to great advantage. In the economic realm, the Pioneer Industries Ordinance allows the technocratic bureaucracy to channel investment capital into desired sectors primarily through the provision of incentives (e.g., tax breaks and subsidized financing) rather than through restrictions. For example, when Singapore decided to direct the economy into more sophisticated and higher-value-added

Table 4.6   Role of Foreign Capital in Singapore's Manufacturing, 1982

	MNC share percentage
Total GDP	26
Total investment	41
Number of firms	25
Number of employees	55
Total employee pay	57
Capital expenditures	63
Output	63
Value added	65
Exports	72
Pretax profits	70

Source: Mirza, 1986: 5, 9, 105.

production at the end of the 1970s, it simply withdrew existing tariff breaks for automobile assembly and tire production; this, in effect, closed down these less sophisticated industries. State power over the economy is also exercised through a large sector of state corporations. For example, state corporations, public utilities, and other government bodies constitute 50 percent of GNP and 20 percent of employment—mostly in the finance rather than the manufacturing sector (Chen, 1983; Crone, 1983; Deyo, 1981; Krause, 1988; Mirza, 1986; Rodan, 1989).

The Singapore case (as well as Hong Kong) raises the interesting point that government spending for subsidized housing, education, and other aspects of popular welfare actually constitutes a subsidy for businesses, who can pay lower wages for fairly skilled labor, rather than a "drag" that diverts resources from more productive private investment. In particular, the Central Provident Fund is created by payroll deductions of about 25 percent that are matched by additional employer contributions—equal to slightly over 10 percent of GNP. This is an ingenious invention that ensures a high investment rate, finances subsidized housing and human capital that benefit MNCs using Singapore's work force, and creates a welfare dependency (e.g., withdrawals are used to purchase apartments) that controls labor without resort to direct repression (Castells et al., 1990; Rodan, 1989).

The state in Singapore thus plays a subtle role of both recruiting and regulating the multinationals. On the one hand, the government has explicitly sought MNCs as allies in national development and provided generous incentives for investing in Singapore. The state also underwrites popular welfare, human-capital development, and physical infrastructure to increase its already considerable geographic attraction for MNCs. On the other hand, the state manipulates incentives to channel foreign (and domestic) capital into desired sectors; and the large role of state corporations restricts the space for MNC penetration. Singapore represents a limited partnership between the state and MNCs, with private domestic capital assuming a minor role. In fact, the primarily Chinese small businesspeople often claim that they have been largely excluded from the fruits of Singapore's economic miracle.

Confucian Capitalism Comes to China: Invoking the Singapore Model While Following the Taiwan Path

When Deng Xiaoping consolidated power in China in the late 1970s, he was committed to radically revising the Maoist model in order to promote national economic development; this, he assumed, would make China stronger and the Communist regime more legitimate. As a consequence of

Deng's drive for change, China has undergone a continuing set of reforms over the past fifteen years. As time passed it became clear that Deng wanted fundamental change in the socialist planned economy to make it more productive and dynamic, but also that he wanted this to occur within a framework of continued Communist rule. Thus, it seems natural that the Chinese were quite attracted to the economically successful authoritarian developmental states in East Asia, now epitomized by the Singaporean model of Asian authoritarianism. Despite the periodic pronouncements of the regime that China had adopted such a model, however, the reality of Confucian capitalism in China appears to be much closer to the guerrilla capitalism exhibited by Taiwan and Hong Kong.

The popular alienation in the mid-1970s that resulted from many Chinese feeling "clawed by the tiger" presented a major challenge to Mao's successor, Deng Xiaoping, following the brief interregnum under Hua Guofeng. Deng, for his part, attempted to revive communism by presenting a new, implicit social contract to the Chinese people. Under Deng's reforms the CCP would retain its monopoly of political power but would also make major concessions in other areas. Economic reforms would generate growth and fill rice bowls; the party would allow much greater freedom of speech, economic entrepreneurship, and nonparticipation in political activities (in other words, the party and the citizenry should leave each other alone); and the CCP would reform itself to provide much more effective leadership. Economic success would make China strong, and Deng would act to unify China once again by incorporating the Chinese *irredenta* of Hong Kong, Macao, and Taiwan into the nation and by repressing the demands of national minorities within China (e.g., Tibetans and Central Asians in Xinjiang). In short, whereas Mao had viewed legitimacy essentially in ideological terms (defined by his own interpretation of Marxism-Leninism-Mao Zedong thought), the more pragmatic Deng tried to base the legitimacy of his government on nationalism and the material well-being of the Chinese citizenry.

In the political realm, Deng pushed hard to create a more pragmatic and effective state administration by replacing older and less educated cadres in both the party and the state; this also helped his personal consolidation of power. During the 1980s a wholesale turnover of top and middle-level officials occurred as Deng evidently tried to create a developmental state similar to those in Taiwan and the other East Asian NICs. For example, an almost 90 percent turnover in ministers, Central Committee members, and provincial party leaders occurred between 1978 and 1988. In other respects the political reform was more episodic and less successful. Deng did end the practice of "campaigning" (i.e., mass mobilizations often directed against an enemy of the regime), but the periods of political relaxation and enlarged freedom of speech inevitably stimulated criticism that Deng and his more conservative colleagues found intolerable, and set off repressive backlashes (e.g., the campaigns against Democracy Wall, spiritual pollution, and bourgeois liberalism).

The major problem, however, was that Deng's insistence that the CCP, and himself as leader, retain a monopoly over political power inevitably clashed with the forces unleashed by his successful marketization reforms in the economy. With the failure of Maoism, debate over economic policy in the CCP turned to a new cleavage. On the one hand, party conservatives led by Chen Yun wanted to return to the orthodox Marxist economic policies of the 1950s. On the other hand, more radical reformers, such as Hu Yaobang and Zhao Ziyang, usually with Deng's backing, wanted to pursue more decentralized and market-based policies in order to provide incentives to the Chinese people to work for the development of their country.

Under strong pressure from Deng, far-reaching reforms were enacted, and these helped stimulate the strong economic performance over most of the 1980s that is documented in Chapter 2. However, their partial nature ultimately created the crisis of the late 1980s. The new pragmatic spirit of the CCP under Deng was strongly reflected in the experimental approach taken to these reforms. That is, reforms would be tried in one area or province or gradually expanded—agricultural reform in Sichuan and Anwei, foreign investment in special economic zones (SEZs), and marketization in the industrial and urban realm in Guangdong—and only implemented nationwide after they had proved themselves in practice (Chang, 1988; Dittmer, 1994; Harding, 1987; Pearson, 1991; Prybyla, 1987; Shirk, 1993; Solinger, 1993; Wu, 1994).

Perhaps the most radical reforms occurred in the realm of agriculture, where the responsibility system in essence duplicated Taiwan's land reform of the 1950s by informally creating small-scale privatized agriculture based on long-term leases. In addition, the freeing of the rural economy permitted the "natural" development of rural industries based on local resources and comparative advantage. The results, at least in the short term, were almost spectacular; food production and rural earnings soared. This occurred not just because individuals and families were given greater incentives to be productive, but also because the reforms were consistent with the existing social and political structures. In particular, rural CCP cadres were integrated into existing family-based networks in the villages and, moreover, were the only ones with the resources and political connections to take over the emerging rural industries. Although they had to yield their direct power over agricultural production, they gained a profitable outlet that could benefit both themselves and people connected to them by clientelistic ties (Oi, 1989). Other aspects of privatization and marketization had some success as well. These reforms included the solicitation of foreign capital (especially in SEZs), the privatization of small-scale businesses and services in urban areas, the decentralization of power to provinces and enterprise managers, the much more extensive reforms that were implemented in Guangdong Province, and the "coastal" strategy of targeting eastern China for export industries (Harding, 1987; Lardy, 1992; Rosen, 1992; Shirk, 1993; Vogel, 1989; Wu, 1994).

However, for the most part, attempts to change the urban and industrial economy bore little fruit because they challenged basic political and social interests. Those particularly affected were top-level CCP members who favored the Chen Yun strategy of orthodox socialist planning; urban and industrial cadres who did not have the "escape hatches" open to their rural colleagues if they lost direct control over production; and much of the industrial work force, whose iron rice bowl was threatened if the mostly inefficient state enterprises were subjected to market discipline. Thus, the Chinese economy moved toward a dualistic structure: Basic industry remained planned within a network of Communist neotraditionalism while market or at least quasi-market forces predominated in agriculture, small-scale businesses, foreign-invested firms, and a few progressive provinces (Harding, 1987; Rosen, 1992; Vogel, 1989; Wu, 1994).

Despite (or, more accurately, at least partially because of) China's extremely impressive aggregate growth during the 1980s, even the economy was not problem free. Rapid growth set off inflationary surges, which were exacerbated by financial decentralization's producing "overinvestment" by competing localities that were trying to maximize their own growth. Liberalized foreign trade brought huge increases in imports, which created balance-of-payments crises every few years. The result was a rapid business cycle that set off deflationary retrenchment in 1982–1983, 1986, and 1988. The marketization reforms began to produce pronounced inequality because many could not take advantage of market opportunities. This ultimately turned to the disadvantage of agriculture and the rural areas as urban market power developed, and led to declining grain production because more-profitable alternatives existed in the countryside.

The dualistic economy and the partial nature of the reforms created additional problems that increasingly strained the PRC's social and political fabric. Because there were essentially two markets, one with state-dictated prices and one with market-dictated prices, tremendous opportunities arose for arbitrage (buying cheap on one and selling dear on the other). Officials and those with official connections had the greatest opportunity to reap windfall profits. Thus, there was a tremendous increase in corruption, and CCP leaders and their children (the so-called crown princes' faction) became very rich. This provoked escalating resentment because many people in China, such as honest officials, intellectuals and students, and workers, had to live on fixed incomes that were translated into a declining standard of living as inflation took off in the late 1980s. Dissatisfaction arose on many sides: from those who thought the reforms had gone too far, and those who thought they had not gone far enough; from those who wanted economic security, and those who wanted entrepreneurial freedom; and from those at the top, and those at the bottom of the Chinese social and political hierarchies. The result was the social and political explosion that led to the Tiananmen tragedy (C. Y. Cheng, 1990; Harding, 1987; Tinari and Lam, 1991; Wu, 1994).

The nature of post-Tiananmen China's political economy appears to be a more extreme version of Deng's original dualistic model of economic reform coupled with political orthodoxy. Instead of tolerating a more relaxed political atmosphere as long as it was not directly challenged, the central leadership in Beijing clamped down in the political realm and enforced orthodoxy, at least in public. Even some ideological vestiges of the Cultural Revolution were reimplemented (ironically so, because even the "eight ancients" in the Forbidden City suffered under Mao). However, economic reform continued, and in several important ways even intensified. What seems to have happened is that the central authorities reached an uneasy truce with provincial leaders; the latter traded off superficial respect for the center's reactionary political position for greater autonomy in the sphere of economic policy (Harding, 1987; Lardy, 1994; Shirk, 1993; Wu, 1994 & 1995).

In fact, the trend toward marketization continued apace. Table 4.7, for example, illustrates the revolution that occurred in price setting. At the beginning of the reform era, the state set almost all prices in the Chinese economy. Just fifteen years later (four years after Tiananmen), the state role in setting prices was approaching the minuscule, even in the area of capital goods. The results of marketization and decentralization were probably the most profound in the area of foreign trade. Here, the regime elected to hold the course for a drastic change of strategy in the market-conforming direction taken just before Tiananmen. In 1988 Beijing changed its strategy toward foreign investment in the hope that it could emulate the export booms of the Little Dragons by producing labor-intensive goods for

Table 4.7   Percentage of Commodities Sold at State-Set Prices

	1978	1993
Retail commodities	97	5
Agricultural goods	94	10
Capital goods	100	15

Source: Lardy, 1994: 11.

markets in the advanced industrial societies and, thus, end its periodic balance-of-payments crisis. Previously, Beijing had viewed foreign capital as a source of technology to aid in the nation's industrial upgrading; now it relaxed regulations enforcing joint ventures and discouraging low-tech investments.

The results of this reorientation were spectacular. Capital inflows from Hong Kong and Taiwan jumped, stimulating a rapid rise in exports and an attenuation of the PRC's balance-of-trade problems that is reflected in the data on total exports and trade balances in Table 4.8. Table 4.8 also confirms that MNC-produced light-industrial goods led China's great expansion of trade in the late 1980s and early 1990s. The share of manufactured products in China's exports jumped from 50 percent in 1985 to over 80 percent in 1993; the labor-intensive categories of textiles, apparel, toys, footwear, sporting goods, and electronics jumped from 31 percent to 51 percent of total exports over this period. Finally, the contribution of foreign firms to China's exports multiplied more than fivefold in just five years, from 5 percent in 1988 to 27.5 percent in 1993; they accounted for approximately two-thirds of the growth in the PRC's exports during the early 1990s (Lardy, 1992 & 1994; Wu, 1994 & 1995).

Reform also commenced in the state industrial sector, in a little-noticed manner that Cheng-Tian Kuo (1994) has termed "privatization within the Chinese state." The government is extremely reluctant to close

Table 4.8   China's Export Performance

	Total exports ($ billions)	Trade balance ($ billions)	Percent exports	
			Manufactures	Foreign firms
1978	9.8	−1.1	—	—
1979	13.7	−2.0	—	—
1980	18.1	−1.9	49.2	—
1981	22.0	0.0	53.3	—
1982	22.3	3.0	55.1	—
1983	22.2	0.8	56.6	—
1984	26.1	−1.3	54.3	—
1985	27.4	−14.9	49.5	1.1
1986	30.9	−12.0	63.8	1.6
1987	39.4	−3.8	66.4	3.0
1988	47.5	−7.8	69.7	5.2
1989	52.5	−6.6	71.3	8.3
1990	62.1	8.7	74.4	12.5
1991	71.9	8.1	77.5	16.8
1992	85.0	4.4	79.9	20.4
1993	91.8	−12.2	81.8	27.5

Source: Lardy, 1994: 30–31 & 72.

down even highly inefficient and literally bankrupt state enterprises for a variety of reasons: the possible loss of face for socialism, the instability that might result from a massive loss of jobs, and the inability to replace the social-welfare functions performed by state-owned factories. Instead of simply continuing massive state subsidies as in the past, however, marketization has been brought to these firms more subtly and indirectly. State enterprises and even government agencies are decentralized into subunits that are forced to compete for "profits" in any way they can (e.g., People's Liberation Army (PLA) units building and running hotels). Units that continue to lose money are allowed to wither through attrition and a lack of bonuses.

> The exemplar of the military transformation is the Shanghai Aerospace Bureau. . . . In 1980 the Bureau began experimenting with some production of civilian goods. . . . In 1983, after receiving the central government's endorsement, it reduced the amount of work-force involved in military production (but without failing the central government's quotas), established civilian production and service subsidiaries, developed new products, explored the technology market, and formed joint ventures with civilian enterprises. . . . Among its products, refrigerators, refrigerator compressors, washing machines, television sets, and electric fans were the most popular in the Chinese market (Kuo, 1994: 403).

According to Kuo, this process of privatization within the state explains why the economy has been so dynamic despite the maintenance of a large state-industrial sector.

The tremendous growth that China has manifested during the Deng era is ironic in several senses. One of the last remaining socialist states is undergoing an economic miracle similar to those of the other East Asian states. The basis for this, however, has been the introduction of markets into China. Furthermore, despite the regime's identification with the developmental state that has been widely credited with leading Confucian capitalism (Amsden, 1989; Wade, 1990), the central state has had little direct influence. Rather than strong state planning and leadership à la Singapore or South Korea, decentralization that has permitted the flowering of individual effort and guerrilla capitalism has been the centerpiece of the reform. In fact, the similarity to Taiwan's pattern of development is uncanny. The household responsibility system spurred agricultural productivity to start the expansion, just as land reform did in Taiwan. The regime hoped to recruit high-tech MNCs, but ended up with labor-intensive assembly operations, just as in Taiwan's economic processing zones (EPZs). Finally, hustling businesspeople, rather than brilliant bureaucrats, are making the decisions that keep East Asian dynamism going in both China and Taiwan.

Flexibility As the Key to Confucian Capitalism: A Varying Synergism of Market, State, and Society

If there is one key to East Asian dynamism and the success of Confucian capitalism, it is flexibility. These countries had to be quite flexible to take advantage of their initial opportunities for industrialization, and especially to keep up their climb from one niche of the global economy to another. This involved the creation of new industries and the discarding of obsolete economic institutions, neither of which is an easy or automatic process. In many instances East Asia was able to outcompete other developing countries simply because its firms were more flexible and responded more quickly to changes in international market conditions (Morawetz, 1981). This flexibility, furthermore, was not just a function of the economic system. Rather, the state was intimately involved in economic change in all of these nations except Hong Kong. Given the tendency for both politicians and businesspeople to prefer rigidity and rents to flexibility and competition (Olson, 1982), East Asian political and economic flexibility must be considered no mean achievement.

The economic strategy of flexible production has taken three very different forms. In Japan, and to a considerably lesser but probably increasing extent in South Korea, flexible production has meant a continuous and innovative upgrading of both products and production processes. Generally, this is a strategy of large conglomerates and their associated networks of small suppliers who can both concentrate resources and quickly shift production processes and relationships. Flexible production takes a much different form among the small-scale Chinese firms in Hong Kong, Singapore, Taiwan, and most recently China, especially the southern coastal part, where entrepreneurs follow a pattern of guerrilla capitalism. A final type of flexible production involves a major reorientation of an entire domestic economy. The most prominent examples of this come from China. Generally, such major economic reorientations might seem to require a state-controlled or socialist economy. However, other examples are offered by capitalist Singapore, where the government promoted industrialization by recruiting foreign MNCs, and by South Korea's heavy- and chemical-industry program.

Given the strong (albeit varying) role of the state in almost all the East Asian economies (Hong Kong being a partial exception), political flexibility has been a vital component of the East Asian development model as well. At the broadest level, all of these countries have adopted what Steve Chan (1993) calls policies of "comprehensive national security"—that is, giving economic development equal emphasis with military matters in setting these countries' principal goals and priorities (see also Samuels, 1994, on Japan). Political institutions have also been structured to promote informed and flexible policies, although the means to achieve this vary widely: technocratic independence from political pressures in Japan, Singapore, and (much of the time) South Korea; expanding the top levels of the regime by adding first technocrats and then electoral politicians to military leaders in Taiwan; minimizing government's direct economic role in Hong Kong; and decentralizing power in the 1980s in the PRC.

Most of these institutions that promote political flexibility and market-conforming economic dynamism rest not on state autonomy but upon some balance and/or cooperation in state–society relations. In Japan, the key institution is the dense network of consensual and reciprocal relationships that have developed between the business community and the technocrats in MITI and other government ministries. In Taiwan, rather than cooperation, state–society balance has been created by the independence of the dynamic sector of small and medium businesses from state control. Likewise, such balance results from laissez-faire policies in Hong Kong and decentralization in China. Extremely strong state domination and autonomy, in fact, probably prevent economic flexibility; the neoclassical critics of statism are assuredly correct in their argument that government officials simply are not capable of anticipating the market or "picking winners," especially in an era of rapid technological change and a relatively open international economy.

This conceptualization of Confucian capitalism indicates that both market flexibility and effective state policy have made vital contributions to East Asian dynamism. However, there also seems good reason to look beyond the simple, if elegant, postulates of both neoclassical economics and the developmental state model for understanding the dynamics of development in East Asia. Market, state, and society must be considered together. Each is important, and East Asia demonstrates that they can interact in a variety of combinations. Development models should probably be much more contingent and contextual than the worldviews of either statism or neoclassicalism.

5

The Political Economy of
South Asian Stagnation: A Vicious Cycle
of State, Market, and Society

Coauthored with Brian S. Trinque

The discussions in Chapters 2 and 3 suggest that South Asian stagnation forms a counterpoint to East Asian dynamism. This chapter examines the political economy of India, the major nation in South Asia, to reveal and examine the factors that differentiate it from the models of rapid growth that were presented in Chapter 4. Before making such an invidious comparison, however, it is worth noting that India's economic performance is subject to countervailing interpretations. Although the observation that real GNP growth seems to be limited to what Deepak Lal (1988) calls the "Hindu rate of growth" of about 3.5 percent per year (which translates into well under 2% per capita) may connote fatalism and despair (Bhagwati, 1993), this actually compares quite favorably with colonial India over the first half of the twentieth century, when almost no growth at all occurred.

India's position is perhaps best captured by Lloyd and Susanne Rudolph's (1987) conceptualization of the nation's "pursuit of *Lakshmi*" (the goddess of wealth and good fortune) as creating a political economy of fundamental paradox: an economy that is simultaneously rich and poor, and a state that is simultaneously strong and weak. How these paradoxes arose can be traced to a logical sequence of interactions among market, state, and society, analogous to the East Asian patterns that were discussed in Chapter 4. India's economic and political strategies at independence were derived from a reaction against the problems of the colonial era. The general strategy of India's self-consciously developmental state then created a new set of economic and political institutions that provided incentives and channels through which powerful social groups pursued their interests. Unfortunately for India, the political economy that evolved did not generate the economic and political flexibility underlying the several variants of the East Asian miracle. Rather, India's political economy generated increasing institutional rigidity and rent-seeking behaviors.

95

The first section of this chapter summarizes the major trends in India's postwar economy, acknowledging the neoclassical critique of economic policies in India. The second section looks more closely at the ideological principles that guided the development strategy of India's leaders and traces the unfortunate interactions they engendered. The third section argues that the divergence in economic performance between East Asia and South Asia is, to a considerable extent, a result of the distinct fortunes of agriculture in the two regions. The productivity of agriculture in many East Asian economies gave leaders a head start toward successful policies, while the more primitive state of agriculture in India made it difficult to conceive, much less implement, similar policies.

Economic Policy and the Trajectory of Indian Development: Creating a Rich–Poor Economy

India clearly merits the title of a developmental state, despite its not very impressive economic record, in the sense that state policy was explicitly directed toward promoting industrialization and eradicating poverty, and that this policy had a major impact upon economic and social outcomes. The roots of Indian economic policy can be traced to the nation's colonial legacy. In particular, India's strategy reflected four fundamental assumptions. First, the stagnation and poverty of the first half of the twentieth century was blamed on colonial exploitation and produced a commitment to self-reliant development. Second, many of India's leaders, particularly Jawaharlal Nehru, had been schooled in English Fabian socialism, which advocated state domination of the commanding heights of an economy, though not necessarily full-scale nationalization and command planning. Third, industry, especially heavy industry, was seen as the driver of successful development; this view was compatible with the dominant economic thought of both East and West at that time. Finally, because it was assumed that state-led industrialization would "pull up" India's poor, developmental efforts were focused on the industrial rather than the agricultural sector (Bhagwati, 1993; Bhagwati and Desai, 1970; Frankel, 1978; Kohli, 1987 & 1994; Rudolph and Rudolph, 1987).

State leadership of the economy was exercised through the Planning Commission, whose two fundamental tasks were to determine the size of investment and savings and to decide how the investment should be allocated among alternative uses. The first decision depended on the expected level of foreign aid and capital inflow and on the marginal rate of savings that would be economically and politically acceptable. The central debate in the Planning Commission, the government, and public forums was between the "big planners," led by P. Mahalanobis and P. Pant with support by Nehru, and the "small planners," led by the Finance Ministry. The big planners believed that if investments were technically feasible, savings ought to be forthcoming somehow; therefore, the Finance Ministry should tax sufficiently to raise the savings rate up to the desired level. Although the usually conservative Finance Ministry opposed this, the big planners managed to keep their targets almost intact because the boldness of their schemes appealed to Nehru's vision and leadership. This meant that planned investment levels were significantly higher than the quantity of savings that could realistically be expected.

The second issue involved the distribution of investment between the agricultural and industrial sectors and between heavy and light industry. Beginning with the Second Plan (1956), industry was increasingly emphasized over agriculture, and heavy industry was increasingly emphasized over light industry. Both these decisions were to prove controversial. The relative neglect of agriculture created a wage-goods constraint that was exacerbated by the attendant, somewhat exaggerated concern with building up the industrial sector to break the capital-goods constraint. Together these strategic decisions would have unfortunate and harmful consequences for India's subsequent economic development (Bhagwati and Desai, 1970).

Various policy instruments were used to guide industrialization into the desired patterns. The most important of the domestic instruments was the powerful and comprehensive industrial-licensing system, which was occasionally combined with price and distributional controls. In addition, the rapid growth of the public sector provided a significant means for influencing the pattern of new investments. In terms of foreign instruments, the government imposed considerable controls over foreign capital and instituted detailed trade and exchange controls via comprehensive quantitative restrictions that shielded domestic production from foreign competition. The framework of import and export policies in turn produced an incentive system that affected the direction of India's industrialization to a considerable extent (see Chapter 3 for a more detailed discussion of these policies).

At the beginning of the First Five-Year Plan in 1951, India's industrial base was quite narrow, employing only 12.5 percent of the total work force (see Roy, 1988, for a discussion of colonial industrialization). The picture changed dramatically during the first ten years of development planning. As Table 5.1 illustrates, industry grew at accelerating rates from just over 5 percent annually during 1951–1955 to 9 percent during 1961–1965. Beginning in the mid-1960s, however, industrial growth slowed noticeably, and considerable excess capacity developed in many industries. After a decade-and-a-half of doldrums, growth picked up again in the 1980s (Government of India, 1990a; World Bank, 1990). The emphasis on heavy industry is clear as well, with basic and capital goods generally having the most rapid growth, along with the very small sector of consumer durables. For example, the share of such traditional light industries as food processing and textiles in total manufacturing output was ap-

Table 5.1   Growth Rates of Industrial Production (percent of total industry)

	1960 weight	1951–1955	1955–1960	1961–1965	1965–1970	1970–1975	1975–1976	1976–1980
Basic goods	25	4.7	12.0	10.4	6.2	5.4	14.7	2.8
Capital goods	12	9.8	13.1	9.7	–1.4	5.6	10.6	4.0
Intermediate goods	26	7.8	6.4	6.9	2.4	2.8	7.5	3.6
Consumer goods	37	4.8	4.4	4.9	4.1	1.5	8.3	4.0
Consumer durables	(6)	—	—	11.0	8.4	1.6	13.2	8.0
Consumer nondurables	(31)	—	—	3.8	2.7	1.5	9.8	3.1
Total industry	100	5.3	7.4	9.0	3.3	3.7	9.8	3.6

Source: Balasubramanyam, 1984: 119.

proximately cut in half, from 68 percent to 35 percent, between 1951 and 1978 (Balasubramanyam, 1984: 113). This trend continued during the 1980s, despite the commitment of the Sixth and Seventh Plans to change the perceived overemphasis on heavy industry and underemphasis on consumer products. Nonetheless, the most significant achievement of the Sixth and Seventh Plans during the 1980s was the growth of "sunrise industries" in such fields as semiconductor chips, computers, microprocessors, communications and broadcasting equipment, microelectronics, electronic materials, and components (Government of India, 1990b & 1990c; Joshi and Little, 1994; World Bank, 1990).

Agriculture followed almost the opposite pattern. With limited investment in agriculture, growth of output was slow through the mid-1960s, averaging less than 3 percent annually over the period 1950–1966, and India's vulnerability to weather-induced food crises emerged as a major problem. Under some pressure from the United States, India made a strong commitment to promoting the green revolution (e.g., using high-yield varieties of wheat and rice and applying fertilizers) in the late 1960s. The results in terms of India's ability to feed itself were little short of spectacular, as was shown in Chapter 2. However, despite an impressive increase in wheat production, the growth rates of output and productivity in agriculture were not much improved from the mid-1960s through the early 1980s (Balasubramanyam, 1984). The failure of the green revolution to transform much of Indian agriculture accounts for the high rates of poverty; estimates vary widely, but at least 40 percent of the population was living in absolute poverty through the mid-1980s (Balasubramanyam, 1984; Centre for Development Studies, 1986; Roy and Tisdell, 1992b; Rudolph and Rudolph, 1987).

One commonly accepted reason for the Hindu rate of growth is that India's strategy of self-reliance distorted resource allocation. At independence, India was ready to reject all vestiges of British imperial rule and economic domination as an affront to Indian dignity and a potentially dangerous mechanism for continuing unequal and exploitative relationships. This economic nationalism was summed up in the slogan "Be Indian! Buy Indian!" As a result of this orientation, India embarked upon a strategy of rapid industrialization based on import substitution, technological independence, and (it was hoped) progress toward greater social equity. Any loss of pure economic efficiency (e.g., higher prices, lower-quality goods, and shortages) that this strategy of self-reliant import substitution entailed in the short run by opting out of the international division of labor was considered worthwhile to avoid the long-term implications of continued foreign domination of the economy. In addition, geography was favorable for such a strategy, because the subcontinent's huge population made import substitution more viable than in small nations, such as the four Little Dragons in East Asia.

Walling off the Indian market from foreign trade and foreign investment allowed rapid indigenous industrialization, but it also created the
protectionism that allowed established industries to remain relatively inefficient and rent seeking (Bhagwati, 1993; Bhagwati and Desai, 1970;
Joshi and Little, 1994; Lal, 1979; World Bank, 1990). However, the
foreign-exchange crisis of 1957 made continuation of this political economy untenable by confronting the regime with the difficult choice of either
opening the economy or foregoing the foreign technology that appeared
necessary to maintain the pace of industrialization. The government decided that opening the economy was the lesser of the two evils and became
more permissive in allowing foreign direct investment with majority or
sole ownership when the equity was tied to desired technology. Consequently, a huge inflow of FDI occurred over the next decade, and the share
of assets controlled by FDI doubled from one-tenth to one-fifth of India's
corporate assets. The changed policy toward MNCs did not mean that
India had adopted laissez-faire policies, however. In fact, one of the major
attractions for MNCs was the potential for substantial monopoly rents that
the closed and uncompetitive Indian market created.

These concessions to foreign capital were not particularly popular in
India. Thus, the government moved to increase its own economic and political capabilities, especially through several nationalizations in the financial industry, so that it could exert more leverage vis-à-vis the MNCs.
India then began to apply this power to "dislodge multinationals" (Encarnation, 1989) beginning in the late 1960s and culminating with the Foreign
Exchange Regulation Act (FERA) of 1973. This measure limited MNCs to
40 percent minority ownership in their Indian subsidiaries unless they
were in a priority industry, introducing critical new technologies, or exporting most of their product. By the early 1980s the share of foreign capital in India's total corporate assets had been cut to about a third of what
it had been at its high-water mark in the 1960s. Unfortunately, the success
of economic nationalism generally reinforced domestic inefficiency and
rent seeking, rather than creating effective national champions as in the
South Korean case discussed in Chapter 4 (Bhagwati and Desai, 1970; Encarnation, 1989; Evans, 1995; Grieco, 1984; Jannuzi, 1989; Joshi and Little, 1994; Lucas and Papanek, 1988).

The blame for India's checkered record of economic development is
likewise often attributed to its large and generally inefficient public sector,
which was developed in accord with the government's socialist ideology
(Bardhan, 1984; Bhagwati, 1993; Bhagwati and Desai, 1970; Evans, 1995;
Frankel, 1978; Lal, 1988; Roy, 1991b; Rudolph and Rudolph, 1987). The
public sector dominates major industrial undertakings, accounting for approximately two-thirds of the jobs in the large-scale "organized sector"
(Government of India, 1990a). The importance of the state sector for the

functioning of the economy, moreover, exceeds its simple share of assets or GDP. Over half of total investment in central public enterprises is in steel, coal, minerals and metals, power, and petroleum—basic inputs to a host of other industries. Therefore, the efficient performance of the public sector is crucial to the efficient performance of the industrial sector and to the overall performance of the economy. However, India's public sector has performed quite poorly, especially in operating state corporations and in conducting fiscal policy (Bhagwati, 1993; Roy and Tisdell, 1992a).

State-owned enterprises (SOEs) in India have been widely decried for their economic inefficiency. The data in Table 5.2 provide strong support for this criticism and neatly fit the neoclassical stereotype of the inefficient government-run industry. The state sector in India has about 60 percent of the industrial capital but produces only about 30 percent of the value added, whereas the opposite is true of the private sector. Moreover, given the capital-intensive nature of state enterprises and the somewhat disproportionately high wages that they pay, they represent "inappropriate technology" for a nation with massive underemployment. The SOEs in India constitute a major impediment to improving the nation's economic performance.

The inefficiency of the public sector produced three of the central phenomena associated with sluggish growth in India. The first is an escalating capital-output ratio that indicates that investment has become increasingly inefficient over time (Rudolph and Rudolph, 1987). The second phenomenon is the comparatively low rates of capacity utilization that mark the Indian economy. In particular, unused capacity has been traditionally highest in the high-priority basic and capital-goods industries; a major reason for lower capacity utilization for most of the industries within this group was inadequate availability of power, which is directly tied to public-sector inefficiency (Reserve Bank, 1985/86).

The poor performance of SOEs, furthermore, constituted a major force in the escalating government budget deficits over the 1980s that culminated in the financial crisis of 1990 (Bhagwati, 1993; Joshi and Little, 1994; Rudolph and Rudolph, 1987). For example, the annual budget

Table 5.2   State and Private Shares of Industry in India, mid-1980s

	Percent state sector	Percent private sector	Percent joint sector
Factories	4.5	93.0	2.5
Fixed capital	60.8	29.2	10.0
Workers	28.0	65.3	6.6
Wages	38.3	53.1	8.6
Net value added	33.3	56.5	10.2

Source: Brahmachari, 1992.

deficit jumped by nearly a half, from 6.4 percent to nearly 9 percent of GNP, during the 1980s (Bhagwati, 1993; Roy and Sen, 1991). Subsidies to SOEs and interest payments together generally accounted for about a quarter of total expenditures and almost three-quarters of the overall deficit during this decade (IMF, 1988: 503–508), indicating the central role of state-corporation inefficiency in driving up the government's deficit. Thus, ironically, public-sector inefficiency created the crisis that forced substantial economic reforms upon the government.

A substantial foreign-exchange crisis erupted in 1990 when the escalating public debt of the 1980s was exacerbated by a number of unforeseen factors. For example, the Gulf War drastically increased India's oil-import bill and forced the expenditure of substantial amounts of foreign exchange to bring Indian workers and their families home from the war zone. As a result, India's foreign-exchange reserves fell to only $1 billion, roughly equivalent to three weeks of import payments. The danger that India might have to default on the repayment of its foreign debt forced the government in 1991 to implement a set of economic reforms in collaboration with the IMF and the World Bank (Bhagwati, 1993).

India's economic reforms consisted of short-term stabilization measures and long-term structural reforms. Probably the highest priority in 1991 was to improve the nation's foreign-exchange-reserve position. The government therefore obtained a sizable loan from the IMF and, in consultation with both the IMF and the World Bank, imposed temporary restrictions on imports. The more fundamental structural-reform program consisted of measures to improve the performance and efficiency of the economy. The most important measure in this regard was liberalization by removing the various controls and restrictions on prices, such as subsidies, trade and foreign-exchange controls, and producers' and procurement prices for agricultural outputs. These reforms were accompanied by demand-side measures to reduce the size of the public sector substantially. In addition, the Indian currency was devalued sharply to reduce the deficit in the external accounts, and the notorious industrial and import-licensing systems were dismantled (Andersen, 1995; Bhalla, 1995).

These reforms had considerable success. During the 1994/95 fiscal year, for instance, India's foreign-exchange-reserve position improved markedly, reaching $17 billion in August 1994 compared to only $1 billion in June 1991 (*Economic Times*, 1994). However, major problems remain. The government still owns about 75 percent of industrial assets; the public sector is still bedeviled by bureaucratic controls and political interference; and the program for privatizing or liquidating poorly performing state enterprises has not been implemented. Moreover, union opposition has forced the shelving of plans to reform the company and labor laws that have made it impossible to dissolve bankrupt companies, sell assets of sick companies, or lay off workers. There has been no move to cut generous power and water subsidies for fear of angering politically powerful farmers. Sluggish 3 percent industrial growth and the consequent shortfall in government revenues kept the budget deficit at 6 percent of GDP during 1993/94, a level considerably higher than the government had projected (*The Australian*, 1994).

The limited success of India's liberalization reflects two very different factors. First, liberalization challenged the interests and perquisites of important vested interests, including the bureaucracy and protected domestic groups that possess significant abilities to resist change. Second, liberalization can benefit only those segments of the population poised to participate in and benefit from a market economy. Unfortunately, as emphasized in the later sections of this chapter, many Indians, especially in the rural areas, lack the education and other resources necessary to seize market opportunities. Thus, the 1991 reforms, though helpful, will not prove to be a panacea for overcoming the Hindu rate of growth (Ghosh, 1995).

Despite the inefficiency and rent seeking that permeate India's economy, there are significant success stories too, as documented by several recent case studies of India's informatics industry (computers, semiconductors, software, etc.). Peter Evans (1995) and Joseph Grieco (1984) have found a pattern reminiscent of the East Asian miracles: A synergism of state, market, and society has promoted rapid development and the emergence of an internationally competitive industry.

The development of the informatics industry in India is all the more surprising because India's strategy for developing this key industry paralleled its dysfunctional approach to other advanced products: relying upon a large state corporation, the Electronics Corporation of India, Ltd. (ECIL), to lead the nation's advance into this high-tech industry. Nevertheless, the informatics industry in India has been quite successful, as indicated by the rapid growth and export competitiveness implied by the data in Table 5.3. Perhaps the primary reason for this success was that India did not persist in its initial strategy of protecting a few large state enterprises. Rather, it switched to a policy, something like Taiwan's guerrilla capitalism, of unleashing the entrepreneurial drive of small enterprises, some of which became quite sizable (Evans, 1995; Grieco, 1994).

The largest informatics firm is now a private enterprise, Hindustan Computers Ltd. (HCL), whose very beginning resulted from entrepreneurial verve. The firm was started by several engineers who worked in marketing for Delhi Cloth Mills Data Products (part of a large business family). The bureaucratic and hierarchical Delhi Cloth Mills (DCM) group provided a poor base for jumping into the new computer industry, and the engineers had little personal capital and no license to manufacture computers, so in 1975 they started to hustle. They quit DCM and pooled about

Table 5.3   India's Performance in Computer and Software Industries (in millions of U.S.$)

	1984	1986	1988
Computer production	66	200	347
Hardware exports	1	3	34[a]
Software exports	17	30	61

Source: Evans, 1995: 169.
Note: a. Figure misleading because of huge sales to USSR; in 1989 hardware exports were only about half of those in 1988.

$20,000 to start a company making electronic calculators as a means to raise capital for the computer business, which they entered through the back door via a partnership with a small state firm having the necessary licenses. By 1990 they led India with $133 million in sales. Their operations combine manufacturing with a substantial software business, particularly commercial applications of UNIX (used primarily for engineering).

State enterprises are also important in India's informatics industry but do not operate in the manner of most Indian SOEs. ECIL ranks fourth in total sales; the second-ranking firm, with 1990 sales of $89 million, is the Computer Maintenance Corporation (CMC), which was formed in 1975 with a legal monopoly over servicing computers not manufactured in India as a result of India's conflict with IBM. The success of these state corporations, however, did not result from following their initial mandates—the development and manufacturing of computers for ECIL and computer maintenance for CMC (for which maintenance accounted for less than a quarter of total revenues by 1990). Rather, both found an internationally competitive niche in large-scale systems-integration projects. For example, CMC computerized the reservations systems for Indian Railways and won contracts with the London subway system and the Syrian government, while ECIL developed a computerized integrated-control system for a state-owned steel mill and automated monitoring systems for India's oil and gas production (Evans, 1995; Grieco, 1984).

Market, state, and society interacted in this instance to create a virtuous rather than vicious cycle. State policy ultimately proved to be market conforming; both private and public firms found niches of competitive advantage in the domestic and international markets. This is not in labor-intensive assembly work, at which Indian firms remain fairly inept, reflecting in Evans's (1995) opinion societal problems in manufacturing. Rather, India's comparative advantage turned out to be low-paid but world-class engineers, a result of India's overemphasis on higher education. This situation is not entirely positive: Software exporters derive much of their profits from "bodyshopping" (i.e., sending low-paid Indian engineers to work as consultants in industrialized nations). Still, India at least has a foot in the door of a high-value-added segment of the informatics industry that rewards the development of human capital.

Given the similarity between India's development in this one key industry and the East Asian experience, one might wonder what makes it different from the many other sectors in which the "Hindu equilibrium" (Lal, 1988) has prevailed. Peter Evans (1995) argues that the informatics field possesses two central characteristics that set it apart from more traditional industries and explain the different governmental tack that emerged. First, informatics is a highly technical field whose attraction in India seems more limited to the technically competent than are most other areas of the economy. Second, opportunities for patronage are limited (most employees must be well educated and technically trained), so it holds little attraction for dishonest bureaucrats. Consequently, even the relevant government agencies have attracted skilled technocrats who are committed to the development of the computer, semiconductor, and software industries in India. When state entrepreneurship proved insufficient for this task, they were willing, therefore, to promote private initiatives. In short, India's informatics industry represents the market-conforming state-in-society model; unfortunately, most other industrial sectors depart markedly from this effective synergy.

The Indian economy, to sum, continues to be a paradoxical one that is simultaneously rich and poor (Rudolph and Rudolph, 1987). It has an advanced industrial base that is the envy of most Third World nations, including some internationally competitive high-tech industries (Evans, 1995; Grieco, 1984), and the green revolution has permitted foodgrain output to grow somewhat faster than the population. More important, there is a large, well-educated middle class to support further development and industrial upgrading. However, much of its heavy industry is relatively obsolete and inefficient, and rural poverty and underemployment still form a massive obstacle to Indian development.

Creation of the Strong–Weak State:
From Developmentalism to Distortions

The discussion of the evolution of India's economy in the previous section is consistent with the neoclassical critique of the country's development strategy, in that government interventions clearly distorted market outcomes. Yet the success of developmental states in East Asia suggests that government intervention per se cannot explain why India has been limited to the Hindu rate of growth. It is necessary to probe the dynamics of India's economic policies to understand why its developmental state turned in such a lackluster performance.

The process by which India developed its "strong–weak state" (Rudolph and Rudolph, 1987) is certainly an interesting one for anyone with an appreciation of irony or paradox. This perspective on the evolution of India's polity provides an explanation for how economic policy came to structure the rich–poor economy outlined in the previous section. In essence, India's central political goals and historical legacies at first pushed the nation in the direction of a strong state with much greater capacity for policymaking and implementation than most Third World nations possess. Unfortunately, these political structures and goals then set off political dynamics that over time progressively undercut the capabilities of the central government while simultaneously increasing the social problems and demands confronting it. Consequently, many of the nation's economic policies became ineffectual and even counterproductive.

At independence there were several historical forces that might well have been expected to expedite the creation of a strong central state. The subcontinent had a long history of overarching empire above the regional kingdoms, and centuries of Moghul and British rule had consolidated the structures for a single polity. Historical traditions are far from deterministic, but in India's case they reinforced the nature of the contemporary political institutions and policy agendas. The long struggle for independence and the economic stagnation associated with the last-half century of British rule engendered a nationalism with both negative (an aversion to foreign rule, influence, and exploitation) and positive (a belief that Indians, if left to their own devices, can do much better for their country and society) elements that implied the need for strong governmental leadership (Kohli, 1987 & 1994; Rudolph and Rudolph, 1987).

The regime's economic commitment to self-reliant, state-led industrialization fit within a broader set of political assumptions or ideas. Lloyd and Susanne Rudolph (1987) argue that the three central principles were: (1) democracy to ensure that the government would act in the interests of the people, (2) socialism to promote rapid industrialization and prevent the continued exploitation of the poor by indigenous capitalists, and (3) secularism to prevent local communal conflicts from erupting and threatening social gains. These principles can be seen as both a reaction against British authoritarian colonial rule and imperialist economic domination, and a reflection of the Fabian socialism of Nehru and other Indian leaders—acquired, ironically, through British education. They can also, perhaps, be considered a "holy trinity" in the sense that, at least at the theoretical level, they promised to create an Indian government capable of leading the nation to freedom, prosperity, and an important role in world affairs.

These political goals implied a strong central state that would take the leading role in directing India's development strategy. Though lofty goals do not necessarily translate into political reality, the implications of historical traditions and political aims were consistent with institutional reality at the time of India's independence. That is, there were two organizations already in place that made the creation of a centralized state not just a hoped-for ideal but a realistic goal well within the capabilities of the incoming regime. One was the Congress Party, which had led the opposition to British colonial rule. The Congress Party was organized on a nationwide basis; with the partition between India and Pakistan, its dominance of Indian politics created the political basis for unified rule and policy. The British had overseen the establishment of the second crucial organization, the Indian Civil Service (ICS). A highly qualified central bureaucracy, the ICS provided the administrative power and capability necessary for centralized rule. Although Congress had viewed the ICS as part of the oppressive British rule before independence, its acceptance of this central bureaucracy as an important instrument whose expertise and administrative talents could contribute to Indian development brought together the political and bureaucratic institutions necessary for a strong centralized state. The collaboration between Congress and the ICS rested on a more solid foundation than political convenience: Both exemplified a Brahmanical system of enlightened elite rule justified by the elite's supposedly moral character and visions (Frankel, 1990). In fact, rather than resisting the new government (old opposition), India's bureaucratic (technocratic) elite—the ICS and the newly created Indian Administrative Service (IAS)—quickly lent their support for the core values of democracy, socialism, and secularism.

India's historical traditions, political and social goals, and government institutions fit together logically in a manner that seemed a priori to duplicate the developmental states that were to evolve in East Asia. In those cases, however, market, state, and society interacted synergistically. In India, in stark contrast, logical consistencies were transformed fairly quickly by practical contradictions, setting in motion a vicious cycle that undercut economic performance. Two such contradictions were critically important. First, the central political goal of democracy itself proved incompatible with Congress's organizational logic, thereby setting off several fissiparous chains of institutional change. Second, the economic strategy of self-reliant socialism distorted India's economy in an unproductive fashion and focused socioeconomic demands upon an increasingly ineffectual state. In each of these cases, political logic drove India away from its holy trinity toward a dysfunctional and interlinked "unholy trinity" of deinstitutionalization, bureaucratism, and monopoly exploitation in both the public and private sectors.

Contradictions Between Democracy and Congress's Patronage-Based Organization

Given Congress's role in leading India to independence, and the absence of a coherent opposition, the ruling party's support for democracy appears quite natural and, in fact, self-interested. However, Nehru's coalitional strategy for retaining power and controlling the party proved inconsistent with democracy's need to appeal to the general populace. The Nehru coalition had three primary components. Middle-class professionals, many directly tied to the state sector, formed one key component naturally attracted to the philosophy of democracy, socialism, and secularism. The participation of the other two groups reflects more concrete incentives. Business interests profited from the monopoly position that India's closed economy created for them, while rural "big men" shaped agrarian reforms so as to minimize any threat to their status (Kohli, 1987 & 1994; Rudolph and Rudolph, 1987).

Figure 5.1 outlines three major results of this contradiction between the dynamics of democracy and patronage-based unity. First, the organizational logic of Congress contributed to the substantial federalism of India's polity. The retention of significant powers by India's states continued a British legacy. In contrast to the centralized colonial administration that worked through the ICS and the army, Great Britain had maintained power by ruling indirectly, as well as through dispersed authority granted to local rajahs and *zamindari* ("intermediaries" who controlled large blocks of agricultural land). Ironically, Congress perpetuated this divide-and-rule strategy of the British (Frankel and Rao, 1990).

Federalism, in turn, contributed to two major problems. One was competition among the states for industrial projects. Similarly to Chinese provinces during the 1980s (Harding, 1987; Shirk, 1993; Wu, 1994), industrialization and economic development led to wasteful duplication and overbuilding of capacity as Indian states followed the logic of self-interest without regard to the discipline of either the market or the central authorities (Bhagwati and Desai, 1970). More indirectly, federalism is also associated with the rising level of communal conflict and nationalist strife that began in the late 1970s.

The large-scale violence between Hindus and Muslims that broke out at the time of independence and partition, despite the efforts of the Congress Party and the Muslim League, had showed that a commitment to secularism on the part of the elites would not necessarily solve the problems of communal conflict. Subsequently, India appeared to do well in ameliorating communal hostilities between Hindus and Muslims and among different castes, while maintaining a functioning democracy (Rudolph and Rudolph, 1987). Yet the ability of India's democracy to hold communal strife in check was clearly eroding by the 1970s, and religious and ethnic conflict became a significant threat to India's polity and economic performance during the 1980s and 1990s (Kohli, 1990). Federalism may have contributed to this problem by re-creating complex party competition and maneuvering in each state; this in turn made local communal

Figure 5.1   Model of How Patronage/Democracy Contradictions Undercut State Power

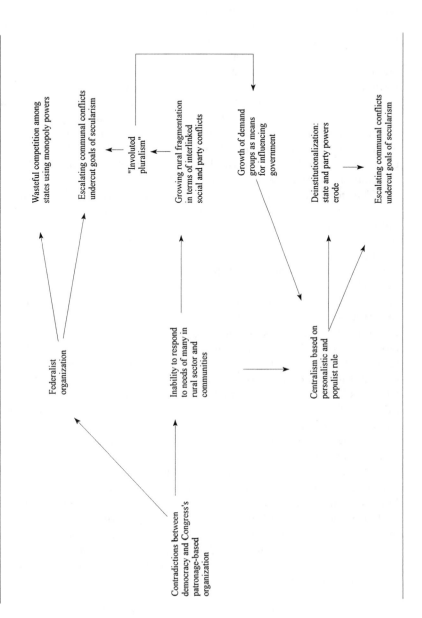

tensions an inviting target for partisan manipulation, thereby exacerbating rather than attenuating these hostilities.

A second counterproductive evolution set off by the contradiction between democracy and patronage involved instability in rural areas. Here, the connection was quite direct in that the need for a mass appeal to voters gradually made Congress's patronage links to big men untenable. Land reform after independence removed the zamindari but did little for the majority of agricultural households who remained either landless or land poor. Problems of agricultural poverty and low productivity were exacerbated, moreover, by Nehru's strategy of concentrating investment in industry based on what turned out to be the mistaken belief that rapid industrial growth would pull the rural areas out of poverty (Bhagwati, 1993; Balasubramanyam, 1984; Rudolph and Rudolph, 1987).

The combination of democracy, widespread rural poverty, and the Nehru strategy of basing Congress's rural support on the influence of rural big men made Congress increasingly vulnerable to contrasting appeals by opposition parties. Indeed, the medium farmers referred to as "bullock capitalists" by Rudolph and Rudolph (1987) played an important role in the Janata Party's formation of the first non-Congress national government in 1977. More significantly, the failure of land reform to alter the economic circumstances of the majority of the population in agricultural areas set off a process in which the patronage-based government and Congress could not adequately respond to the pleas for ameliorative policies that democratization unleashed. This produced a growing rural fragmentation in terms of socioeconomic and party conflicts that were interlinked in complex and idiosyncratic ways in different states and regions. This created what has been termed "involuted pluralism," or the "excessive multiplication and fragmentation" of political groups and arenas (Rudolph and Rudolph, 1987; see also Frankel, 1978; Frankel and Rao, 1990; Kohli, 1990). The increase over time of involuted pluralism was a major factor stimulating the escalation of communal conflict.

The third set of relationships modeled in Figure 5.1 is of broader importance, because it provides the central explanation for the evolution of India's strong–weak state. The involuted pluralism resulting from the contradiction between the huge number of groups mobilized by India's democratization and the limitations of Congress's patronage-based organizational dynamics resulted in the emergence of "demand groups" whose growing power and importance in Indian politics actively undercut normal government institutions.

> Formally organized interests work in institutionally defined policy arenas. They attempt to influence legislatures, bureaucratic agencies, and sometimes party policy. . . . Demand groups, by contrast, do not work

primarily in institutionally-defined policy arenas. They rely less on expertise and lobbying skill than on symbolic and agitational politics. The tactics and style of demand groups have become a highly elaborated political art form that speaks to India's indigenous political culture, mobilizes support, influences public opinion, and gains bargaining advantage. Its ad hoc and spontaneous tactics include public dramas such as *padyatras* (political pilgrimages), *hartals* (shutdowns), *rasta rokos* (road blocks), and *gheraos* (lock-ins) (Rudolph and Rudolph, 1987: 252–253).

The vicious cycle among rural fragmentation, involuted pluralism, and the rise of demand groups increasingly undermined the Nehru formula for ruling India democratically, thereby creating pressures for a new political formula. Nehru's daughter, Indira Gandhi, found such a formula in the late 1960s and early 1970s. She challenged the Congress establishment or "syndicate" (which, ironically, had initially supported her for prime minister because it saw her as relatively pliant) by appealing directly to the people with her slogan of "Abolish poverty!" The success of Gandhi's populist appeals allowed her to centralize party and government power by subordinating the normal hierarchy and organization to her personalistic desires and coterie (Frankel, 1978; Kohli, 1987 & 1994; Rudolph and Rudolph, 1987).

Centralization of power is usually associated with increasing state strength and capacity. In India, however, exactly the opposite happened. The rise of personalistic rule led to the deinstitutionalization of the state and Congress party hierarchies, whose power flowed to the personal retinues of Gandhi and other leaders (Frankel, 1978 & 1990; Rudolph and Rudolph, 1987). Consequently, centralization actually resulted in decreased state capacity as the government became increasingly concerned with personalistic battles for political power and spoils, as opposed to competent administration and service provision. Atul Kohli (1994) conceptualizes this process of degeneration neatly as a double paradox: Rural fragmentation stimulated national centralization; because of the personalistic nature of rule, centralization of power decreased rather than increased the strength and capacity of the Indian state.

In particular, the rift within Congress between Indira Gandhi and the syndicate, and the alternation of governments between parties that commenced in the late 1970s, combined to destroy the integrity and competence of the IAS. Beginning with Gandhi, many of India's top politicians no longer accepted the IAS as a neutral and highly skilled technocracy committed to the development and well-being of Indian society. Rather, pressure was exerted to be responsive and loyal to individual political leaders who decided rewards and punishments accordingly (Rudolph and Rudolph, 1987). Such a transformation not only attacked state capacity directly by subordinating policy implementation to personalistic political whims but, more seriously, created incentives for bureaucratic corruption and the growth of a predatory state (Evans, 1995) by destroying the legitimacy of technocratic administration.

Self-Reliant Socialism

Just as democracy in the subcontinent ultimately stimulated several counterproductive outcomes, India's commitment to self-reliant socialism, as modeled in Figure 5.2, set off a second chain reaction of political and economic consequences that helped shape the Hindu rate of growth. For Nehru (1954), self-reliance meant that individuals can and should be free of dependence on capitalist relations of greed and competition. He believed that it is possible for people to act from a spirit of service to the community, so long as a responsive and competent government takes the lead in providing the material and cultural foundations.

The material foundation for self-reliance was to be found in the power of industrial machinery. A concise summary of the government's strategy was drafted by Mahalanobis.

> We have to produce more and more machinery and tools and energy per person so as to increase the productivity of each individual worker, and also to supply more and more people with machinery, tools and power. In India, with our abundant supply of iron ore we should obviously install new steel plants every year. Instead of importing machinery to install these new plants it would be obviously desirable to make such machinery within the country. We must therefore have factories for the production of heavy machinery and heavy electrical equipment. Once we succeed in establishing these basic heavy industries it would be possible to produce more and more essential capital goods out of our domestic resources; and using such capital goods, to increase modern industrial investment at a rapid rate. A rapid industrialization of the country is thus the only radical cure of unemployment (Bose and Mukherjee, 1985: 215).

Many have noted the similarity between India's planning effort in the 1950s and 1960s and the intellectual currents flowing in both the Soviet Union and the West. It should be acknowledged, however, that much of the underpinning of India's policies represents an independently conceived attempt to confront the complex of problems and ambitions facing India.

Nehru and Mahalanobis considered employment generation to be the primary goal of planned development (Bose and Mukherjee, 1985). They insisted, however, that productive employment is possible only when workers have modern machinery and tools. Because many years would pass before India was able to produce capital goods for more than a small fraction of its labor force, a "diffuse" sector of small-scale and village industries would be needed to provide the majority of jobs. Thus, the strategy

Figure 5.2 Model of Economic and Political Consequences of Self-Reliant Socialism

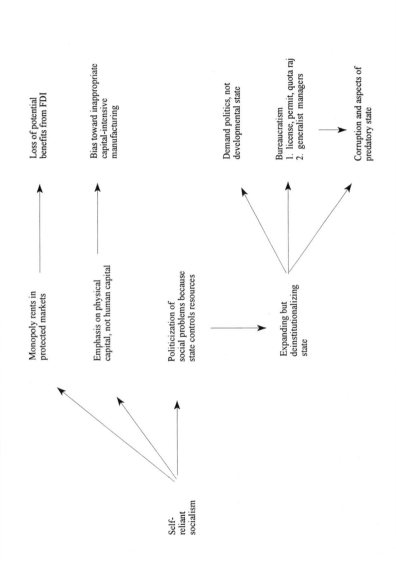

was to develop India by expanding the modern sector of a classic dual economy. Although government would take direct responsibility for forward-looking, capital-intensive investments, support for the diffuse sector would be limited to "institutional changes, spread of education, improvement of communication, etc., and, above everything else, by carrying conviction to the masses that Government is doing its best for national development" (Bose and Mukherjee, 1985: 157). Nehru (1954) chided those who expected much government assistance for these handicraft activities and made it clear that their expansion was dependent on their own inherent strength and vitality. The diffuse sector served as a temporary shelter where workers were to await the construction of the modern economy.

Nehru and Mahalanobis included agriculture in the diffuse sector. On the one hand, substantial improvements in agricultural productivity were not expected until the industrial sector was able to provide modern inputs. On the other hand, immediate increases in agricultural output were to be achieved "by intensive cultivation of land by hand and by improving conditions of living in rural areas through community projects, land reform, consolidation of holdings, village cooperative [sic] etc." (Bose and Mukherjee, 1985: 156–157).

The paramount objective of the central government was to ensure that the modern economy would remain free of the influence of self-interested individuals or groups who would divert the nation from its ultimate goal of extending the full benefits of modernity to every citizen. The support of the masses was to be achieved through political means, rather than direct economic assistance. Specifically, the government was to exercise control over the distributional effects of the growth process: "planning should be deliberately aimed at achieving a broad parity in the level of production and of living in the different regions of India and preventing the formation of depressed areas" and "avoid . . . heavy concentration of financial power in the hands of a small number of monopoly capitalists" (Bose and Mukherjee, 1985: 118 & 121). Despite self-reliance, however, a substantial foreign influence on India's growth path did emerge in the common practice of tying foreign aid to particular projects involving imports of material and/or expertise from the donor country. This undoubtedly strengthened the government's bias toward large, capital-intensive projects that are easier to administer and observe than a larger number of small and diverse projects.

Whether one's perspective is a neoclassical appreciation for market forces, or the recognition that an effective developmental state utilizes, rather than attempts to override, market incentives, India's policies are a striking example of a government's ability to generate inefficiencies, rent seeking, and economic stagnation, as depicted in Figure 5.2. The absence of competitive markets was used by both state corporations and domestic businesses in India to sustain increasingly inefficient and obsolete operations, and to pursue other goals in place of economic efficiency—such as patronage employment opportunities for the public sector and higher than normal profits (i.e., monopoly rents) for the private sector. Indeed, the relationship of mutual rent seeking between the Congress Party and the big business houses has been described as "a flabby and heterogeneous dominant coalition preoccupied in a spree of anarchical grabbing of public resources" (Bardhan, 1984: 70).

In addition to general economic inefficiency, self-reliant socialism generated an inappropriate industrial structure. In the belief that an indigenous capital-goods sector is a cornerstone of a nation's economic independence, India's industrial and trade policies were targeted on capital-intensive heavy industries. This strategy offered no relief for India's high poverty and unemployment rates, but was consistent with the policymakers' belief that only a dramatic demonstration of modernity by the state could be sufficient to rouse the tradition-bound masses of India. One result was that India lagged behind many other developing nations in its commitment to literacy and mass education, a gap to which its modest economic performance is often attributed. This problem was exacerbated by another British legacy, that of devoting scarce educational resources to elite higher education. In fact, India has a considerable oversupply of university students and graduates, especially in the humanities and liberal arts, thereby creating another vocal and powerful demand group (Bhagwati, 1993; Rudolph and Rudolph, 1987; Weiner, 1991).

Neoclassicists would generally expect state intervention in the economy to produce such distortions. Yet the governments of Japan in the 1950s and South Korea in the 1960s made expensive commitments to, respectively, maintaining and developing domestic steel industries. Except for Hong Kong, all the East Asian Dragons, big or little, had significant periods of highly protectionist import-substitution industrialization. The key difference was that in East Asia some combination of market forces (e.g., the need for small economies like those of the Little Dragons to participate in international trade, or the stiff competition among Japanese keiretsu) and government policy (e.g., South Korean performance standards for chaebol to retain state-controlled financing) served to promote efficiency. In India, in sharp contrast, the government's ideology blinded it to the importance of economic efficiency, while economic rents were large enough to keep the major economic actors satisfied.

India's commitment to self-reliant socialism also generated another set of consequences that undermined both state capacity and economic performance. Their effects, as summarized in the bottom half of Figure 5.2, can be considered indirect because they resulted more from unintended effects than from the logic of self-reliant socialism per se. The state accounts for over two-thirds of the jobs in what Indians call the organized sector of medium and large industrial, commercial, and financial establishments. The state's control over such a large proportion of society's resources makes it the focus of attempts to alleviate many social problems. Whereas Indian socialism views such calls for state activism favorably, the low capabilities of government to respond effectively to the social problems emanating from the huge "unorganized" sector resulted in Kohli's two-stage paradox of an "expanding but de-institutionalizing" state.

Perhaps most seriously, this situation vitiated an important initial advantage for India: a well-trained and highly motivated civil service that could have provided technocratic leadership of the national-development project, as occurred in Japan, Singapore, and South Korea. Instead, bureaucratization became a drag on economic performance. Although India eschewed a full command economy based on the planning of physical production for the entire economy, it implemented a detailed system of regulation as a means for industrial policy and to prevent large-scale capitalists from abusing their economic power. This evolved into the "license, permit, quota raj" (Encarnation, 1989; Evans, 1995), which is now almost universally condemned, even by those sympathetic to socialist goals. This vastly expanding regulatory state was driven not only by the logic of regulation itself but by pressures to expand the state bureaucracy as a means for creating middle-class employment: More bureaucrats need at least a minimum of something to do, so they create more regulations.

More broadly, the very nature of the IAS—well-educated generalist managers—proved inappropriate and counterproductive when the civil service was given the task of managing state corporations. Management of technical enterprises by generalists without any expert knowledge, who nevertheless would not defer to the advice of their technically trained subordinates, led to incompetence, ad hocism, routine-mindedness, and endless red tape in policy decisions (Bhagwati and Desai, 1970). In short, the IAS, reflecting its British colonial heritage, was trained and probably well qualified to supply enlightened public administration. When this management philosophy was transferred to the sphere of running economic enterprises, it became a sure recipe for disaster. Furthermore, civil servants were affected by the intrusion of political factors in economic and administrative decisionmaking, such as burgeoning corruption and the gross inefficiencies that resulted from using SOEs as patronage bases for both management and unskilled labor.

India's status as a rich–poor economy, therefore, can be explained to a considerable extent by the political dynamics that created its strong–weak state. The initial goals of India's political elite entailed a strong developmental state, and the combination of its development strategy and the changes set off by democratization led to a centralization of political power. Rather than promote development, however, this centralization weakened state capacity and was associated with a variety of counter-productive economic policies by the government and the encouragement and protection of rent-seeking activities by private business. The line between making decisions on political rather than economic criteria, and outright corruption and plundering was crossed easily and often. This resulted in a political economy dominated by the unholy trinity of deinstitutionalization, bureaucratization, and rent seeking.

This section has described how an interweaving of political and economic processes sustained for nearly a half-century a self-defeating pursuit of Lakshmi. Although it is plausible that the errors of India's policymakers were in themselves sufficient to propel the country onto this unfortunate path, it is not clear that a greater respect for market forces, whether in themselves or as tools of a developmental state, would have been sufficient to set in motion sustained and widely shared economic progress. Indeed, the previous chapters showed that the success of development efforts in East Asia was due at least as much to the quality of private-sector behaviors as to the wisdom of government policies. Societies in East Asia were able to both influence and respond to government policies, because of generally high levels of wealth, income, and education, compared with the norm in India at independence. What accounts for this fundamental disparity between East and South? Why did India's elite not realize the folly of attempting a self-reliant socialism that failed to equip the majority of Indians to make any contribution to the nation's economic progress? The answers have much to do with the productivity of agriculture, to which attention is turned in the next section.

Agriculture, Public Policies, and Private-Sector Capabilities

Excepting those rare economies in which there is little or no crop production, a productive agriculture is universally acknowledged as a requirement for sustained economic growth. Nonetheless, it is easy to underestimate the full and lasting implications of agricultural performance. In his recent monograph outlining the origins of India's present economic challenges, Jagdish Bhagwati (1993) includes barely ten words of commentary on agriculture. Although Deepak Lal (1988) presents an insightful history of India's agriculture, he draws the implication that further development of agriculture is of secondary importance compared with measures to promote labor-intensive exports. This policy advice seems reasonable, but it fails to appreciate a major lesson of the Asian development experiences reviewed in the present work: No government is likely to succeed in promoting labor-intensive exports unless its citizens are able to respond effectively to the opportunities and incentives the state may provide. Creation of this ability is the principal contribution of a productive agriculture to a nation's overall development.

More serious than the tendency of scholars to overlook the importance of agriculture is the real neglect of the majority of people by government policymakers. Enriching the peasantry has rarely been a top priority of government strategists, and success in this area is rarer still. There may be more at work here than a deficit of compassion or a desire to exploit others. Increasing the productivity and incomes of those who work the land is expensive, the benefits accrue only slowly, and the contribution to overall economic development is likely to be visible only in hindsight. It is not surprising, therefore, that meaningful support for agriculture in government policies is determined largely by the degree to which the sector has become an annoying constraint on growth.

Japan As an East Asian Model

The economic history of Japan illustrates both the essential role of agriculture in development and the reluctance of policymakers to provide the sector with commensurate support. Moreover, a comparison of Japan's experience with that of India lends insight into the relative failure of the latter country's development efforts.

When Japan's Meiji leaders began the process of rapid modernization of the economy in the final decades of the nineteenth century, they had at their disposal the most productive foodgrain sector in Asia. In fact, by the middle of the twentieth century, only South Korea and Taiwan had achieved average rice (paddy) yields per unit of land exceeding the most conservative estimate for Japan around 1880 (Hayami and Yamada, 1970). This remarkable productivity was the result of more than two centuries of economic and social evolution during the Tokugawa period (Smith, 1959). More specifically, by 1880, about 60 percent of Japan's cultivated land—including nearly all the paddy area—received some degree of irrigation (Kikuchi and Hayami, 1985). Although high yields were, in part, a reflection of population densities well above the Asian average, the Meiji government received in taxes an average of nearly 15 percent of agriculture's net product until 1900 (Hayami, 1988), whereas the retained output was sufficient both to maintain the agricultural population and for landlords to invest a considerable portion of their rental income in the nation's industrialization.

Throughout the period before World War II, Japan's agriculture bore a tax burden several times greater than that imposed on nonagriculture, while it financed private investments in other sectors. Equally significant, cheap food was provided for the growing industrial labor force. These contributions of agriculture to Japan's industrial-military goals did not require, at first, much public expenditure. Prior to 1900, rice yields were improved primarily through local-government-sponsored innovation and diffusion of traditional techniques and inputs among progressive farmers (*gono*). By the turn of the century, however, the diffusion of existing technology had begun to reach a limit imposed by the available agronomic knowledge, seed varieties, and water-control infrastructure. The need to expand the scope of government support for agriculture was articulated most forcefully by the representatives of the gono, who became the principal beneficiaries of the gradual increase in government expenditures on agriculture that occurred during the decades preceding World War II (Hayami, 1975).

Before diverting any great amount of scarce financial capital to assist agriculture, Japan imported increasing quantities of rice from its colonies in Taiwan and Korea. The investments required to maintain an adequate supply of rice were concentrated in Japan's colonies, rather than in Japan proper, because further improvements in water-control infrastructure in Japan were far more expensive (Kikuchi and Hayami, 1985). The relatively low-cost engineering projects in Japan had been completed prior to the Meiji Restoration in 1868 and during the first few decades thereafter. Imports of colonial rice had risen by 1929 to 14 percent of Japan's domestic production (Allen, 1981) and to 20 percent of domestic production by the mid-1930s (Hayami, 1988). This, along with an industrial depression and unusually good harvests in Japan, caused rice prices to plummet in the late 1920s and early 1930s.

The government perceived the danger of serious disruption in its domestic agriculture and so reduced the volume of rice imports, but not by nearly enough to turn the terms of trade in favor of agriculture. Further action on behalf of agriculture was considered necessary, however, to confront the alarming rise in peasant disputes that had begun in 1918 and continued into the early 1930s (Napier, 1982). The tax rate on net agricultural output was reduced from around 12 percent during the first two decades of the century to under 7 percent by the late 1930s. During the same period, government subsidies received by agriculture rose from negligible to more than 1 percent of net product. Beginning in 1931, the subsidy to agriculture (as a percentage of net sectoral product) exceeded the subsidy to nonagriculture (Hayami, 1988). With the aid of these subsidies, the area of land served by irrigation infrastructure rose by more than 1 million hectares between 1920 and 1940, compared with an increase of only 546,000 hectares between 1880 and 1920 (Hayami, 1975). Confirming the increased cost of the more recent irrigation expenditures, the marginal capital-output ratio in agriculture, which had averaged 1.36 between 1900 and 1920, rose to 5.00 during the years from 1920 to 1942 (Hirashima, 1986).

The impact of the food constraint on government policies toward agriculture went beyond taxes and subsidies. As early as 1924, Japan's leaders began to recognize that commercialization of agriculture and expansion of investment opportunities outside the sector had resulted in a widespread phenomenon of landlords renouncing direct oversight of agricultural operations to become absentee (parasitic) landlords (Hayami, 1975). At the same time, tenant farmers were gaining in literacy, were sending family members to work in factories or with the military, and were exposed to bureaucratic procedures and the rule of law rather than tradition (Smethurst, 1986). They were thus prepared to perceive changes in their power relative to the once-revered landlords and to pursue their own interests to the extent possible. In this climate, the national interest would be served better by assisting small farmers and tenants directly to increase their productivity (Waswo, 1982). This view was strengthened when food shortages reappeared in the late 1930s despite rising imports from the colonies (Hayami, 1988). The shift in political support from landlords to tenants ought not to be exaggerated. It reveals, nevertheless, that the government was coming to understand that cheap food for industrialization now depended on creating incentives for cultivators to innovate and invest in growth-inducing inputs.

The government began providing financial assistance to tenants who wished to buy the land they were cultivating. Between 1926 and 1937, 115,000 hectares of land were acquired by tenants, far exceeding the government's target (Hayami, 1975). Although this represented only 4 percent of farmland under tenancy, the government later implemented a two-tier pricing structure for land that allowed tenants to buy land at lower prices than landlords, with the result that the conversion of land from tenancy to owner-cultivated accelerated during World War II (Smethurst, 1986). In 1939 the first legislation to place a ceiling on land rents was passed (Waswo, 1982). According to Smethurst (1986: 104), "The striking transformation of the countryside between 1868 and 1948 turned peasants into farmers. General MacArthur and his land reform only iced the cake."

It is evident that the strength of agriculture on which Japan built its early industrialization was neither a laissez-faire outcome nor the result of an enlightened government's respect for the sector. In fact, the industrialization strategy of Japan's leaders early in the twentieth century, with its logic of cheap food and cheap labor, seemed designed to prevent the rise of the large middle class on which a successful synergy between state and society depends. Oshima (1987: 111) emphasizes the contrast between the exploitative militarism of Japan's prewar growth and the initial postwar period in which

> new technologies and institutions increased [crop] yields; then came rises
> in real wages and farm incomes, domestic demand, crop diversification,

and off-farm employment, all of which contributed to full employment, and these accelerated wage increases, mechanization, and migration in the 1950s.

From this dynamism, triggered by widely shared agricultural productivity, arise competitive domestic markets, increasingly educated workers, and industrial firms capable of meeting international standards of efficiency (Adelman, 1984; Grabowski, 1994; Johnston, 1970; Mellor, 1976; Mellor and Johnston, 1984; Oshima, 1987; Trinque, 1992).

This brief account of early modern economic growth in Japan provides additional support for the claim made in earlier chapters that an economic "miracle" requires both a developmental state and a society able to recognize and pursue opportunities to improve the productivity of economic resources. More important, it resolves the "chicken or egg" quandary implicit in the need for state and society to interact synergistically. How can a society with low economic productivity give rise to an effective developmental state? How can a developmental state, if it should appear, accomplish anything, when its ability to choose and implement correct policies relies on a social dynamic that does not yet exist? The paradox is resolved in the recognition that the state need not—indeed, cannot—predetermine the course of economic change. Foresight and discipline are commendable qualities. Fortunately, the rather more common errors of judgment and pursuit of short-run rents create strains and dislocations—disequilibria—that present both state and society with opportunities to rethink their policies and behaviors. Thus, a low-productivity economy can "pull itself up by the bootstraps."

More specifically, Japan's experience confirms the important role of agriculture in economic development. In Taiwan and South Korea, also, productive farmers—an ironic legacy of Japan's hesitancy to invest in the further development of its own agriculture—made substantial contributions to each economy's industrialization, while a combination of economic and political incentives motivated land reforms and subsequent investments. Taiwan is often cited as the ideal example of what Irma Adelman (1984) has called "agricultural-demand-led industrialization" because of the state's early and consistent commitment to developing agriculture. The evolution of policies in South Korea more closely resembles the Japanese pattern of an initial focus on industrialization followed (in the late 1970s) by increased public spending on agriculture (Oshima, 1993).

India and the East Asian Model

The evolution of economic policies in independent India parallels Japan's prewar experience. The developmental state in each country concentrated its attention and resources on industrialization; a serious commitment to the modernization of agriculture was accepted only gradually and without enthusiasm. In Japan the process culminated dramatically in a land reform imposed by an occupying army, while India continues to get by with limited reforms and limited modernization of a generally low-productivity agriculture.

When independence from the British was achieved in 1947, India's leaders felt acutely the need to end what they believed to have been a long period of exploitation of their people by imperialist and capitalist forces. It was imperative that political independence be followed as quickly as possible by economic independence. Thus, as in Japan, India's rulers were committed to industrialization and, to a somewhat lesser extent, militarization. In India, unlike in Japan, this was to mean a rapid adjustment to autarchy. It may be that India's decision not to promote international trade served neither its goal of economic strength nor the welfare of its citizens. India's leaders believed, however, that trade with the West had impoverished their country and would continue to do so if not tightly controlled. In this they may well have been mistaken, just as Japan's leaders may have been mistaken in their belief that increasingly aggressive imperialism was the best way to further Japan's interests. What is important is that these beliefs were firmly held not only by each country's leaders, but by powerful segments of their societies as well. The pressure on India's leaders to implement policies regardless of their negative impact on the nation's export potential was as great as the pressure in Japan for policies to maximize exports.

Of greater significance, probably, than India's distrust of international trade was the need of the central government in New Delhi to create and preserve a unified nation. Whereas Japan's greatest threats were external, India was most vulnerable to destruction from within. It is instructive that the major internal disturbance to confront the Meiji leaders in Japan, the civil war of 1877, was inspired by a belief that the government was failing in its responsibility to protect Japan from foreign domination (Lehmann, 1982). India's leaders did not have the benefit of an obvious external enemy to inspire commitment to the national interest above all else.

In its first years of independence, India had to overcome the horror of partition, incorporate the princely states, and somehow counterbalance the "centrifugal forces of diverse language, culture, and objectives on the Indian subcontinent" (Mellor, 1976: 4). Addressing India's parliament in 1952, Nehru (1954: 93) emphasized the link between India's economic planning and the nation's plural character.

> Our plan for future progress must cope with the amalgam and variety we have in India. When I see these two heavy volumes of the Report of the Planning Commission, my mind conjures up the vision of something

vast—the mighty theme of a nation building and re-making itself. We are, all of us, working together to make a new India—not abstractly for a nation but for the 360 million people who are wanting to progress as individuals and as groups.

Nehru (1954: 940) went on to urge that the government's "objective must be to put an end to all differences between class and class, to bring about more equality and a more unitary society—in other words, to strive for economic democracy." If the goal of economic democracy were kept always in view, Nehru believed, divisive impulses might be held in check. Moreover, the very attempt to approach the goal of economic democracy through central planning

> has made people think of this country as a whole. I think it is most essential that India, which is united politically and in many other ways, should, to the same extent, be united mentally and emotionally also. We often go off at a tangent on grounds of provincialism, communalism, religion or caste. We have no emotional awareness of the unity of the country. Planning will help us in having an emotional awareness of our problems as a whole. It will help us to see the isolated problems in villages or districts or even provinces in their larger context (Nehru, 1954: 97).

Whereas it was important for a strong center to offer positive proposals with nationalist appeal, it was equally necessary to avoid as much as possible providing any grounds for regional or sectoral interests to organize against the center. Chakravarty (1987: 16) argues, for example, that a decision was made not to promote textile exports because this "would have required supporting a particular regional group of industrialists at the expense of others." Chakravarty goes on to note that growth of a modern textile industry was offensive to those who endorsed the Gandhian vision of renewing India's ancient textile handicrafts. The decline of this highly labor-intensive industry during the nineteenth century was one of the principal indictments against capitalism among India's nationalist writers.

The goal of national unity was, in fact, served by the chosen policy of capital-intensive industrialization. Before any attempt could be launched to promote industrialization, however, some measures had to be taken to improve the productivity of India's agriculture. Agricultural output had grown at a meager annual average rate of 0.6 percent between 1891 and 1941, roughly the same as the population-growth rate over the period (Reynolds, 1985). Apart from importing food to meet immediate needs, the government addressed the needs of agriculture with a Community Development Program, investments in land infrastructure, and land reform.

A dominant feature of the attitude of India's leaders toward agriculture was their belief that low productivity in the sector was primarily a social problem. Narrowly economic requirements—physical infrastructure, demonstration of improved practices, current inputs such as seeds and fertilizers, and development of new technologies—were either considered of secondary importance or simply overlooked. The ambitious Community Development Program launched in 1952 had as one goal the freeing of India's villages from exploitation by moneylenders and grain merchants; the parallel goal of removing exploitation by landlords was to be accomplished through reformist legislation. Liberation of the peasant economy was to be combined with education to undermine the cultivators' fatalism and resistance to change that had resulted from exploitation and was responsible for their failure to make full use of existing technical knowledge. Most important, community development was seen as a means of bringing India's rural villages into the unified, modern India that was being created. In Nehru's words, "These Community Projects appear to me to be something of vital importance, not only in the material achievements that they would bring about but much more so because they seek to build up the community and the individual and to make the latter a builder of his own village centre and of India in the larger sense" (Nehru, 1954: 85).

Mellor (1976) considers that India's Community Development Program was responsible for at most a negligible amount of the acceleration of growth that occurred in agriculture during the 1950s. Expansion of irrigation, however, was responsible for about 20 percent of foodgrain-output growth during the period from 1949/50 to 1956/57 and 14 percent of the growth between the latter year and 1960/61. Expansion of unirrigated land area contributed about 46 percent of increased foodgrain production during the early 1950s, then declined to 20 percent between 1956/57 and 1960/61. The other major source of output growth was intensification of the labor input, which accounted for 26 percent of growth up to 1956/57 and 55 percent during the period ending in 1960/61 (Mellor, 1976: 32). Irrigation expenditures were focused, not surprisingly, on large projects that contributed to the central government's prestige and avoided the difficulties inherent in administering small projects in a heterogeneous environment.

Among India's early policies toward agriculture, the Community Development Program may be viewed as a reflection of ideology and cultural presumptions regarding the peasantry. Irrigation expenditures were a simple pragmatic necessity. It is in the area of land reform and the related issue of taxation of agricultural incomes that one finds evidence of the influence of political reality on economic policies.

India's zamindari (landlord) abolition, effected during the First Five-Year Plan (1951–1956), parallels in some respects the dispossession of the *daimyo* in Japan in 1872. In each case the action was politically easy—in Japan because the reform was symbolic of the restoration of power to the emperor; in India because the zamindari system was associated in the public consciousness with the period of British rule. Also in each case, the reform consisted of lopping off the head of a hierarchy of rights in land, rather than a true transfer of "land to the tiller." A final similarity is that both reforms made some contribution to improving incentives and productivity in agriculture.

The differences between zamindari abolition and daimyo dispossession are far more significant than the similarities, however. First, the prime motivation for and result of daimyo dispossession was the transfer to the national government of the considerable land revenues that had sustained the daimyo during the earlier feudal period. The dispossession was followed by an extensive Land Tax Revision that began in 1873. Agriculture provided no less than 75 percent of combined national and local tax revenues in Japan prior to 1900. Not until after World War I did agriculture's share of the tax burden fall below 50 percent (Hayami, 1988). In contrast, revenue generation for the central government was no part of India's zamindari abolition.

A second major difference between zamindari abolition and daimyo dispossession is that the former was advertised as a transfer of land to the tiller, whereas the latter was responsible for a significant increase in tenancy. The proportion of total arable land cultivated under tenancy in Japan rose from less than 30 percent in the early 1870s to nearly 50 percent by 1930 (Hayami, 1975).

In India, according to the frequently cited estimates of Ali Khusro, zamindari abolition reduced the proportion of land under tenancy from 60 percent to 25 percent (Mellor, 1976). The potential significance of zamindari abolition was greatest in India's eastern region; many other parts of the country have historically been dominated by owner cultivation. Although the reform had a real impact in some instances, Herring (1983: 128) points out that

> ground rent as an institution was not attacked or abolished; old owners ("intermediaries") were allowed to retain large amounts of land for "self-cultivation," which often meant continuation of sharecropping, and new owners (former superior tenants) were—in fact if not in law—free to engage sharecroppers as well. . . . The reforms did not assure that cultivators would obtain land nor that new proprietors would not function as parasitic rentiers.

Despite the limited nature of land reform in India, it is plausible that, as Mellor (1976: 34–35) asserts, these reforms "may well have helped increase the rate of growth of foodgrains production from the 0.11 percent in the pre-independence decades to the 2.5 to 3.0 percent of the first two five year plans." However, it is officially acknowledged in India that the implementation of zamindari abolition and, to an even greater extent, later attempts to redistribute land through ceilings on landholdings, have been disappointing. The failure of India to effect meaningful land reform is intimately related to the decision of the central government not to rely on agriculture as a significant source of tax revenue. Each reflects the limits of central authority within India's federal polity.

The most significant effect of the daimyo dispossession in Japan was that the former *han* (feudal domains) were transformed into prefectures thoroughly subordinate to the national government. Such a degree of centralization was not possible in India, and this is the final point of contrast between daimyo dispossession and zamindari abolition. Land revenue and, indeed, the bulk of government responsibilities with regard to agriculture had been placed under the authority of India's provinces as part of a limited autonomy granted during the period of British rule. In drafting the constitution of independent India, it was necessary to continue this sharing of powers between the central and state governments. Agriculture and land revenue were especially assured of remaining state subjects because of the heterogeneous character of agriculture in the subcontinent and the dependence of the ruling Congress Party on the political support of the landholding elite.

In addition to the constitutional separation of powers between the center and the states, significant taxation of agricultural land in India has been blocked by the fact that a land-tax revision such as occurred in Japan would require the government to produce detailed records of land ownership from which to calculate the taxes owed. This would obligate India's leaders to take sides, in practice and not merely in rhetoric, between the landlords and the cultivators. As it is, the center has the luxury of declaring its solidarity with the mass of peasant voters without directly threatening the interests of the agrarian elite. If one follows Jannuzi's (1989) suggestion to label India's agrarian policies as "revenue reform" rather than "land reform," the impact of the policies, as regards India's central government, remains as weak.

As a final note on this topic, it must be remembered that securing land revenue in India would have been considerably more difficult and expensive than it had been in Japan. For one thing, Hayami (1975) has estimated that India's agricultural output per male farm worker on average between 1957 and 1962 was less than 85 percent of the comparable figure in Japan around 1880; yield per unit of agricultural land in India around 1960 was less than 40 percent of the yield eight decades earlier in Japan. The rulers of Meiji Japan acquired from the daimyo a landholding class accustomed to paying taxes. Nonetheless, Japan spent nine years and nearly an entire year's land revenue on the cadastral surveys required to implement the Land Tax Revision (Hayami, 1975). In India land revenue had declined steadily under British rule, representing only 1 percent of national income on the eve of independence (Lal, 1988). In 1960/61, taxes from agriculture amounted to 5.6 percent of income in the sector (Mellor, 1976), barely a third of the tax rate imposed in the early years of Meiji rule in Japan. Resistance to and evasion of attempts to increase land revenues in India would likely have been as effective as they have been in the case of land reforms. Given these considerations, it is not difficult to understand why India's government did little either to implement reforms to encourage greater productivity in agriculture or to exploit the sector as a source of finance for economic growth.

India's leaders thought it best to treat agriculture as a *"bargain sector, a sector with large unexploited potential which can provide the requisite surplus with relatively low investment and in a comparatively short time after, of course, a certain minimum infrastructure has been developed"* (Chakravarty, 1987: 94). The planners of India's modernization expected of agriculture only that it provide cheap food to support the creation of an industrial sector in which advanced machinery and technology would provide the most rapid growth of output and productivity. The demand on agriculture was further softened by the availability of food imports. Finally, a significant boost to the desire of India's leaders to concentrate their efforts on developing industry came from the apparent early success of the agricultural policies: Foodgrain output grew at an average rate of 4.8 percent during the First Plan period, and foodgrain prices declined relative to all other commodities (Mellor, 1976).

India's attempt at rapid industrialization focusing on heavy industries under government control began with the Second Five-Year Plan (1956–1961) and remained dominant through most of the Third Plan period (1961–1966). The decision to pursue this course was a result of India's peculiar form of self-reliant socialism, of the need to bind the country into a cohesive nation, and of the factors discussed earlier that militated against any significant reliance on agriculture to contribute to modernization. Despite the inefficiencies and negative consequences of India's strategy, the industrial sector grew at an average annual rate of 6.2 percent between 1951 and 1960, with an accelerating trend to a 9 percent growth rate from 1961 to 1965 (Mellor, 1976). This compares favorably with the average annual growth of industry in Japan between 1885 and 1940, 6.6 percent (Oshima, 1987).

Among the goals guiding the formulation of India's Second Five-Year Plan was the elimination of unemployment within ten years. Estimates of unemployment, including disguised unemployment, in the mid-1950s ranged from ten to thirty million workers. It was estimated also that more than two million new job seekers would be entering the labor force each year. Employment generation during the Second Plan was inadequate to absorb even the new entrants, prompting calls for massive increases in plan expenditure for the Third Plan and beyond (Bose and Mukherjee, 1985). Frustration over the employment performance of the government's policies strengthened the resolve of India's policymakers, and public outlays nearly doubled from 46.7 million rupees in the Second Plan to 85.8 million rupees in the Third Plan (Pendse, 1988).

The poor performance of agriculture at the close of the Third Plan period exposed a serious weakness in the government's strategy. Growth of agriculture had seemed adequate during the Second Plan years; the growth rate of agricultural output per capita in the 1950s averaged 1.3 percent, compared with Japan's slightly negative per capita growth from 1901 to 1937 (Oshima, 1987). Agriculture in India remained heavily dependent on favorable weather, however, and a drought in 1965/66 caused foodgrain production to decline by 19 percent below the previous year's harvests. Output of foodgrain in 1966/67 was still nearly 17 percent below the level of 1964/65 (Barker, et al., 1985). As a result of rising prices for food and raw materials and stagnant consumer demand, industrial growth fell sharply and averaged only 5.4 percent during the 1960s, declining further to 4.5 percent during the 1970s. The growth rate of agriculture fell from 3.2 percent during the 1950s to 1.9 percent on average during the 1960s and 1970s (Oshima, 1987). Thus, India encountered, as had Japan about 45 years earlier, a food crisis that was to produce a significant revision of government policies.

India's initial response to the food crisis of the mid-1960s was to increase foodgrain imports, which already had risen from 3.5 to 7.5 million tons between 1961 and 1965, to 10.4 million tons in 1966 (Mellor, 1976). Because there was no chance of sustaining such a level of imports, a major effort was launched both to increase food output and to reduce vulnerability to unfavorable weather.

The new policies toward agriculture adopted in the late 1960s were largely conditioned by developments under way prior to the droughts of the mid-1960s. Mellor (1976) points out that the encouraging growth of agriculture during the First Plan period had been an illusion. Once adjusted for differences in weather conditions between the initial and terminal years of the period, the average annual growth rate of foodgrain output is shown to have been not the 4.8 percent proclaimed officially, but 2.2 percent. A poor performance in 1957/58 strengthened doubts as to the health of agriculture in India and gave impetus to the creation of the Intensive Agricultural District Programme (IADP) in 1961 (Barker, et al., 1985).

Although the IADP is not credited with much success in directly improving the performance of agriculture, it represented a growing recognition by the government that low productivity was a result of real constraints faced by farmers, rather than their ignorance. A direct corollary of this idea is that significant advances in agricultural productivity are possible only with the provision of the full set of complementary inputs, including improved seeds, fertilizers, controlled and adequate irrigation, and knowledge of the proper use of these inputs. This new thinking was embraced by C. Subramaniam (1979), who was appointed minister of food and agriculture in 1964 and launched the High-Yielding Varieties Programme in 1966.

Even before the green revolution began in the late 1960s, experience with the IADP had revealed that, compared to the western states of Punjab and Haryana, progress was going to be very slow in the eastern rice belt, where operational holdings were small and fragmented, tenancy was widespread, and water-control infrastructure was grossly inadequate and particularly expensive to create. The receptivity of India's northwest region to the green revolution had its roots in the irrigation investments of the preindependence period (Trinque, 1992). The course of agricultural growth in India since the mid-1960s has enlarged the gap between this favored region and the rest of the country, with the eastern region lagging especially.

The proximate causes of India's green revolution were the allocation by the government of considerable foreign exchange for the purpose of importing chemical fertilizers, and the subsequent decision to allocate adequate funds to import, adapt, and distribute dwarf wheat varieties that had been developed in Mexico. As a result of the first move, the value of fertilizer imports rose from $20 million in 1960/61 to $186 million in 1968/69 (Mellor, 1976). Readier access to fertilizers at reasonable prices resulted in an increase in their contribution to output growth from 11 percent between 1956/57 and 1960/61 to 59 percent between 1964/65 and 1970/71 (Mellor, 1976).

The marked increase in fertilizer use would not have been possible without the introduction of hybrid plant varieties capable of converting the additional nutrients into grain production rather than vegetative growth. Experimental adaptation of dwarf wheat varieties to Indian conditions was begun in the winter of 1963, and the improved seeds were widely available by 1968. Output of wheat increased by more than 11 percent per year on average between 1964/65 and 1970/71. The availability of fertilizers and the dwarf wheat created incentives for farmers to invest in private tube wells to assure irrigation, with the result that irrigated area under wheat increased at an average annual rate of 6.4 percent between 1960/61 and 1967/68 (Mellor, 1976).

The dramatic success of wheat did not provide a quick resolution to the crisis in agriculture. Wheat comprised only 14 percent of total foodgrain output in 1964/65, whereas rice, with a 44 percent share of output, is described by Mellor (1976: 50 & 56), as "the orphan of the revolution." As Subramaniam (1979) notes, rice is grown in India under widely diverse conditions, each requiring specific plant varieties and practices to achieve optimal yields. Also, the existing water-control systems in India's rice-growing regions are generally incapable of providing the precise irrigation requirements of the improved varieties.

It was the rice crop, the principal crop of the eastern region, that had suffered most during the droughts in 1966 and 1967. By 1969 the central government was sufficiently alarmed by increasing organized violence in the eastern region to issue an internal memorandum on "The Causes and Nature of Current Agrarian Tensions" (Jannuzi, 1989). This was followed in 1970 by the convening of a Central Land Reforms Committee. "In its report, published in May 1972, the urgency of new agrarian reforms was explained in terms of the dramatic increase in landlessness and growing tensions in rural areas, exacerbated by technological change that accentuated income differentials" (Herring, 1983: 136).

It is possible to argue, as does Mellor (1976), that land reform is not itself a prerequisite for high-productivity agriculture. It is essential, in fact, to recognize that land reform by itself can have at most a limited impact on productivity and living standards. At this time, however, government leaders had begun explicitly to link land reform with other measures, such as water-control investments, provision of credit to enable the purchase of modern inputs, and research into rice and other food crops, that would allow farmers throughout the country to participate in the green revolution.

As always, implementation of reforms required the cooperation of the state governments, which were not quick to act. Prime Minister Indira Gandhi had made land reform part of her Twenty-Point Programme for poverty elimination and cited the states' failure to move forward with redistributive programs among the reasons for declaring a state of emergency in 1975 (Herring, 1983). Gandhi's slogan of "Abolish poverty!" was subsequently contaminated by its association with the repressive policies of the Emergency. During the political turmoil in which the Congress Party lost and regained control of the center, the government's commitment to land reform decayed into inadequately funded programs to create rural employment on infrastructure projects and to provide low-interest loans to the poor to buy productive assets. These programs serve in practice, if not in intent, as a revival of the low-capital, low-efficiency informal-sector jobs that Mahalanobis had suggested might occupy the poor until there was room for them in the "real" economy.

After a setback arising from a sharp increase in fertilizer prices during the early 1970s, India has made continued progress in raising food output. In addition to continued growth in the core area comprising Punjab, Haryana, and the western part of Uttar Pradesh, modernization of agriculture is occurring gradually in eastern Uttar Pradesh, Gujarat, Andhra Pradesh, and isolated areas of other states, including some in the eastern region. Moreover, growth of agricultural incomes in these areas has produced an economic dynamism involving continued investments to raise productivity, diversification into noncrop agriculture, growth of the nonagricultural economy, and improvements in average levels of education and skills (Leaf, 1984; Sharma and Poleman, 1993; Upadhya, 1988). This is clear evidence that India is capable of engendering the positive synergies responsible for economic progress in East Asia.

The principal beneficiaries of improved agriculture are medium and large farmers with access to sufficient land and other resources; the larger proportion of the rural population who own little or no land receive a minimal benefit or, in some cases, suffer a decline in real income as their access to common-property resources is constrained by privatization and environmental degradation (Jodha, 1986; Roy and Tisdell, 1992b; Tisdell, 1990 & 1991). Nonetheless, agricultural income and wages are higher and the incidence of poverty is lower in those regions in which green-revolution technologies have been applied (Mellor, 1988; Tisdell, 1990 & 1991; Vohra, 1982).

In 1985/86 India imported no foodgrain for the first time since independence, prompting a pronouncement of food self-sufficiency by Prime Minister Rajiv Gandhi. Food imports were required, however, following a severe drought in 1987/88. India's domestic food production is at best barely sufficient; the demand for food is limited by the approximately 40 percent of the population below a nutritionally defined poverty level; and the supply of food remains vulnerable to weather-induced fluctuations.

The significance of this sequence of events is that India's leaders were for a time seriously concerned about the economic and, especially, political implications of a largely stagnant agricultural sector. The irony is that the technology of the green revolution has such power that its geographically limited application has removed the urgency for measures, whether inclusive of land reform or not, to enable the spread of modernization to a majority of India's cultivators. Thus, an enduring obstacle to the adoption in India of a growth strategy in which progress in agriculture enables the majority to contribute to the building of an efficient and dynamic economy is that the technologies on which such a strategy must rely are readily appropriated to serve the needs of a dualistic growth strategy.

The bullock capitalists spawned by high-productivity agriculture play contradictory roles in the process of economic change. On one hand, as noted earlier, they are alert to opportunities to invest farm incomes and diversify the family's economic activities. As a political demand group, on the other hand, their interests lie in maintaining a pattern of subsidies for and minimal taxation of agriculture that limits the government's ability and incentive to invest on behalf of the majority of cultivators who still await a green revolution.

The government has noted with some satisfaction that the severe drought of 1987/88 appeared to have a much smaller impact on the industrial sector than previous droughts, and recent trends in government policy and industrial performance suggest a willingness to promote growth on the basis of a rising demand for consumer durables (Kurien, 1991). If India succeeds in reducing further the linkages between rural incomes and industrial growth, it may be quite some time before it is again confronted with the unfinished business of agricultural modernization.

Although the process of economic growth is unique in each country, the need to develop agriculture so that economic change can involve a majority of the population is a robust generalization. Nonetheless, policies to promote agriculture seem everywhere to take second place, at best, behind support for industrialization. Fortunately, even the most narrowly conceived industrialization effort can be hindered by a weak agriculture, which may then come to the attention of policymakers. In the meantime, a state committed to development, even if not actively seeking to broaden participation in the process, can learn from its mistakes and find its policies shaped by elements of society with the ambition, education, and flexibility to seek higher incomes through investment and improved productivity.

The Hindu Rate of Growth: How Ideas, Institutions, and Interests Interacted to Produce Rigidity and Rent Seeking

The process by which India's political economy produced the Hindu rate of growth becomes easy to understand when one looks at how it evolved. As suggested by recent theorizing about the impact of *ideas* on international relations and political economy (Goldstein, 1993; Goldstein and Keohane, 1993; Hall, 1989), the basic philosophies of India's leaders at the time of independence did much to structure the nation's political and economic *institutions*—a democratic polity unified by the Congress Party, an economy with a large and expanding state sector, and an emphasis upon heavy industry as the driver of development. This, in turn, channeled the means by which groups with shared *interests* pursued their goals in certain distinct ways.

As institutional economics is wont to argue (Clark and Lam, 1995; March and Olsen, 1989; North, 1990; Steinmo et al., 1992; Teece, 1990), these institutions did much to shape India's subsequent economic performance. Unfortunately, rather than flexibility and synergism among market, state, and society, many of these institutions encouraged rigidity and rent seeking. Such institutions include a huge bureaucracy of elitist generalists, an ultimately "malign neglect" of agriculture, a self-reliant development strategy whose protectionism made rent seeking more profitable than entrepreneurship, a contradiction between democracy and patronage politics that set off a chain of political dynamics undermining the state's capacity to formulate and implement economic policies, and a growing state sector that acted as a magnet for demand politics. Despite such problems, however, there is also more than a ray of hope when one considers that the institutions in India's political economy can also create incentives for "virtuous cycles," as indicated by the exceptions of the green revolution and informatics industry, limited as their impacts still are. Institutional legacies are complex and potentially changeable; this implies that many different types of interactions among market, state, and society are possible.

PART 3

Development:
More Than Market,
More Than State

6

The Role of the State in Development: Contributions and Limitations

The success of the East Asian capitalist nations discussed in Chapter 4 certainly implies that strong state leadership need not be inimical to economic performance, as neoclassical economics contends, and may well play a key role in promoting development. Yet the need for "bringing the state back in" to the analysis of development (Evans et al., 1985) should not blind us to the many counterexamples that neoclassicists can justly cite in which state intervention in the economy produced exactly the distortions and perversions that they predicted, as the case of India discussed in Chapter 5 indicates. What seems to be needed, then, is a more balanced view of the state's role in development. Just as the neoclassical view that turning loose "the magic of the marketplace" will produce riches seems oversimplified, so too does the analogous assumption that turning loose a developmental state will produce rapid growth. This chapter, therefore, seeks to move beyond the neoclassical view of development by examining another crucial variable for developmental outcomes: the role of the state and its policies. However, it should soon become clear that the state should not replace the market as a unicausal explanation for whether developing nations grow rich or stay poor or muddle along somewhere in between. Both state and market contribute to economic outcomes, and there appears to be a need for "bringing society back in" as well.

The Logic of the Developmental State

The model of the developmental state rests upon two assumptions concerning the processes of development in the Third World. First, most developing nations are at such a disadvantage in terms of their position in the world economy that market forces themselves preclude significant growth. Second, states in at least some of these nations possess the power to overcome the barriers facing late developers. These two assumptions reflect what might respectively be termed the demand for and the supply of state economic leadership in the political economies of developing nations. The empirical and analytic question, of course, is how valid these assumptions are. The government moved vigorously to promote industrialization in Japan, Singapore, South Korea, and Taiwan; many, if not most, observers believe that their growth trajectories would have been far less dramatic without large-scale state intervention.

However, if these cases suggest that state power can overcome developmental barriers, they do not answer two more fundamental questions. First, is state intervention really necessary? After all, laissez-faire Hong Kong grew just as rapidly. Therefore, if the statists are to contend that a developmental state is a normally necessary condition for development, they must explain such anomalies. Second, does a developmental state always work? Here, the rejection of a developmental state as a sufficient condition for economic success can be instantaneous. The nations in South Asia and the communist countries in East Asia established what must be considered developmental states, and they are universally considered to have undermined economic vitality.

Without the demand for a product—be it coking coal, sex toys, or state economic leadership—the supply of it becomes immaterial. Thus, the first step in constructing the statist model is to justify the need for special state activism as a necessary condition for most developing nations' achieving what W. W. Rostow (1960) has termed "economic take-off." It is best to begin with a series of postulates about economic activities, which are probably noncontroversial (with the partial exception of how markets work) across a broad spectrum of economic thought from Marxists to Misesites:

1. Increased economic productivity is necessary to improve the national welfare (popular standard of living, defense capability, etc.).
2. Specialization in economic activities both within and among national markets promotes economic efficiency and productivity.
3. Markets, *when operating freely,* promote specialization and allocate resources effectively.
4. Nations or subnational areas should specialize in their abundant resources.

Both statists and neoclassicists would almost certainly agree with these four assumptions, as would more than a few Marxists whose criticism of capitalism focuses upon the inevitability of markets being perverted by dominant economic interests. At the next step, however, statists, Marxists, and many conventional economists depart from what may be called the neoclassical penchant for static comparative advantage:

5a. National comparative advantage is economically neutral in terms of sector and product composition, primarily determined by general resource endowment (i.e., land, labor, and capital), and, therefore, fairly static.

The classic example of comparative advantage was that British cloth should be traded for Portuguese wine. The objection from those who criticize the "equilibrium" focus of neoclassical economics is that such a division of labor, if perpetuated for sustained periods of time, would keep the agricultural country poor, while the industrial country got ever richer— which is at least in the ballpark of what happened to Britain and Portugal over the course of nearly two centuries.

In short, according to the critics, some economic activities are far more desirable than others for a specific nation because they are more productive, lead to technological gains in productivity, and produce positive side effects, such as promoting mass education. For all these reasons, industrialization is normally believed to be almost essential to development, giving rise to the alternative perspective:

5b. Nations must change their dominant economic activities, normally replacing primary with industrial production, if they are to develop.

Assumption 5b, one should hasten to add, would not be considered a challenge to conventional economics. For example, it forms a central premise in Rostow's *Non-Communist Manifesto* (1960).

In fact, the theory of the international product cycle, sketched in Chapter 3, explains how industrialization spreads from the developed to the developing world, periodically giving more and more nations at least the opportunity to achieve "economic take-off." In essence, the international product cycle refers to the life cycle of a particular good or product. Generally, new products are developed and produced in the most advanced industrial nations because they involve the latest (and most expensive) technologies, are produced by very capital-intensive processes, and require highly skilled production workers. Over time, however, the production of the item becomes more standardized and labor-intensive. Consequently, as an industry (e.g., textiles and apparel) matures, the product cycle works to diffuse its production to areas with low labor costs. This allows a few developing countries to begin the industrialization process, provided that they have access to a minimum level of investment capital and to a potential work force with at least a basic level of education. Once capital and technology began to spread rapidly around the world during the postwar era as a result of the transportation and communications revolutions, an ever accelerating diffusion of production commenced, first to other industrialized countries and ultimately to nations with semiskilled, low-cost labor. This explains Third World industrialization and the growing competition faced by mature economies. Moreover, the product cycle is dynamic in that those countries that succeed at the first level eventually price themselves out of this niche in the global economy because growth leads to rising real wages (Gilpin, 1987; Vernon, 1966).

The idea of the international product cycle can form the foundation for a series of assumptions that challenge neoclassical trade theory. The first (which is not incompatible with neoclassical theory) is that a focus on static comparative advantage ignores the dynamic effects of the international product cycle upon national economies—that is, the problem of maturing industries. A second, slightly more controversial proposition is that certain economic activities are more desirable than others because of their extensive linkages to other industries or their role as a technological driver; textiles, steel, automobiles, and high-tech production have taken on such prominence at various times over the last two centuries. Third, and clearly more controversial, is the idea that comparative advantage is not fully (or perhaps even largely) determined by fixed economic factors but results from "competitive forces," including entrepreneurial skills and policy manipulation (Porter, 1990). These three premises led to the highly contested assumption justifying the developmental state—that state activities and policies form a key part of competitive advantage because they create a more or less productive business environment (Clark and Lam, 1995; Gilpin, 1987; Graham, 1992).

The conception of the developmental dynamics produced by the international product cycle, in turn, suggests several fundamental prerequisites for development. First, there needs to be a basic stock of investment capital. Second, even given adequate financial resources, human skills are essential, both for entrepreneurship and for at least a minimally skilled work force (whose skill requirements escalate quickly as a nation moves up the international product cycle). Finally, development activities in the Third World (generally sooner rather than later) come into competition or conflict with foreign corporations and/or countries that wield considerable market power. Thus, an ability to deal with external forces must be created as well.

Statists and neoclassicists differ greatly on whether state policy or market operations will be more efficacious in surmounting these three barriers to a nation's moving up the product cycle, and whether the operations of global capitalism or government interventions pose a greater threat to economic development (see Table 3.1 in Chapter 3). From the statist perspective, perhaps the basic obstacle is that resource scarcity exacerbates high entry barriers to new economic activities; that is, entrepreneurs in a developing nation cannot freely float into a new industry that might be profitable simply because they lack the requisite capital, knowledge, marketing contacts, and so forth. Moreover, the problems of resource scarcity and high entry barriers, which would exist in perfectly functioning markets, are compounded by the existence of market imperfections. Oligopolies exist in many industries that can use their market power to prevent new entrants, creating a situation in which only a state's countervailing power based on political sovereignty can offer hope for potential new competitors from the developing world.

In such a situation, a government can mobilize and concentrate the necessary resources by providing subsidized capital from public revenues, obtaining foreign loans for development purposes, searching out information about business opportunities and foreign markets, using trade policy to extend infant-industry protection to new plants, licensing technology, recruiting and regulating foreign-invested corporations, building the basic infrastructure necessary for an industrializing society, getting the prices wrong in order to stimulate sunrise industries that can become internationally competitive in the future, establishing education and training programs to develop human capital, and establishing state corporations to develop industries for which private capital is not forthcoming. Thus, at least according to the statists, there is a considerable demand for state activities supporting industrial transformation and economic development (Amsden, 1989; Evans et al., 1985; Johnson, 1982; Onis, 1991; Wade, 1990; White, 1988).

From this perspective, incidentally, the anomaly of Hong Kong's laissez-faire development in a political economy in which state support for industrialization appears necessary for most late industrializers should no longer appear particularly anomalous, because several of the key features necessary for industrialization came together quite fortuitously in the Hong Kong of the early 1950s. The fleeing Shanghai textile manufacturers provided industrial expertise and capital that are rare in nonindustrial societies; and the British merchant houses, cut off from their traditional entrepot trade by the Chinese Communist victory, had a strong incentive to collaborate with the new small firms in finding market opportunities overseas. Finally, the British colonial administration had long before established the legal infrastructure undergirding commercial activity. This rare combination of conditions allowed Hong Kong to respond to market forces that would have sailed past most developing societies.

Even accepting the first stage of the statist argument—that there is a demand for state developmental activities—a second stage in the line of logic is needed to justify the presumption that there is a supply of such economic-policy help available for economies attempting to cast their fate to the international product cycle. According to the statist paradigm, strong and autonomous developmental states are able to meet this challenge. As suggested by the outline of such a state in Table 6.1, each of these three institutional characteristics—strength, autonomy, and developmental commitment—must

Table 6.1   Structural Characteristics of a Developmental State

State strength
Strong capability to implement policies
   Coercive authority
   Popular acceptance and legitimacy
Capacity for making and implementing decisions
   Leading role for bureaucracy staffed by expert technocrats
   State structure extensive enough for requisite actions
Strong commitment to development
   Not predation
   Not bureaucratic and patronage politics
   Not exclusively military security
State acts in unitary fashion

State autonomy
Protection by a strong leader who reigns rather than rules
Independence from both dominant and subordinate classes

Results
Takes long-term view of national interest
Resists rent-seeking behavior
Makes investments for long-term payoffs and structural transformations that would not
   occur under short-term market pressures

Questions this approach must answer[a]
Q: Why are government technocrats better able to formulate business strategies than
   owners and managers?
A: Because their ability to take a strategic viewpoint is more important than business
   acumen.
Q: Why does the state not use its monopoly powers to extract rents, as businesspeople are
   assumed to do?
A: Because of some combination of professional values, cultural conditioning, and democratic
   responsibility.

Note: a. Answers represent standard responses by statists.

be present if a government hopes to supply the developmental support that its society and business community may demand.

According to this model, developmental states are viewed as strong in the sense that they can effectively implement their policies. This capability is in turn based on two factors. First, the policies must be accepted by the broader society because of some combination of personal benefit and self-interest, belief that the government is acting legitimately, and fear of the repressive might of the regime. Second, the policies themselves must be well designed and appropriate. Some of the important conditions include the existence of a well-educated bureaucracy, the state's commitment to treating development as a high priority, and the absence of debilitating bureaucratic infighting.

The second characteristic, autonomy, means that state officials can act independent of pressures from social groups, especially dominant classes that try to use their influence to prevent change that would threaten their vested interests (Rueschemeyer and Evans, 1985). This can occur when the bureaucracy is both protected and respected by a strong executive leader who, to use the words of Chalmers Johnson (1982), chooses to "reign but not rule." As a result of such a situation, economic decisionmakers within the government are able to take a long-term perspective on national interest, resist pressures for rent seeking, and make long-term investments that could not be justified by short-term market logic.

Moon and Prasad (1994: 362–363) summarize this stereotype of the East Asian capitalist states nicely.

> Executive dominance allows political leaders to create and expand spaces for bureaucratic rule. Bureaucratic agencies in the East Asian developmental states are highly structured and competently staffed. . . . The organization is composed of highly capable individuals screened and recruited through cut-throat open competition. They are analytically adept, and technically competent. Bureaucrats in the developmental states are also united in purpose, and show an unusually high degree of congruence with organizational and national goals. Such unity of purpose minimizes bureaucratic in-fighting and enhances inter-agency consensus and coordination. Furthermore, meritocratic practices originating from the Confucian tradition and elite social status prevent public bureaucrats from being "captured" by rent-seeking social groups.

As indicated in the last section of Table 6.1, there are two potentially embarrassing questions that this approach must answer. The standard responses are presented as well, but only a moment's thought, if that, should be necessary to conclude that these rationales are not entirely convincing. The first is: Why are government bureaucrats better than businesspeople at making strategic economic decisions? Statists argue that they are better educated and trained, have more resources at their disposal for gathering information, and are more concerned with promoting the national interest than pursuing individual wealth. Yet, even accepting that they might be able to take a more strategic perspective, their training and duties do not make them particularly qualified to make predictions about technology and product trends in a global economy in which the product cycle is moving quite rapidly. Thus, their competence for selecting worthy industries to promote, at all but the grossest level, is exceedingly questionable.

Second, the assumption that strong and autonomous political leaders and technocrats will be interested in constructing a developmental state is far from self-evident. In fact, it flies in the face of the very market-imperfection logic used to justify it—that state intervention in the economy is justified because some private businesspeople will use their almost inevitable market power to collect monopoly rents. Why, therefore, does the state not use its power for profit and plunder, following the pattern of what

Evans (1995) calls the predatory state? Or become a "bureaucracy" concerned with status, deadening procedural rituals, and/or patronage politics? Or subordinate economic performance to other desiderata, such as military security? The statists refer to leaders' professional training or cultural values but really do not make much of a case for those in the public sector being substantially less self-serving than those in the private economy.

In short, if one applies the economic logic used by the statists to establish the demand for state economic leadership, the a priori conclusion is that its adequate supply would probably be fairly limited in most societies. This is not to deny that a successful developmental state could emerge. Rather, its creation would probably require a fortuitous combination of historical circumstances, analogous to the factors that permitted Hong Kong's laissez-faire development pattern. The next section evaluates the developmental state model in terms of the experiences of East and South Asia.

Evaluating the Developmental State: State and Development in East and South Asia

Our basic conundrum in using South Asia and East Asia to evaluate the developmental state model is that, with the exception of Hong Kong, all of these states—those whose economic records were spectacularly successful and those who recorded pitiful performances—superficially appear to be strong and autonomous. Certainly, this should give one considerable pause before joining the statist camp! This section provides an overview of the strengths and limitations of the statist approach by comparing both the successes and failures to the abstract model outlined in Table 6.1. It begins by showing how the Confucian-capitalist states both conform to and depart from the characteristics of a strong and autonomous developmental state, and then asks why the strong and autonomous states in South Asia and communist East Asia lagged behind in the race toward economic development.

The idea that the six East Asian capitalist regimes—Dengist China, Hong Kong, Japan, Singapore, South Korea, and Taiwan—are strong and possess executive leaders who provide political insulation for the technocracy has considerable face validity. Most of these governments have been fairly authoritarian in nature; and many had or have strong individual leaders (Hofheinz and Calder, 1982; Pye with Pye, 1985). The best exemplar here is Singapore's Lee Kuan Yew, who has presided over a strong and paternalistic state whose policies brought extremely rapid economic and social growth and who has of late become the leading spokesman for the superiority of "Asian authoritarianism" (Friedman, 1995). Even in democratic Japan, where the electoral politicians are comparatively weak, an ingenious system evolved in which the bureaucracy was protected in areas involving international trade, while substantial amounts of patronage were funneled into such areas as agriculture, construction, local government, and domestic retail (Calder, 1988).

This stereotype of strong and generally authoritarian government is beginning to unravel outside Singapore, however. Taiwan and South Korea have made major strides toward democratization, and their current governments appear far from strong and revered in the eyes of their populations (Chan and Clark, 1992/93). The Japanese political structure broke down in the early 1990s, with both politicians and bureaucrats looking weak and indecisive. In the PRC, despite the regime's authoritarian nature and stated interest in following the model of the Singaporean developmental state, rapid growth in the 1980s and especially in the early 1990s has been associated with the radical *de*centralization of economic power and policymaking.

Similarly, the idea of a unified technocracy strongly committed to the nation's development project strikes several responsive chords but falls far short of a full description. The Confucian-capitalist states, except Dengist China, all qualify for a high ranking on bureaucratic competence. Yet this is far from the whole story. The mere existence of a strong technocracy does not necessarily mean that it will be used well or act in a unified fashion. In the Philippines, for example, Kuo's (1995) comparative study found a highly sophisticated and skilled elite executive bureaucracy that was equal to Taiwan's in terms of its capacity for becoming a developmental state. However, it was ignored and pushed aside by the "crony capitalism" of the Marcos regime. Even in such reputed developmental states as Japan and South Korea, bureaucratic politics can affect and stalemate policy (Moon and Prasad, 1994; Okimoto, 1989; Prestowitz, 1988). Leon Hollerman (1988), for example, has termed this a transformation to "Japan, Disincorporated." Furthermore, a perverse combination of democracy and prosperity (two normatively desirable national characteristics) has led to burgeoning corruption in China, Japan, South Korea, and Taiwan (Moon and Prasad, 1994)—this corruption is the antithesis of a developmental state.

The process of economic change itself is undercutting the power for technocratic leadership of national economies. As economic policy becomes more complex and the speed of the international product cycle accelerates, autonomy evidently becomes a dysfunctional burden for economic decisionmakers because government officials simply do not have the expertise to make competent business decisions. That is, a developmental state may be well situated to mobilize the resources for entering the iron and steel industry, but it cannot plot out a coherent strategy for fluxing high-tech sectors. Thus, rather than autonomy, interaction or balance between the state and the private business sector (society) is most advantageous in promoting international competitiveness. For instance, MITI's advantage in the 1980s and 1990s does not lie in its ability to dictate industrial policy to Japanese corporations, but in its tight reciprocal relations with top-level management that result in a consensual style of decision-making (Okimoto, 1989). However, the very need to make rapid strategic business decisions is beginning to render obsolete MITI's style of making industrial policy through building a time-consuming consensus with business leaders, or the time-consuming process of consensus building within keiretsu or individual businesses, for that matter (Boulton, 1995; Gereffi, 1996).

More fundamentally, the globalization wrought by the transportation and communications revolutions has eroded the autonomy of national economies and, most especially, the identification of many firms with specific national headquarters (Harrison, 1994; Reich, 1991). This has resulted in what Gary Gereffi (1995 & 1996) has termed "global commodity chains" (GCCs) in which the multistage production and distribution of goods are organized across national lines by networks of Western and Japanese transnational corporations and allied firms in such Little Dragons as South Korea and Taiwan. The GCCs are driven by the pressures of the international product cycle, which pushed standardized manufacturing from the First World to the Little Dragons and, subsequently, to the currently low-wage economies of China, Southeast Asia, and elsewhere in the Third World. Enterprises at the intermediate level take the lead in finding and managing the new production sites. Many of these transnational linkages, furthermore, are not simply the result of market conditions or attractive state policies but derive from embedded social ties, such as the linkages among Chinese business communities throughout East and Southeast Asia (Bernard and Ravenhill, 1995; Chan, 1993; Gereffi, 1995 & 1996). Consequently, developmental success now hinges much more on the ability of private business to manage complex networks than on specific state policies.

The East Asian capitalist nations (Hong Kong excluded as usual), in sum, possess the characteristics of a strong and autonomous state, but only to a limited extent. Moreover, several long-term secular trends all appear to be gradually undercutting the capacity of their developmental states. First, the "third wave" of democratization (Huntington, 1991) that is washing over East Asia, Lee Kuan Yew notwithstanding, increases the constraints on state autonomy and flexibility. Second, the increasing rapidity of the international product cycle is overtaking traditional methods for the exercise of economic leadership by the state. Finally, these countries' very success in promoting rapid growth and industrial transformation has created economies whose complexity and intricacy have moved them beyond the position at which the state's comparative advantage in mobilizing and concentrating resources is effective or, perhaps, necessary. Thus, there is clearly more at work in East Asian dynamism than just the inspired and effective leadership of strong and autonomous developmental states.

In contrast to capitalist East Asia, the communist command economies of that region and the planned economies of South Asia have been far less effective in promoting economic growth, despite their ideological commitment to rapid development and their strong and autonomous states. Two reasons consistent with conventional images of their political economies may be adduced for this failure that have somewhat different implications for the statist–neoclassicist debate. First, they may have faltered economically because their socialist ideologies led them to divert resources from productive uses to social welfare, thereby promoting equity at the cost of growth. Yet this line of reasoning is not particularly convincing for several reasons. First, as discussed in Chapter 4, East Asian dynamism shows that the growth–welfare trade-off is not inevitable. Second, among the South Asian and communist countries, as seen from the data in Chapter 2, only Sri Lanka really made a strong commitment to welfare; and Sri Lanka's conversion to laissez-faire at the end of the 1970s did not produce a more vibrant economy.

The second and far more convincing reason that communist East Asia became a felled hare and South Asia became a tortoise that waddled is that they soon degenerated into bureaucratic states—where "bureaucracy" does not connote the efficient organization of Weber but the leaden, overbearing, and patronage organization of Reaganomics. In both types of systems (much more extensively in China and North Korea than in South Asia and Vietnam), there was an initial push into heavy industry. However, these economies atrophied over time as subsequent change was held back by bureaucratic inertia. Chapter 5, for example, described how public agencies and state corporations became bureaucratized patronage networks in India; somewhat analogous patterns can be found in the other nations.

The varying validity of these two reasons for communist and South Asian stagnation has some relevance for evaluating the "I told you so" citation of them by neoclassicists as support for their critique of the developmental state model. The first (growth–equity trade-off) presents a sharp challenge to advocates of state economic leadership because it posits a considerable constraint upon government activity; its seeming inapplicability is probably good news for the statists. The second would be fatal for the statist model if it confirmed the universal validity of neoclassical theory's prediction that such degeneration is inevitable. However, the success of the East Asian capitalist states demonstrates that this is certainly not the case.

Rather than simply dismiss statism, one may ask what differentiates the successful and unsuccessful states examined here. One answer emerges from harking back to their two very different policy packages discussed in Chapter 3: export promotion/market conforming/entrepreneurship/agricultural development (capitalist East Asia) vs. import substitution/market distortion/bureaucratism/agricultural disdain (South Asia and communist East Asia). The key driver appears to be a commitment to export promotion. Once a nation casts its fate to the international marketplace, the state is disciplined to be developmental rather than bureaucratic because the economic degeneration that bureaucratism brings is directly and quickly punished. Thus, rather than choosing between state and market, the best path to development may be integrating their special capabilities into international markets.

Policies and Activities of the East Asian Developmental States

The previous section considered how the macro structural characteristics of the various states in South and East Asia conformed to the postulates of the developmental state model. It is also valuable to take a closer look at the more micro policies and activities that are attributed to developmental states. According to the theory of the developmental state, government technocracies can perform a valuable leading role for several central tasks in the national development project. As illustrated in Table 6.2, these encompass three different types of government activities. A perhaps initially confusing array of examples and counterexamples can be cited concerning how well the putatively developmental states in East Asia performed here. These contrasting findings are consistent, however, in their implication that we must look beyond *both* state and market to understand these political economies.

The Tasks of a Developmental State

The first group of activities involves the creation and maintenance of a sound environment, without which a market economy could not operate. Most of these, incidentally, are accepted as necessary by neoclassical economists. Such governmental functions include maintaining political order (including holding political corruption and "squeeze" on businesses to an acceptable minimum), creating a stable legal order for market relationships, using macroeconomic (fiscal and monetary) policy to curb inflation and dampen the business cycle, and financing expensive physical infrastructure projects (e.g., highways, railroads, harbors, and airports) that are vital for commerce and business expansion. Another policy falling under this rubric may be termed "state deactivism" in the economy, such

Table 6.2   State Roles in Development

Creating a conducive business environment
Maintain political order
Create and maintain legal order underlying private property and market relations
Maintain macroeconomic stability
    Monetary and fiscal policies
Provide physical infrastructure
Sponsor market liberalization after import-substitution controls and privatize state
    enterprises
Minimize drain on private resources
    Limit size of state, unnecessary defense spending, and huge welfare programs/
        bureaucracy

State economic activism
Macroeconomic stimulation
    Monetary and fiscal policies
Control and channel finance into vital sectors
Industrial policy
    Target key industries
    Force high performance standards on industry
    Promote basic structural transformations of economy
    Economic planning
Trade policy
    Protection for import-substitution industrialization
    Divert protectionism of trading partners
Regulate MNCs
    Recruit foreign capital
    Prevent denationalization of economy
    Channel foreign capital and technology into key sectors
State entrepreneurship
    State corporations in key industries
    Partnerships of state with foreign and local capital
Policy incentives for general structural transformation

State social activism
Provide human-capital infrastructure (education)
Anti-poverty redistributional policies (spending for health, nutrition, and other social
    services)
Safety and environmental protection
Protect population from economic power of business class

---

as the privatization of state corporations and market liberalization, which is a common method for moving from import substitution to export-led growth (Balassa, 1981). More broadly along these lines, the state can minimize the drain of resources away from the private sector by limiting government size and unproductive activities such as military spending and welfare programs. This is something of a paradox if we equate strong government with big government.

Direct state activism in the economy represents the second category in Table 6.2. It is these policy areas that create the fundamental divide between the statist approach and neoclassical assumptions that governments simply cannot perform such functions effectively and efficiently. Statists, in sharp contrast, advocate more stimulative macroeconomic policies than are necessary for stability in the expectation that they can generate a virtuous cycle of self-reinforcing growth. More fundamentally, statists also believe that the government of a late industrializer should take a leading role in financial mobilization and allocation to ensure that it is effectively used and directed into targeted sunrise sectors. Control over finance, in turn, is the first step toward an activist industrial policy because the provision of capital represents one of the primary tools for targeting an industry (along with tax relief, other types of subsidies, R & D assistance, creating actual state enterprises, and trade protection). In addition to providing assistance to selected industries, these tools can be used to enforce performance standards on particular industries and firms. Finally, statists also want governments in the developing world to take a strong role in negotiating with foreign corporations and countries. Trade policy is important, especially with rising protectionism in the industrial world. In addition, statists have a somewhat ambiguous view of foreign capital, viewing it as a source of valuable funds and technology and of fierce and perhaps unfair competition to local industries. Consequently, they advocate state controls over MNCs to ensure that the latter contribute to the national-development project rather than simply exploit local resources. More broadly, the state can move beyond policies toward single industries by promoting general structural transformations (e.g., from import substitution to the export of light-industrial goods, from light industry to heavy industry, etc.) and can create systems for large-scale economic planning.

A third dimension emerges from the work of scholars committed to the basic-human-needs approach who urge what might be called social activism, in addition to economic activism. This can be justified on normative grounds alone—that is, development is not really occurring unless the bulk of the population in a country benefits from economic growth. However, the growing emphasis on human capital as an important source of growth suggests that the creation of an educated and healthy society may actually promote growth in the long term. Recent comparative analysis, for example, does indeed suggest that investment in human capital has a positive long-term effect on economic performance (Moon, 1991; Moon and Dixon, 1992).

In evaluating how well the governments of capitalist East Asia have performed on these policy dimensions, an image or stereotype of success and good performance can certainly be cited. Again, however, enough exceptions and caveats emerge to suggest that something beyond the developmental state must have been involved in the economic success of these countries—and to point the direction for finding this "something." Much of the economic success of these nations must be attributed to the nature of their societies, especially the indigenous business communities. Thus, there seems to be an analytic need for bringing society back in.

Creating a Good Business Environment

In terms of the first task, creating a favorable framework for economic activities, the stereotype of the East Asian capitalist nations is that their outstanding economic records can be explained at least in part by the ability of the developmental states there to create a good business environment. Generally, authoritarian governments have been able to provide political and economic stability, with two exceptions: (1) what appears to be creative economic chaos in Deng's PRC and (2) periodic military coups in South Korea; these, however, seemingly had only marginal impact upon the overall political economy. Two caveats must be noted here, however. First, stability is not a sufficient condition for good economic performance because it does not greatly differentiate the Confucian capitalists from the less successful strong states, although more examples of instability admittedly can be found among the latter (Maoist upheavals, civil war in Sri Lanka and Pakistan, communal conflict in India).

The second caveat is more fundamental. Some scholars view authoritarian rule as an essential part of East Asian development (Cumings, 1984; Deyo, 1989; Hofheinz and Calder, 1982; Zeigler, 1988). Authoritarian governments, from this perspective, can resist pressures from both business and labor (e.g., overcoming business resistance to liberalizing the economy, suppressing labor to keep wages low, and keeping social-welfare expenditures low) and maintain a good environment for business by preserving political stability. If this is true, the growing trend of democratization in East Asia might be expected to undermine the efficacy of the developmental states there.

However, it is also possible to interpret authoritarianism as a cost of economic development that modernization and social change will gradually overcome (Clark, 1989). This argument is consistent with Mancur Olson's (1982) theory that prolonged political stability encourages the rise of "distributional coalitions" among political leaders and interest groups that manipulate the economy to gain monopoly rents, thereby undermining economic performance and ultimately leading to "the decline of nations." Although Olson's theory is based on democratic polities, it might be even more applicable in authoritarian regimes where leaders have greater discretion.

Olson's model does appear readily applicable to recent events in Japan. The successful Japanese system of "crisis and compensation" outlined earlier fell victim to such degeneration in the early 1990s. Over time, it allowed important sectors to become increasingly noncompetitive, thereby raising their costs to Japanese consumers. The external political costs rose, too, because Japan's trade partners became increasingly aggressive in protesting the protection of these sectors in the face of Japan's huge trade surplus (Prestowitz, 1988; Tyson, 1992). Internal decay occurred as well. Corruption became increasingly blatant; bureaucracy–business ties moved toward a greater appreciation of the coziness of sharing monopoly rents; and the LDP succumbed to a gridlock that prevented it from making even the minor reforms that probably would have sufficed to keep it in power (Blaker, 1995; Noble, 1994).

In terms of several of the other components of a good business environment, the East Asian capitalist nations appear particularly remarkable in that they have seemingly escaped several trade-offs that might normally be necessary. First, they have combined small government with assertive developmental states. Almost all (Dengist China excepted) are relatively small compared with other nations at the same level of income per capita. All have managed very good social outcomes with low levels of social welfare spending, thus avoiding the normally assumed trade-off between growth and equity (see the data in Chapter 2). This record challenges the normal assumption that big government is strong government. Big government is almost certain to produce bureaucracy (in the bad sense); if government is to be an effective leader and coordinator, it probably needs to be reinvented as "lean and mean" (Osborne and Gaebler, 1992).

The achievements of the East Asian developmental states in the individual policy areas are impressive as well. The high investment rates that exist throughout the region demonstrate that government is not shutting out investment opportunities but has created effective incentive structures to promote savings and investment. Most of them have made large and productive investments in infrastructure, although rapid growth continues to create problems in this area. For example, anyone who has witnessed rush hour (or almost any time, for that matter) in Tokyo or Taipei should realize that infrastructure bottlenecks do not choke off all growth. Moreover, the states also have good records on inflation, indicating effective macroeconomic policies. In the defense realm, whereas Japan's economic success is often attributed to its low levels of military spending, Singapore, South Korea, and Taiwan have all grown quite rapidly despite high military spending throughout much of the Cold War era.

In one respect, however, several of the states have failed to a significant extent in the central task of creating orderly market conditions and property rights, including holding political corruption to fairly modest levels. Disparate examples include the "Wild West" capitalism now thriving in China and Vietnam in spite of (or perhaps even because of) a surprisingly undefined legal order; the ability of so many small enterprises to flout laws and regulations in Taiwan; and the widespread corruption in all these countries except Singapore and, until fairly recently, Hong Kong.

Such gross examples of developmental state failure certainly imply that there is more to the East Asian miracle than just state performance. The Chinese practice of what might be called *guanxi* capitalism is a good case in point. Operating a business relies to a significant extent on guanxi (or personal connections, usually including payoffs) with government officials; thus, guanxi capitalism is really rent seeking by politicians and bureaucrats. It is prevalent in the dynamic areas of China (C.Y. Cheng, 1990; Harding, 1987; Vogel, 1989), clearly existed during the import-substitution 1950s in Taiwan (Gold, 1986), and is emerging in Hong Kong with the city's gradual absorption into the PRC (Lam, 1990a). It can be argued that the first two instances represented some economic progress in the sense that, despite their distorting effects, they were associated with expanding marketization and greater economic dynamism. However, the growing impact of personal connections as a prerequisite for doing business in Hong Kong can only hurt economic efficiency and long-run competitiveness.

In addition, good aggregate performance may hide substantial instances of mismanagement. In the realm of macroeconomic policy, for example, even the good overall record for price stability recorded by Japan and Taiwan does not mean that several serious policy failures did not occur. The huge influx of money brought on by the burgeoning trade surpluses of the 1980s created the bubble economy whose crashes created Japan's severe recession and Taiwan's growing economic instability in the early 1990s. Moreover, this recession has led to significant strains on the system of lifetime employment and keiretsu–supplier relations (Sender, 1995) that may sunder the economic institutions sketched earlier, regardless of cultural proclivities. This is occurring, ironically, at the precise time that the United States seems to be moving toward adopting many of these institutions.

Economic Activism

The touchstone of most theories concerning the success of the developmental state in East and Southeast Asia (or anywhere else, for that matter) lies in the field of its economic activism and the supposed consequences for economic performance. In particular, the rapid growth of these countries is often attributed to their industrial policies, which push national economies into a series of sunrise industries of increasingly greater sophistication and value added. At the level of gross correlations, this presumed relationship seems to hold. All of these countries, with the exception of Hong Kong, have sought to implement a multitude of industrial policies, and many of the favored industries have prospered. Even analysts sympathetic to the laissez-faire perspective have accepted that the East Asian experience demonstrates the efficacy of market-conforming state intervention (Roumasset and Barr, 1992; World Bank, 1993).

Several important types of industrial policy are usually cited, although the East Asian nations have generally avoided stimulative macroeconomic policy—the first type of policy listed under "state economic activism" in Table 6.2. First, many of these governments have exercised tight control over financial institutions, which in turn has allowed them to direct credit to specific industries and even firms and to impose performance criteria (e.g., export capacity) as a condition for continued credit. This has been seen as a key component of development policy in South Korea (Amsden, 1989; Woo, 1991) and, probably to a much lesser extent, in Japan (Johnson, 1982; Okimoto, 1989).

Such financial control and targeting can probably only work, however, in nations with a fairly high degree of corporate concentration, suggesting that it would not be efficacious in economies of numerous small firms, such as Taiwan's (or Hong Kong's). But although one would expect a much different financial system in Taiwan, the formal financial system is just as centralized and government controlled as South Korea's. Moreover, rather than being praised for enlightened industrial targeting, Taiwan is almost universally condemned for rigidity and bureaucratism and for ignoring the needs of small businesses (Fields, 1995; Wade, 1985; Wu, 1985). The slack was taken up, however, by the informal "curb market" of semilegal but unregulated lending, which constituted a third of the external finance of small businesses as late as 1985 (Chiu, 1992; Fields, 1995; Wade, 1985). The government's tolerance of the curb market, whether from a conscious policy or an inability to control national financial flows to the extent that South Korea could, created a financial system much more congruent with Taiwan's industrial structure than the system that existed on paper. This also demonstrates the efficacy of alternatives to state guidance, however, and provides an instance in which curbing state strength and autonomy probably proved beneficial.

Overall these nations have generally been given very high marks for their industrial policy. As described in Chapters 3 and 4, Japan, Taiwan, Singapore, and South Korea have used a variety of direct and indirect policy instruments to promote the periodic structural upgrading of their economies; Japan and especially South Korea have clearly targeted their guidance to particular industries and even firms quite successfully. In addition, several scholars have attributed East Asia's strong economic record to the ability of such nations as Japan, South Korea, and Taiwan to minimize the harm that Western trade policies do to their businesses. In fact, they developed a reputation for promoting and liberalizing exports while continuing significant protection of their home markets (Bobrow and Chan, 1987; Chan, 1987; Haggard and Moon, 1983; Prestowitz, 1988; Yoffie, 1983). Finally, East Asia's ability to manage foreign capital (e.g., channeling it into specific sectors) is often cited as a key component in the region's economic success (Amsden, 1989; Haggard and Cheng, 1987; Mardon, 1990; Mardon and Paik, 1992; Mirza, 1986). Even in the very controversial area of state corporations, East Asian success stories are easy to tell. State corporations are almost universally condemned by neoclassicists (and many others) for being inefficient because they can use the power inherent in government sovereignty to shield themselves from economic competition. Examples supporting this "iron law" are easy to find in communist East and South Asia, but this is not just a problem of state socialism or of South Asia's bureaucratic rent seeking, because state corporations in Taiwan are widely denounced for being inefficient compared to the private sector (Gold, 1986).

Before dismissing state entrepreneurship on philosophical or ideological grounds, one should consider the story of Pohang Iron and Steel Works in South Korea. When the South Korean government initiated the project to construct a full-scale integrated iron and steel works in the late 1960s, it was turned down for support by the World Bank, which did not like state corporations and did not believe that South Korea had a comparative advantage in steel production. Twenty years later, presumably without a sense of irony, a World Bank report called Pohang (which was built with Japanese aid) "arguably the most efficient producer of steel in the world" (Amsden, 1989; Wade, 1990). Many state enterprises in Singapore and Japan have turned out to be similarly effective and internationally competitive.

This implies that the industrial policies of the East Asian developmental states worked quite well. When one moves to the level of evaluating specific Asian industrial policies, however, the actual mechanisms promoting economic growth become somewhat more ambiguous and problematic. Sometimes states stumble into successful strategies that they subsequently claim to have planned or discovered. Good examples of this are the growth of export-processing zones (EPZs) in Taiwan in the 1960s and the similar development in China (a rather ironic set of twins) twenty years later. In the early 1960s, General Instruments was looking for a site for low-level assembly work in Asia. Because of rising wages in Hong Kong, it negotiated an agreement with the government in Taiwan to provide the basic legal guarantees for such an export platform (e.g., establishing a bonded warehouse for the components that were to be assembled). The government was willing to do this fairly expeditiously because its own program for attracting foreign investment in several specific industries had found no takers. The rest is history: Taiwan retrospectively "discovered" the EPZ; a combination of government negotiations on FDI entry and the dynamics of guerrilla capitalism resulted in a rapid expansion of links to the domestic economy and technology transfer; and the export boom commenced (Lam, 1992; Schive, 1990). The same thing happened in the late 1980s in China when the government hoped to attract high-tech investments but instead attracted producers from Hong Kong and Taiwan who moved their labor-intensive operations to China because of rising wages at home (Wu, 1995).

In many other instances state industrial policy can provide only part of the explanation for the dynamics of a particular industry—even one that is the subject of industrial targeting by one of the strongest developmental states. For example, Japan's MITI has provided a series of plans and state guidance for the key machine-tool industry. Yet in many instances, such as the producers' total deviation from government plans for industrial concentration (which showed that MITI's understanding of the machine-tool industry was somewhat defective), it was clear that industry development had little to do with government planning (Friedman, 1988). Similarly, it was private industry concentrated in large chaebol that pushed ahead with the rapid upgrading of the semiconductor industry in the first half of the 1980s, despite the reluctance of the South Korean government (Hong, 1992).

State Social Activism

The performance of these countries as fantastic overachievers in terms of social outcomes (see Chapter 2) should gladden the hearts of human-capital theorists. Most have strong records in education compared to other nations dating back to the 1960s. They also have relatively low welfare spending, despite good performance on most social indicators, suggesting that human-capital investments teach people to help both the economy and themselves. Moreover, some types of social spending may actually act as subsidies to business, rather than as diversions of funds from productive employment. For example, state-subsidized housing in Hong Kong and Singapore permits the payment of lower wages, which in turn enhances the cost competitiveness of goods produced there (Castells et al., 1990; Schiffer, 1991). Such state policy is effective because it gives people the ability to act for themselves and be productive in individual endeavors. The state is part of the story, but so is society.

The case of Sri Lanka is instructive in regard to the shortcomings of both neoclassicalism and statism. Sri Lanka's excellent record on social outcomes doubtlessly resulted from the broad-ranging social-welfare programs that were established in the 1950s and 1960s, reflecting a political consensus among the major parties. This consensus was strained by declining economic performance during the 1970s; the victory of the more conservative party in 1977 led to a programmatic revolution that cut the role of government and liberalized the economy (Bruton, 1992). This rendition of Sri Lanka's story sounds well in tune with neoclassical orthodoxy. A country made a decision to promote social equity, but the social programs gradually undermined the productive capacities that generated the revenues to pay for them. This conundrum was solved by drastically cutting back the redistributive programs and (à la the four Little Dragons) casting the nation's fate to the tides of the international economy in the belief that the resulting growth would trickle down to the masses.

Such an interpretation of Sri Lanka's political economy does not stand the test of comparative analysis, however. First, Taiwan had a stellar record on meeting basic human needs without creating large welfare programs (although state initiatives in land reform and education were certainly relevant), showing that basic human needs can be met in more than one way. Second, Sri Lanka's switch in economic strategy had somewhat disappointing results. The primary reason for this probably was that liberalization brought an intensification of speculative activities that benefited only the rich, rather than an expansion of productive capacities that might have generated a trickle-down effect (Bruton, 1992).

The marketization reforms in China at the same time had surprising results. Despite the problems of inflation, inequality, corruption, and brutal repression, economic growth skyrocketed, precisely because so much entrepreneurship was directed into productive activities: agriculture, small-scale commerce and services, and ultimately labor-intensive assembly. The implications of the comparison between Sri Lanka and China are far from salutary for either neoclassicists or statists. The former see reforms fail under the type of regime they advocate and succeed in many ways under a regime they abhor. The latter see a strong state succeed but only because society can find ways to escape the political obstacles erected by the state. Thus, neither market nor state alone can explain the differences between China and Sri Lanka. One is again led to bring society back in to discover why one system worked so much better than the other—in this case, why entrepreneurial activities were devoted to speculation in Sri Lanka but more productive concerns in China.

The Ambiguous Nature of the State's Economic Role: A Case Study from Taiwan

The preceding analysis has focused for the most part upon the general characteristics of the political economies in East Asia and South Asia. Such a discussion can only be carried on at a fairly abstract level, which tends to blur the actual interactions between states and private businesses. This section presents a detailed case study from Taiwan to give a better idea of how government policy and business initiative interacted in the development of the plastics industry there. It suggests that the roles of state and society in development are highly unpredictable and interdependent.

The beginning of the plastics industry in Taiwan, as part of its import-substitution effort, has something of a comic-opera air. The government, acting on the 1953 recommendation of a U.S. consulting firm, tried to start up this industry, but even with considerable state subsidy local business-people saw little future for what was to become an important industry within little more than a decade. As Tun-jen Cheng (1990: 152) describes the situation,

> With the aid funds, the state built several plastics plants, protected the market, and advertised them for transfer, but it found no buyers for the plants. The state was compelled to plead for takeover by promising all sorts of lucrative support. Meanwhile new entrants were not prohibited.

Wang Yung-ching, a small businessman who had run rice and lumber businesses in a far from spectacular fashion, offered to purchase a PVC (polyvinyl chloride) plant that the government had built with U.S. aid, allegedly for another entrepreneur who had decided he did not want it. Initially, the Ministry of Economic Affairs (MOEA) was not interested in Wang, reportedly because of his lack of experience in the industry. However, Wang found a more influential partner and lobbyist to plead his case, and MOEA presumably became more concerned about what to do with the plant as time passed. Ultimately Wang became the owner (presumably a proud one) of the PVC plant. He began production but quickly ran into a major problem: He could not sell the PVC that he made; there was even a time when his relatives and employees were storing unsold pellets in their homes (Fields, 1995; Kuo, 1995).

If the story ended here, the result would be a case study in industrial policy failure. Whether intended by the MOEA or not, the image is one dear to the entrepreneurial ethic of P. T. ("there's a sucker born every minute") Barnum: one victim shucking its losses off on another. That is, an international consulting company sold a credulous Third World government a bill of goods that cost them the consulting fee and the state investment in an uneconomical factory. The government then recouped some of its losses by talking an incompetent businessman out of his small stock of capital, thereby decreasing the nation's already low level of capital.

However, the story does not end here because the "missing ingredient" of entrepreneurship came into play. Wang had faith that the second half of the twentieth century would be the age of plastics. The only problem, he probably reasoned, was that his fellow Taiwanese businesspeople did not realize that cheap and readily marketable products could be fashioned from plastic. Unfortunately, Chinese businesspeople tend to be the practical sort who believe their eyes, not theoretical marketing analyses. It was here that Wang's entrepreneurial abilities came into play. Rather than bemoaning his fate and going into bankruptcy, he decided to show potential customers what could be done with plastic by building a small plastics-molding factory. He produced goods that could be sold first on the domestic market and later on international markets (e.g., dolls and dishes, rain boots and toy reindeer, tubes and tables, etc.). To build this plant, however, Wang had to enter the curb market and convince his relatives and employees to put up some of their own property as collateral, indicating the importance of the informal sector for financing even what started out as a state project.

Wang both diversified and created a demand for PVC among copy cat entrepreneurs. But about twenty years later, in the late 1970s, a new problem arose about Wang's capital stock. The government, as governments are wont to do to small businesspeople, demanded that Wang pay more taxes. Luckily for Wang, his "small" business ventures centered on Formosa Plastics made a "minor" contribution to Taiwan's economy estimated at roughly 5 percent of total GNP. When Wang said that he was considering withdrawing all the assets under his control from the state-owned banking system, the government decided that his taxes were in order (Fields, 1995).

A decade later, in the late 1980s, Wang faced another investment problem. He wished to build a naphtha cracking plant in a small village that protested so loudly about potential chemical wastes that they blocked the plant. Wang then turned up across the Taiwan Strait in China—where it was then technically illegal for him to be—and offered to build a $17 *billion* dollar petrochemical complex in Fujian Province. This unsettled Taiwan's authorities. Rather than arresting Wang upon his return, however, the premier visited the village opposing the naphtha cracker and talked them into withdrawing their opposition in return for the government's compensating them for the risks the plant would create. Wang then cited his patriotic duties to Taiwan and withdrew his offer to the PRC (much to the relief of Li Peng, who was queasy about such intrusions of capitalism in the aftermath of Tiananmen Square, if rumor is to be believed). Wang's patriotism seemed finite, however. He developed proposals for $7 billion complexes in both Taiwan and China and was using the threat of canceling them as a means to get more concessions from both governments—infrastructure construction and environmental regulation relief in Taiwan, and permission for domestic sales in China (Fields, 1995; Liu, 1993; Pun, 1992).

This case shows the complex nature of how state, market, and society interact. It began with a combination of state and private investment. It avoided imminent failure, however, not by the state's foresight or direct financial support, nor by the automatic operation of the marketplace. Rather, Wang's entrepreneurial vision and ability created an escalating financial base for him and Formosa Plastics that first made them independent of the government and then seemingly gave them significant leverage over even the regime of a medium-sized industrial nation. This case also shows the difficulty in resolving the debate over whether Taiwan possesses a developmental state. Whereas the regime clearly targeted the plastics industry and built the PVC plant that started Y. C. Wang on the road to Fortune 500 status, it is hard to agree with the interpretation that this represents successful state tutelage and leadership in industrial policy (Gold, 1986; Wade, 1990) because the government had little to do with the development of the Formosa Plastics empire and because Wang's power vis-à-vis the government shifted so radically.

This case study certainly indicates that the state has played a significant role in Taiwan's development, but it is a role that is easy to overstate. The state built a PVC plant for, ultimately, Wang and targeted the plastics industry at the level of official pronouncements. However, it is hard to give the state much credit for the principal dynamics that led to the formation of the Formosa Plastics empire. What turned out to be vital was the nature of the society that created entrepreneurs who were capable of taking advantage of the opportunities that the market or the state may produce. The state's success therefore depended much more on the capabilities of society than vice versa.

Moving Beyond State and Market in Asian Political Economy

While the debate between the statists and the neoclassicists is still going strong, other, much different critiques of the theory of the developmental state are beginning to appear. These argue that the state per se (and in combination with the market) provides an insufficient explanation for readily observable differences in developmental outcomes. Thus, recourse is necessary to additional variables denoting state–society relations and the business environment (e.g., entrepreneurial talents, the foundation of human capital, the incentives and disincentives for various types of economic activities, and, more broadly, the cultural environment in which a political economy operates). In short, just as statist theory added state to market as an important factor shaping developmental outcomes, this nascent approach can be viewed as a call for bringing society back in.

7

Strong States, Strong Societies, and Development: Institutions and Indeterminacy

Over the last several decades, development studies have evolved through a series of dichotomous "dueling debates" between (1) modernization theory and dependency theory over whether capitalism and modernization promote or pervert development; (2) neoclassical economics and the developmental state approach over whether market or state is more important in stimulating the development processes; and (3) the developmental state and state-in-society approaches over whether the state alone or a combination of state and society is more important for supplementing market forces to help a nation climb the ladder of the international product cycle. Their competing logics provide a useful framework for reviewing the postwar developmental histories of East Asia and South Asia. In each case our analysis in this book is consistent with the broader consensus that has emerged (or seems to be emerging in the last debate) in political economy that (1) opportunities for upward mobility in the global economy are far less constrained than dependency theory implies; (2) state policy is a critical component of competitive advantage; and (3) both state and society must generally make key contributions if development is to occur. Yet, in each case, a comparison of these political economies produces some more nuanced specifications as well.

Strong States and *Strong Societies*

The political economies of East Asia and South Asia certainly do not provide fertile ground for dependency theory. In East Asia, poor nations industrialized rapidly and distributed their newly accumulated wealth fairly widely, despite the pessimism of dependency theory about the possibility for such growth with equity. India's much less impressive Hindu rate of growth also holds cold comfort for dependency theory because the Indian government, seemingly taking the dependency critique of international capitalism to heart, proved quite apt at "dislodging multinationals," to use the phrase of Dennis Encarnation (1989). Economic distortions and inequalities in South Asia (and in the more successful East Asia as well) generally represented the power and policies of domestic rather than foreign groups and actors. India, in fact, suggests several ironies regarding dependency theory. The Indian bureaucrats in the ICS under British rule became strong supporters of the postindependence Congress Party policies of democracy, socialism, and secularism; and the rent-seeking MNCs that did invest in India after 1960 simply took advantage of a domestically determined policy aimed at promoting self-reliance.

In short, the penetrative capabilities of external powers was fairly limited in both regions, as compared to Africa or Latin America (Amin, 1974; Bornschier and Chase-Dunn, 1985; Cardoso and Faletto, 1979). The British left India because the Indians kicked them out, and foreign capital was fairly limited in Japan and South Korea because of government laws and regulations. Thus, to generalize, strong states and/or strong societies in East and South Asia prevented the emergence of exploitative dependency linkages.

The conclusion that many states and societies in Asia are fairly strong certainly has implications for the second and third debates. Concerning the clash between neoclassicists and statists, almost all the East Asian economic miracles were promoted by government economic leadership, indicating the need for bringing the state back in (Evans et al., 1985). Even the failures of the developmental states in South Asia and communist East Asia do not necessarily validate the neoclassical perspective. Chapter 5 shows that there is government failure aplenty in India. Yet government strategy in India's informatics industry produced a virtuous cycle similar to those observable in the East Asian developmental states. What this suggests (to paraphrase Marx rather broadly and in an anti-Marxist manner) is that governments make history (development), but not exactly as they choose. In other words, market-conforming policies work, market-distorting ones create a "Hindu equilibrium."

More broadly, markets do not function in isolation. Rather, they exist within political contexts in which state policies inevitably shape market incentives to a significant extent. For example, U.S. businesspeople are often chided for their myopic concern with quarterly profits ("the bottom line") and compared unfavorably to Japanese corporations, which take a longer-term strategic perspective and emphasize market share. These differences, however, are almost certainly not inherent in the two nations' different gene pools or business-school doctrines. They are the result, instead, of the incentives created by the very different financial systems in the two countries (arms-length equity financing in the United States versus debt financing from allied keiretsu banks in Japan), which government policy molded (Prestowitz, 1988; Zysman, 1983).

Yet if the market does not work perfectly in splendid isolation, neither does the state. In fact, economic performance is probably enhanced by the integration, not the segregation, of state and market (Gilpin, 1987). Thus, the many examples that can be found in East and South Asia of state failures and resulting economic distortions—which certainly are inconsistent with the model of the strong and autonomous developmental state—do not necessarily justify a return to the simplicity of neoclassical logic. Rather, the review of the East and South Asian political economies presented in this book implies that whether state and market interact well or ill in a particular country is determined by the broader societal context. Thus, time and again our analysis has suggested that only bringing society back in can explain a particular set of economic outcomes.

Unlike the first two sharply dichotomous debates, the difference between the developmental state model and the state-in-society approach is somewhat more muted because the latter does not deny the efficacy of state action for supplementing market forces. Rather, it makes almost the same arguments about the need to go beyond simple neoclassicalism but then contends that both state and society as independent and interacting entities must be incorporated into political-economy models for several reasons. First, both state policy and nonstate (society) actions usually contribute to economic performance. For example, in Taiwan, government policies created the environment for dynamic guerrilla capitalism, which operated quite independently from the state; conversely, in India monopolistic rent seeking by private firms, state corporations, and corrupt politicians all helped establish a suboptimum Hindu rate of growth. Second, state policy is usually embedded within a more complex societal web. For example, the success of industrial policy in Japan is now attributed not so much to state leadership and economic direction as to effective government–business cooperation and culturally conditioned management practices.

Finally, state and society interact dynamically over time to change the nature and capabilities of a given political economy. In South Korea, for instance, the nature of the political economy ultimately evolved fairly radically in several stages. First, the success of the chaebol undermined government strength and autonomy; second, democratization changed the nature of government. Most recently, under the new president, reformist Kim Young-Sam, the government is responding to popular opinion to crack down on the power and corruption of two of the primary components of South Korea's original developmental coalition: the military regime and the chaebol (Hahm and Plein, 1995; Lee and Sohn, 1995; Moon and Prasad, 1994; Nam, 1995). Such fundamental transformation is very hard to comprehend from the perspective of dependency, neoclassical, or statist theory alone, suggesting a need to turn to the more open-ended and complex visions of the state-in-society approach.

The state-in-society approach also suggests the need for a more sophisticated conceptualization of state–society relations than is usual. Most approaches to the role of state–society relations in a political economy focus upon the balance of power between state and society. For example, Japan, South Korea, and France are seen as having strong states that dominate their societies, whereas the United States is viewed as having a weak state that primarily reacts to the pressures emanating from pluralistic social forces. From the statist perspective at least (neoclassicists would certainly dissent), strong states can (but not necessarily will) exercise the leadership necessary for good economic performance and growth in today's highly competitive global economy (Gilpin, 1987). For example, Japan's industrial policies are widely cited as an advantage in dealing with the laissez-faire United States (Fallows, 1994; Graham, 1992; Prestowitz, 1988; Tyson, 1992); the economic underdevelopment of many Third World countries has been linked to their combination of weak states and strong societies (Migdal, 1988); and the U.S. political economy has been unfavorably compared to those of the internationally open small corporatist states in Europe (Katzenstein, 1985).

Such a measuring of the relative power of state and society is far too simplistic, however, as Thomas Risse-Kappen (1995) has recently argued. For instance, there is far more balance in East Asian state–society relations than most observers, especially from afar, are wont to assume (see Chapter 4). Even in the Middle East, which is often viewed as a prime illustration of the weak state–strong society paradigm, the oil bonanza set off a complex differentiation of power between rulers and merchants (Crystal, 1990). Moreover, the economic "Euro-sclerosis" of the 1980s and 1990s has taken much of the luster off European-style corporatism (Peters, 1991). In contrast, as Jeffrey Hart (1992) concluded in his comparative study of industrialized economies, dominance by either the state (e.g., France) or society (e.g., the United States) can undercut effectiveness. Rather, cooperation between the public and private sectors seemingly provides the best results.

Such cooperation can only be effective if the various participants (e.g., government, business, and labor) are skilled and effective. Thus, entrepreneurship and labor depend on each other for the creation of a competitive corporation, but government plays a key role as well. Without a strong education system, the supply of both skilled entrepreneurs and workers may well be inadequate; business depends greatly upon state-supplied infrastructure; and, in a time of competing industrial policies in an interdependent global economy, government support for domestic corporations can be a matter of life or death for them. For example, although Ronald Reagan regarded industrial policy as a "great satan" (Graham, 1992), his willingness to use sanctions to support the 1986 Semi-Conductor Agreement with Japan provided U.S. firms with the breathing space necessary to regain their competitiveness (Prestowitz, 1988; Smith, 1995; Tyson, 1992).

In short, both a strong state and a strong society appear vital to promoting development and maintaining competitiveness.

Institutions and Indeterminacy in Developmental Effectiveness

Both the neoclassical and developmental state models simplify development theory by attributing to one factor (respectively, market operations and state policy) the role of master causal agent for how well or ill a developing economy fares. Such parsimony is the essence of theory building, yet the question always arises of when simplification becomes oversimplification. According to Thomas Kuhn (1970), scientific theories change when they fail to explain phenomena in which the relevant scholarly community is interested without generating too many anomalies. Many neoclassicists and statists are certainly satisfied with their models, but we believe that the numerous anomalies cited here suggest the need for recasting our approach to development studies.

The state-in-society approach also theoretically challenges the neoclassical and statist approaches in a manner that may explain why they appear oversimplified. In essence, both neoclassical economics and the theory of the developmental state represent forms of rational actor theory (RAT to its detractors). Neoclassical economics is based on the assumption of utility-maximizing individuals; statists make an analogous assumption at the national level. In this perspective, states are conceived as unitary actors that logically consider a range of policy options and select the ones most likely to promote economic development or achieve some other objective. Rational actor theory appears simplistic for at least two important reasons. First, even casual observation indicates that states are not unitary and neither individuals nor states rationally pursue objective economic goals with any great exclusivity. Second (and more profoundly), this is so because individual decisions and state policies are embedded within a much broader and richer institutional context of cultural and social forces that shape both to a considerable extent.

A concern with institutional context turns our attention to an emerging rival to neoclassical economics: institutional economics. This approach argues that economic institutions, even market ones, vary greatly among nations (e.g., debt-based corporate financing in Japan as opposed to the equity-based system in the United States), and that these institutions affect how economies perform. Economic institutions, in turn, are embedded within broader political and social systems. Institutional development, furthermore, is presumed to be historically conditioned and contingent rather than absolutely determined by culture, political/economic philosophy, or divine intervention. Once developed, however, institutions become quite "sticky" and generally are only subject to change under crisis conditions. In essence, this approach contends that the logic of political and economic behavior varies widely among societies because such activities take place within the much different contexts that have been generated by historical, cultural, and social factors (Clark and Chan, 1995; Clark and Lam, 1995; Doner, 1992; March and Olsen, 1989; North, 1990; Steinmo et al., 1992; Teece, 1990). From this perspective, developmental outcomes vary for two fundamental reasons. First, some societies generate more-effective economic institutions than others. Second, economic institutions vary in their congruence with particular national contexts, and inappropriate institutions create barriers to effective action.

This institutional perspective fits quite nicely with the state-in-society argument that society must be added to any explanation of how states and markets operate. However, if institutionalism provides a less simplistic alternative to neoclassicism or statism, it is subject to the opposite criticism that it is so open-ended that it does not really constitute a meaningful framework at all. Most narrowly, although it brings in additional factors, it does not necessarily serve the vital theoretical function of indicating what should be excluded as irrelevant. More fundamentally, unlike with states and markets, even defining or isolating institutions may be problematic. Institutions are usually defined as ongoing and fairly permanent arrangements in the society, economy, and polity that set the rules and routines by which policies are made and markets operate. They exist at a number of levels.

- Fundamental social and cultural norms that shape economic and political values in a society
- The central structures and statutes defining and governing the market in an economy
- The formal organizations and more informal decisionmaking processes in a polity that are involved, directly or indirectly, in economic policymaking
- The business culture that prevails in individual enterprises or industry segments
- Specific government policies that affect how well an economy performs.

It would be a daunting task to specify every type of institution; many of them involve informal patterns of interaction that may prove difficult to observe. Moreover, it is easy for disagreements to arise over just what composes a specific set of institutions. To scholars versed in the dominant positivist epistemology of political science and economics, therefore, this call for incorporating more complexity into our theories of development suggests the danger of playing tennis without a net (as blank verse was once described). Such a danger cannot be denied. However, at a time when the previously dominant paradigms (neoclassical, dependency, and statist theory) seemingly provide oversimplistic straitjackets for interpreting reality, the necessity to rethink the methods of conceptualizing development cannot be gainsaid either.

More broadly, institutionalism, unlike the other three perspectives, calls attention to the inherent indeterminacy of how political economies evolve. Sociocultural, economic, and political institutions are complex and, almost inevitably, historically contingent. That is, institutional context shapes state policy and economic performance. By the standards of logical positivism, such an approach is an admission of failure. Yet the importance of indeterminacy in social science is being increasingly recognized (Bohman, 1991). It mirrors and, in fact, lags similar trends in the physical and life sciences, such as quantum and chaos theory, from which the positivists in the social sciences take their Newtonian standards (Becker, 1991). This line of argument leads very quickly to abstract levels. We conclude, therefore, by providing an illustration of the institutionalist approach through a brief sketch of political culture in the political economies of East and South Asia.

Political Culture: Institutions, Indeterminacy, and Development as an Open-Ended Process

Students of political economy tend to think in terms of universal theories, such as the neoclassical and developmental state models. Area-study specialists, in contrast, tend to think in terms of unique and disparate cultural areas. Just as neoclassical economics can differentiate East Asia from South Asia in terms of market-conforming export promotion versus market-distorting import substitution, such eminent area specialists as Lucian Pye (with Pye, 1985) divide the two regions between the "pragmatic secularism" underlying Confucian capitalism and the "otherworldly" Hindu and Muslim cultures of South Asia. This provides a neat explanation for their radically different growth rates; from this perspective, Dengist China is simply returning to the Confucian fold after three decades of mistakenly following an inappropriate route plotted by a bastardized version of a European philosophy.

Before we accept such easy cultural determinism, however, it is good to remember that not so long ago Max Weber's (1951) association of Confucian culture with economic stagnation was taken as scholastic orthodoxy. This certainly suggests some indeterminacy. That is, there are apparently several components of Confucianism, which have differing implications for economic and political performance. Depending upon the circumstances, Confucian culture may either stimulate or inhibit economic activities; which ones become most influential in a given situation depends upon historically contingent factors (Clark, 1989; Wong, 1986). Moreover, whatever the fatalism implicit in references to the Hindu rate of growth, Indian political culture possesses some interesting and surprising parallels with Confucianism. Both can create or undermine strong states and strong societies.

The concept of political culture has been used in many ways. We adopt one of the simpler definitions: a set of widely shared social values impinging upon a nation's political economy. At the abstract level these values include beliefs about what is valuable, what a person's role in the world should be, how people should relate to each other, and what constitutes legitimate authority. In more concrete or operational terms these values concern whether hard work and economic enterprise are valued, whether human (especially political) relationships are seen as hierarchic or more egalitarian, whether political office primarily involves decisionmaking power or status, how (or if) an individual can achieve socioeconomic mobility, and to what social and/or political institutions loyalty is owed. Thus, political culture is embodied in enduring patterns of production, consumption, and distribution and consequently is not easily changed. At the same time, it permeates the political economy, setting norms of expectation and behavior for both the elite and the masses. These norms underlie and shape official policies, entrepreneurial decisions, and ordinary daily behavior in work, learning, spending, and recreation. Taken together such values form broad patterns of what Lucian Pye (with Pye, 1985) terms the "cultural dimensions of authority," which, he argues, are more or less functional for various tasks, such as promoting industrialization, fighting wars, or maintaining the status quo in a primitive society.

East Asia's Confucian philosophy was initially developed in China from the thought of an actual scholar/philosopher who lived about five hundred years before the birth of Christ, although it was greatly elaborated and probably radically changed over the centuries. It was in essence a secular philosophy aimed toward creating the good society through the leadership of a benevolent state staffed by the most educated and moral men in the land, who would use their knowledge and virtue to take care of their people. This would create a social and political hierarchy, but it would be based on merit and on reciprocal obligations between those in authority, in government or the family, and those below them. The practice, however, could be very different, representing what Pye (1991) calls "sweet and sour Confucianism" (benevolent theory versus malevolent practice). Power was abused in the sense that a major goal of power was the ability to derive satisfaction from mistreating one's dependents (e.g., oppressive gender roles within the family). Broader cultural traits, moreover, were reflections of fundamental socialization that occurred in the family; this inculcated a belief in the father as an omnipotent authority figure and in the necessity to limit one's trust to the family circle.

In terms of the government, positions were staffed through competitive examinations for a thousand years, but merit was determined by knowledge of arcane Confucian theory whose relevance to daily administrative tasks was questionable; there were constant conflicts among bureaucratic factions whose personalistic nature created deep-seated uncertainty and insecurity among officials; debates and conflicts were carried on in moral rather than practical terms; the mandarins, or bureaucrats, were contemptuous of merchants and excelled at "squeezing" them; and there was a tremendous bias to hold back rather than promote change and reform (Pye, 1981 & 1991; Pye with Pye, 1985). These aspects of Confucianism led theorists such as Max Weber (1951) to conclude that this culture would almost inevitably be associated with economic backwardness and stagnation; that judgment seemed to be confirmed by Chinese history during the nineteenth and early twentieth centuries.

Such pessimism, however, ignores many other aspects of Chinese Confucian culture. First, orthodox Confucianism itself contains important elements that can be quite functional for promoting economic transformation. The government was exhorted to protect and promote the national good; respect for authority provided more maneuverability for a government; a high premium was placed upon education; an individual's fate was linked to his or her own talents and efforts; and strong family ties created incentives for family-based entrepreneurialism.

Second, whereas Confucian orthodoxy forms one pole of Chinese culture, other dimensions of that culture also can be discerned. The stifling restrictions and stereotyped behavior of Confucianism have always engendered a strong underground counterculture manifested by Taoism and rebellious secret societies (Pye, 1988). This is expressed culturally in the folk hero of the Monkey, Sun Wukong, who still delights Chinese opera goers by discomfiting pompous officials and upsetting the bureaucratic hierarchy. Outwardly conforming to the rituals of Confucianism, many Chinese harbor secret desires to break out of the social order and strike out on their own. Whereas Confucianism stresses order and authority, the heterodox cultures reject the primacy of central authority and legitimize rebellion as a means to escape domination. Such a culture has helped stimulate the guerrilla capitalism of Hong Kong and Taiwan (Lam, 1990b; Lam and Clark, 1994; Tai, 1989). However, just as with orthodox Confucianism, the implications of the heterodox culture for economic performance are contingent and ambiguous. For example, revolutionary Maoism and the economic disaster that it brought may be viewed as another manifestation of the heterodox culture.

Third, feudal Confucianism overcomes some of the problems associated with the patriarchal Chinese variant. Japan and Korea imported their essentially Confucian cultures from China. However, unlike China, both these nations had long periods of feudalism, which evidently created a significantly different variant of Confucianism. The feudal Confucian cultures in Japan and Korea share many of the central values of Chinese Confucianism, such as strong group loyalties, respect for authority, concern with achievement, and a high regard for education. Their feudal histories, however, give them some additional values that appear important for promoting development. Feudalism forced Japanese and Koreans to work and fight together in large groups that extended beyond kinship lines; thus they are much less concerned with abstract philosophy and more practical than many aspiring Chinese mandarins. Feudal Confucianism also promotes cooperation in the large organizations; this has been used to explain the strong developmental states and huge corporate conglomerates that distinguish the Korean and Japanese political economies from the Chinese ones (with the exception of Singapore's strong developmental state). Somewhat different child-rearing practices from the Chinese reinforce these behavioral differences as well. In Japan, for example, the father is far less authoritarian (and often absent from the family); close physical contact with the mother promotes group dependency; family lines are not so rigid as in China; and children are trained to succeed in the world outside the family (Pye with Pye, 1985; Reischauer, 1988).

The rapid development and industrialization of postwar Japan and South Korea, the two principal Confucian feudalists among today's capitalist nations, offer a strange counterpoint to the modernization approach. In the West, at least according to modernization theory, the destruction of feudal society and linkages was a prerequisite for the unleashing of the entrepreneurial verve and technological transformations that explain "how the West grew rich" (Rosenberg and Birdzell, 1986). This is a view, incidentally, that laissez-faire economics shares with Marxism. In the East, in contrast, the feudal heritage of Japan and South Korea seems to have contributed to their superstar performance on the economic playing field. This suggests two conclusions about indeterminacy. First, the interactions between an economy and its social and political environment are complex and contingent. Second, the economic implications of a given set of social patterns or institutions may change drastically depending upon the historical circumstances; compare, for instance, the tremendous dynamism of Meiji Japan with the preceding shogunate.

As would be expected, India has a much different culture, resulting from its religious and historical antecedents. This has been used by theorists such as Lucian Pye (with Pye, 1985) to explain the contrast between the Hindu rate of growth and East Asian dynamism. In terms of its cultural basis, the essence of Hindu philosophy is that every human soul has to go through a process of rebirths before ultimately being reunited with the supreme power from which it originated. The more morally justified actions one performs, the greater chance one will have of shortening the process of rebirth. Love for wealth and the pursuit, acquisition, and enjoyment of luxury and comfort are discouraged. This philosophy, unlike the more secular Confucianism, therefore discourages the motivation for the activities normally associated with economic dynamism. It also fosters the belief that destiny is predetermined, which creates feelings of helplessness and apathy.

According to Pye's (with Pye, 1985) model, the central elements of Hindu culture have combined in the current Indian political economy in a particularly perverse manner (analogous to the "sour Confucianism" of the late Qing Dynasty). The caste system smothers the need for individual achievement and goal seeking and separates political and religious leadership—the former being quite amoral and pragmatic. The emphasis on the inner world of the self leads to moralistic posturing. This has created an ineffectual postindependence leadership style that combines grand national-development plans, which are not seriously meant to be carried out (the moral dimension), with an extensive patronage-style distribution of resources (the amoral dimension). This is just the reverse of the Japanese pattern of keeping patronage politics out of the central issues in the domestic political economy. In India, therefore, the "caste-bureaucratic" culture stresses status rather than performance in both economic and political activities and legitimates considerable inequality (despite India's ostensibly Gandhian philosophy) and the neglect of rural regions.

If the impact of Confucianism upon East Asian political economies is subject to considerable indeterminacy, the same can be expected of India's political culture. As argued in Chapter 5, the ideology and nationalism of India's top political leaders at the time of independence shaped the evolution of the country's political economy to a considerable extent—certainly far more than occurred in East Asia. It is ironic that, although this ideology was put in the service of nationalism, it was primarily derived not from the indigenous culture but from what might be called the counterculture of the occupying imperial power (Fabian socialism), while some of the bureaucratic perversions that emerged seemingly represented a continuation of British administrative theory.

Just as there are several major variants of Confucianism, each having somewhat different implications for development, India too has a variety of cultural, philosophical, and historical traditions. Despite the legacies and cultural traits supporting centralized rule and limiting socioeconomic mobility, India also has a far more democratic historical tradition than do the East Asian nations. Ancient Indian kingdoms, although ranging from oligarchies to republics, tended to be fairly decentralized; district, town, and village councils were granted extensive powers or had large central assemblies. Moreover, despite the caste system, intercaste marriages were fairly common. These democratic traditions, which continued until 1000 A.D., when the Muslim rule in India began (Altekar, 1977), were valuable in helping India become the world's largest democracy. They also make Indians far more militant and less tolerant of political and business authority than are East Asians, thus stimulating the rise of dysfunctional demand politics (Rudolph and Rudolph, 1987).

Despite the sharp distinction drawn between the Chinese and Indian political cultures by Lucian Pye (with Pye, 1985), parallels can also be drawn between India's political culture and Pye's conception of Confucianism as a philosophy that advocated enlightened elite rule though it was often distorted into oppressive "sour Confucianism" in practice (Pye, 1981, 1988 & 1991; Pye with Pye, 1985). In Francine Frankel's (1978 & 1990) interpretation, Gandhi advocated an essentially Brahmanical system of rule in which the educated and skilled elites had a moral obligation to take care of the interests of the poor and of those in lower castes. Therefore, he was not receptive to advocates of empowering the marginal members of India's society so that they could promote their own interests. A similar logic motivated the British creation of the ICS. From this perspective, the patronage-based Congress system and the exclusion of many peasants from the fruits of land reform can be seen as the "sour" practical results of the attempted reliance on "Brahmanical benevolence." Similarly, the rise of demand politics is analogous to manifestations of the Chinese heterodox culture, albeit much less functional than the guerrilla capitalism of Hong Kong and Taiwan.

The impact of culture on a political economy therefore involves significant indeterminacy. Every culture has a variety of components whose specific influence on social, political, and economic institutions can vary greatly, depending on the historical circumstances that make them operative or inoperative. From this state-in-society perspective, East Asian dynamism occurred because, in a variety of ways in different nations, the cultural context facilitated the emergence of strong states and/or strong societies whose talents then promoted rapid development. In India, in contrast, the basis was laid for the creation of a strong state; however, the development policies of the state then ignored or stifled considerable segments of society. This process generated the problems and institutional responses that ultimately debilitated the state's capacity.

Strong States, Strong Societies, and Development: Transcending One Trade-off but Facing Another

The concluding section of Chapter 4 argued that the key to the success of the East Asian political economies lay in the flexibility of their businesses and their governments. Chapter 5 described how India's political economy degenerated into rigidity and rent seeking as the problems of a weak society generated a dynamic that undercut state strength. The arguments adduced in this chapter link such flexibility (or the absence of it) to the strength of a nation's society and state. Strong institutions have the capacity to be flexible; weak ones cannot adjust. In addition, unlike many analyses of state–society relations, which seek to assess the balance of power between state and civil society, the study of the political economies in East and South Asia suggests that both a strong state and a strong society may be necessary if the requisite economic and political flexibility is to be created and protected. In most cases, both state and society clearly contributed to East Asian dynamism; India shows how a weakness in one sector can undermine the efficacy of the other. Even the two seemingly unidimensional East Asian success stories are not totally clear-cut cases: The strategy of Singapore's strong state depends on a highly skilled and motivated work force, whereas the guerrilla capitalism of Hong Kong's strong society was facilitated by the colonial administration's provision of infrastructure, guarantees of free markets, and strength in trade negotiations.

Development emerges as an open-ended process, based upon the recognition by the state-in-society approach of the significant indeterminacy in how institutions shape economic and social outcomes, on the one hand, and how they are shaped by their cultural and historical contexts, on the other. Today's successful political economy may degenerate tomorrow, and a current problem child can revitalize its society and state, transforming itself into an economic dynamo. The highly statist strategy of Singapore is quite vulnerable to a change in the nature of the regime. Democratization in Taiwan has brought more ties between business and government elites, but rather than stimulating more sophisticated industrial policy, it has generated gross corruption and increased the openness of Mainlander–Islander tensions (Chu, 1992; Kuo, 1997; Wachman, 1994); this is almost certainly to the detriment of Taiwan's future economic performance. In contrast, the demand politics that are normally viewed as threatening India's stability and policy effectiveness may also be taken as a sign of the awakening of formerly marginalized groups (Frankel, 1990) who may ultimately help build a stronger society.

Finally, the argument that both strong states and strong societies contribute to development has countervailing implications about the trade-offs and bottlenecks associated with industrialization and economic growth. This approach is optimistic in that it suggests that the normally assumed trade-off between growth and equity, or meeting basic human needs, may not be all that severe. When critics of neoclassical theory argue that it ignores more well-rounded conceptions of development (Griffin, 1989; Nafziger, 1990), they may not really be suggesting killing the goose that lays the golden eggs. Rather, in many (but certainly not all) instances, government programs for meeting basic human needs evidently create the human capital on which further development depends, rather than stifling initiative by diverting resources from the "efficient" private sector.

Although the possibility for transcending this traditional trade-off may be greater than is generally recognized, however, the state-in-society approach suggests another, far less recognized problem. The logic of self-interest suggests that strength can be used for self-aggrandizement. For example, in the mid-1980s, Japan was generally seen as having an effective set of collaborative and mutually reinforcing relationships among corporate leaders, the permanent civil servants in the key ministries, and electorial politicians in the LDP. Yet these soon contributed greatly to Japan's political and economic crisis of the early 1990s because their vested interests made them increasingly inflexible.

Mancur Olson (1982) formalized this logic in a model assuming that long periods of political stability in democracies (the same could be said for dictatorships) stimulate the emergence of "distributional coalitions" of businesspeople, politicians, and labor unions that use their political power to distort the economy in order to reap particularistic benefits or monopolistic rents for themselves. Strong states and strong societies therefore have the capability to enhance economic performance. Yet this very strength also creates incentives to abuse power for economic gain or to shield oneself from the discipline of the market. As implied by Olson's title, *The Rise and Decline of Nations,* this suggests that economic success is not always self-reinforcing. The open-ended nature of development means that even the strong states and strong societies in successful economies must keep on their toes, and social and political change in currently lagging nations may create the basis for the take-off to a new economic miracle.

REFERENCES

Adelman, I. 1984. "Beyond Export-Led Growth." *World Development* 12: 937–949.

Aghazadeh, E. and H. D. Evans. 1988. "Price Distortions, Efficiency, and Growth." Brighton: IDS mimeo, University of Sussex.

Agherli, B. B., I. S. Kim, and H. Neiss. 1987. "Growth and Adjustment in South Asia." *Finance and Development* 23: 12–15.

Alam, M. S. 1989. *Governments and Markets in Economic Development Strategies: Lessons from Korea, Taiwan, and Japan.* New York: Praeger.

Allen, G. C. 1981. *A Short Economic History of Modern Japan.* London: Macmillan.

Altekar, A. S. 1977. *State and Government in Ancient India.* New Delhi: Motilan Baranasidas.

Amin, S. 1974. *Accumulation on a World Scale: A Critique of the Theory of Underdevelopment.* New York: Monthly Review Press.

Amsden, A. H. 1989. *Asia's Next Giant: South Korea and Late Industrialization.* New York: Oxford University Press.

An, T. S. 1989. "North Korea: The Cost of Self-Imposed Isolation." Pp. 145–167 in C. Y. Chennault, ed., *Modernizing East Asia: Economic and Cultural Dimensions of Political Change.* New York: St. John's University Press.

Andersen, W. K. 1995. "India in 1994: Economics to the Fore." *Asian Studies* 35: 127–139.

The Australian. 1994. August 9.

Bagchi, A. K. 1981. "Export Incentives in India: A Review." Pp. 297–327 in A. K. Bagchi and N. Banerjei, eds., *Change and Choice in Indian Industry.* Calcutta: Centre of Studies in Social Science.

Balassa, B. 1981. *The Newly Industrializing Countries in the World Economy.* New York: Pergamon.

Balasubramanyam, V. N. 1984. *The Economy of India.* London: Weidenfeld and Nicholson.

Balasubramanyam, V. N. and D. R. Basu. 1990. "Export Promotion Policies and Export Performance." Pp. 213–232 in C. Milner, ed., *Export Promoting Strategies: Theory and Evidence from Developing Countries.* New York: Harvestor Wheatsheaf.

Bardhan, P. 1984. *The Political Economy of Development in India.* Oxford: Basil Blackwell.

Barker, R., R. W. Herdt, and B. Rose. 1985. *The Rice Economy of Asia.* Washington, DC: Resources for the Future.

Bates, R. H. 1981. *Markets and States in Tropical Africa: The Political Basis of Agricultural Policies.* Berkeley: University of California Press.

175

Becker, T., ed. 1991. *Quantum Politics: Applying Quantum Theory to Political Phenomena.* New York: Praeger.

Bernard, M. and J. Ravenhill. 1995. "Beyond Flying Geese and Product Cycles: Regionalization, Hierarchy, and the Industrialization of East Asia." *World Politics* 47: 171–209.

Bhagwati, J. N. 1978. *Foreign Trade Regimes and Economic Development: Anatomy and Consequences of Exchange Control Regimes.* Cambridge, MA: Ballinger.

Bhagwati, J. N. 1993. *India in Transition: Freeing the Economy.* Oxford: Clarendon.

Bhagwati, J. N. and P. Desai. 1970. *India: Planning for Industrialization.* London: Oxford University Press.

Bhagwati, J. N. and T. N. Sririvasan. 1975. *Foreign Trade Regimes and Economic Development.* New York: Columbia University Press.

Bhalla, A. S. 1995. "Recent Economic Reforms in China and India." *Asian Survey* 35: 555–572.

Blaker, M. 1995. "Japan in 1994: Out with the Old Order: In with the New?" *Asian Survey* 35: 1–12.

Bobrow D. B. and S. Chan. 1987. "Understanding Anomalous Successes: Japan, Taiwan, and South Korea." Pp. 111–130 in C. F. Hermann, C. W. Kegley, Jr., and J. N. Rosenau, eds., *New Directions in the Comparative Study of Foreign Policy.* Boston: Allen & Unwin.

Bohman, J. 1991. *New Philosophy of Social Science: Problems of Indeterminacy.* Cambridge, MA: MIT Press.

Bornschier, V. and C. Chase-Dunn. 1985. *Transnational Corporations and Underdevelopment.* New York: Praeger.

Bose, P. K. and M. Mukherjee. 1985. *P. C. Mahalanobis: Papers on Planning.* Calcutta: Statistical Publishing Society.

Boulton, W. R. 1995. "Japan's Product Development Strategy: Roadmaps for Technology Development." *Business & the Contemporary World* 7: 104–118.

Brahmachari, S. 1992. *Impact of Incentives on Productivity in Public Enterprises: An Economic Analysis of Case Studies.* Calcutta: Ph.D. Dissertation, University of Calcutta.

Bruton, H. J. 1992. *Sri Lanka and Malaysia.* New York: Oxford University Press.

Burns, J. F. 1995. "Bombay's Bleak Nationalism: 'Hindustan' for Hindus Only." *New York Times* (November 3) pp. A1 & A6.

Butterfield, F. 1982. *China: Alive in the Bitter Sea.* New York: Times Books.

Calder, K. 1988. *Crisis and Compensation: Public Policy and Political Stability in Japan, 1949–1986.* Princeton: Princeton University Press.

Campbell, R. W. 1991. *The Socialist Economies in Transition: A Primer on Semi-Reformed Systems.* Bloomington: University of Indiana Press.

Campbell, R. W. 1992. *The Failure of Soviet Economic Planning: System, Performance, and Reform.* Bloomington: Indiana University Press.

Caporaso, J. A. and D. P. Levine. 1992. *Theories of Political Economy.* Cambridge: Cambridge University Press.

Cardoso, F. H. 1973. "Associated Dependent Development: Theoretical and Practical Implications." Pp. 149–172 in A. Stepan, ed., *Authoritarian Brazil: Origins, Policy, and Future.* New Haven: Yale University Press.

Cardoso, F. and E. Faletto. 1979. *Dependency and Development in Latin America.* Berkeley: University of California Press.

Castells, M., L. Goh, and R. Y. W. Kwok. 1990. *The Shek Kip Mei Syndrome: Economic Development and Public Housing in Hong Kong and Singapore.* London: Pion.

Centre for Development Studies. 1986. "Between Need and Greed: The Wasting of India, the Greening of India." New Delhi: Presentation to the Union Council of Ministers, May 21.

Chakravarty, S. 1987. *Development Planning: The Indian Experience.* Oxford: Clarendon Press.

Chan, S. 1985. "The Impact of Defense Spending on Economic Performance: A Survey of Evidence and Problems." *Orbis* 29: 403–434.

Chan, S. 1987. "The Mouse That Roared: Taiwan's Management of Trade Relations with the U.S." *Comparative Political Studies* 20: 251–292.

Chan, S. 1993. *East Asian Dynamism: Growth, Order, and Security in the Pacific Region,* 2nd ed. Boulder, CO: Westview.

Chan, S. and C. Clark. 1992a. *Flexibility, Foresight, and Fortuna in Taiwan's Development: Navigating Between Scylla and Charybdis.* London: Routledge.

Chan, S. and C. Clark. 1992b. "The Rise of East Asian NICs: Confucian Capitalism, Status Mobility, and Developmental Legacy." Pp. 27–48 in C. Clark and S. Chan, eds. *The Evolving Pacific Basin in the Global Political Economy: Domestic and International Linkages.* Boulder, CO: Lynne Rienner.

Chan, S. and C. Clark. 1992/93. "The Price of Economic Success: South Korea and Taiwan Sacrifice Political Development." *Harvard International Review* 15: 24–26 & 64.

Chan, S., C. Clark, and D. Lam, eds. 1997. *The Role of the State in Asian Development: Beyond the Developmental State.* London: Macmillan.

Chang, D. W. W. 1988. *China Under Deng Xiaoping: Political and Economic Reform.* New York: St. Martin's.

Chen, P. J. S., ed. 1983. *Singapore Development Policies and Trends.* Singapore: Oxford University Press.

Cheng, C. Y. 1982. *China's Economic Development: Growth and Structural Change.* Boulder, CO: Westview.

Cheng, C. Y. 1990. *Behind the Tiananmen Massacre: Social, Political, and Economic Ferment in China.* Boulder, CO: Westview.

Cheng, T. J. 1990. "Political Regimes and Development Strategies." Pp. 139–178 in G. Gereffi and D. L. Wyman, eds., *Manufacturing Miracles: Paths of Industrialization in Latin America and East Asia.* Princeton: Princeton University Press.

Chiu, P. C. H. 1992. "Money and Financial Markets: The Domestic Perspective." Pp. 121–193 in G. Ranis, ed., *Taiwan: From Developing to Mature Economy.* Boulder, CO: Westview.

Chu, Y. H. 1989. "State Structure and Economic Adjustment of the East Asian Newly Industrializing Countries." *International Organization* 43: 647–672.

Chu, Y. H. 1991. "Industrial Change and Developmental State in the East Asian NICs: A Case Study of the Automobile Industry in South Korea and Taiwan." Paper presented at the Annual Meeting of the American Political Science Association, Washington, DC.

Chu, Y. H. 1992. *Crafting Democracy in Taiwan.* Taipei: Institute for International Relations.

Clark, C. 1989. *Taiwan's Development: Implications for Contending Political Economy Paradigms.* Westport, CT: Greenwood.

Clark, C. and D. Bahry. 1983. "Dependent Development: A Socialist Variant." *International Studies Quarterly* 27: 271–293.

Clark, C. and S. Chan. 1994. "The Developmental Roles of the State: Moving Beyond the Developmental State in Conceptualizing Asian Political Economies." *Governance* 7: 332–359.

Clark, C. and S. Chan. 1995. "MNCs and Developmentalism: Domestic Structures as an Explanation for East Asian Dynamism." Pp. 112–145 in T. Risse-Kappen, ed., *Bringing Transnational Relations Back In: Non-State Actors, Domestic Structures, and International Institutions*. Cambridge: Cambridge University Press.

Clark, C. and D. Lam. 1995. "The Competitiveness Debate: Recognizing and Reforming the Institutional Context of National Economic Behavior." *Business & the Contemporary World* 7: 12–27.

Coble, P. M. 1980. *The Shanghai Capitalists and the Nationalist Government, 1927–1937*. Cambridge, MA: Harvard University Press.

Commerce. 1968. May 9.

Crone, D. K. 1983. *The ASEAN States: Coping with Dependence*. New York: Praeger.

Crystal, J. 1990. *Oil Politics in the Gulf: Rulers and Merchants in Kuwait and Qatar*. Cambridge: Cambridge University Press.

Cumings, B. 1984. "The Origins and Development of the Northeast Asia Political Economy: Industrial Sectors, Product Cycles, and Political Consequences." *International Organization* 38: 1–40.

Deyo, F. C. 1981. *Dependent Development and Industrial Order: An Asian Case Study*. New York: Praeger.

Deyo, F. C., ed. 1987. *The Political Economy of the New Asian Industrialism*. Ithaca: Cornell University Press.

Deyo, F. C. 1989. *Beneath the Miracle: Labor Subordination in the New Asian Industrialism*. Berkeley: University of California Press.

Dittmer, L. 1994. *China Under Reform*. Boulder, CO: Westview.

Doner, R. F. 1992. "Limits of State Strength: Toward an Institutionalist View of Economic Development." *World Politics* 44: 398–431.

Eckstein, A. 1977. *China's Economic Revolution*. Cambridge: Cambridge University Press.

Economic Times. 1994. March 1.

Eisenstadt, S. N. 1973. *Tradition, Change, and Modernity*. New York: John Wiley.

Encarnation, D. J. 1989. *Dislodging Multinationals: India's Strategy in Comparative Perspective*. Ithaca: Cornell University Press.

Evans, H. D. 1990. "Outward Orientation: An Assessment." Pp. 40–58 in C. Milner, ed., *Export Promoting Strategies: Theory and Evidence from Developing Countries*. New York: Harvestor Wheatsheaf.

Evans, P. B. 1979. *Dependent Development: The Alliance of Multinational, State, and Local Capital in Brazil*. Princeton: Princeton University Press.

Evans, P. 1995. *Embedded Autonomy: States and Industrial Transformation*. Princeton: Princeton University Press.

Evans, P. B., D. Rueschemeyer, and T. Skocpol, eds. 1985. *Bringing the State Back In*. Cambridge: Cambridge University Press.

Fallows, J. M. 1994. *Looking at the Sun: The Rise of the New East Asian Economic and Political System*. New York: Pantheon.

Fei, J. C. H., G. Ranis, and S. W. Y. Kuo. 1979. *Growth with Equity: The Taiwan Case*. New York: Oxford University Press.

Fields, K. J. 1995. *Enterprise and the State in South Korea and Taiwan*. Ithaca: Cornell University Press.

Frank, A. G. 1969. *Capitalism and Underdevelopment in Latin America*. New York: Monthly Review Press.

Frankel, F. R. 1978. *India's Political Economy, 1947–1977: The Gradual Revolution*. Princeton: Princeton University Press.

Frankel, F. R. 1990. "Conclusion: Decline of a Social Order." Pp. 482–517 in F. R. Frankel and M. S. A. Rao, eds., *Dominance and State Power in Modern India: Decline of a Social Order*, Vol. II. Delhi: Oxford University Press.

Frankel, F. R. and M. S. A. Rao, eds. 1990. *Dominance and State Power in Modern India: Decline of a Social Order*. Delhi: Oxford University Press.

Frieden, J. 1981. "Third World Indebted Industrialization: International Finance and State Capital in Mexico, Brazil, Algeria, and South Korea." *International Organization* 35: 407–431.

Friedman, D. 1988. *The Misunderstood Miracle: Industrial Development and Political Change in Japan*. Ithaca: Cornell University Press.

Friedman, E. 1995. "The Subtext of Asian Authoritarian Discourse: Can East and Southeast Asia Join to Build an International Human Rights Regime?" Paper presented at the Conference on the Politics and Economics of Regional Cooperation in East and Southeast Asia, University of Wisconsin, Milwaukee.

Friedman, M. and R. Friedman. 1980. *Free to Choose*. New York: Harcourt, Brace, and Jovanovich.

Galenson, W., ed. 1979. *Economic Growth and Structural Change in Taiwan: The Postwar Experience of the Republic of China*. Ithaca: Cornell University Press.

Gereffi, G. 1990. "Paths on Industrialization: An Overview." Pp. 3–31 in G. Gereffi and D. Wyman, eds., *Manufacturing Miracles: Paths of Industrialization in Latin America and East Asia*. Princeton: Princeton University Press.

Gereffi, G. 1995. "Global Production Systems and Third World Development." Pp. 100–142 in B. Stallings, ed., *Global Change, Regional Response: The New International Context of Development*. New York: Cambridge University Press.

Gereffi, G. 1996. "Commodity Chains and Regional Divisions of Labor in East Asia." Durham: Duke University Papers in International Political Economy.

Gereffi, G. and D. Wyman, eds. 1990. *Manufacturing Miracles: Paths of Industrialization in Latin America and East Asia*. Princeton: Princeton University Press.

Gerlach, M. L. 1992. *Alliance Capitalism: The Social Organization of Japanese Business*. Berkeley: University of California Press.

Gerschenkron, A. 1962. *Economic Backwardness in Historical Perspective: A Book of Essays*. Cambridge: Harvard University Press, 1962.

Ghosh, A. 1995. "Economic Liberalization in India: An Assessment." Paper presented at the Third International Conference on Development and Future Studies, Helsinki, Swedish School of Economics.

Gilder, G. 1984. *The Spirit of Enterprise*. New York: Simon & Schuster.

Gillies, M., D. H. Perkins, M. Roemer, and D. H. Snodgrass. 1987. *Economic Development*. New York: Norton.

Gilpin, R. 1987. *The Political Economy of International Relations*. Princeton: Princeton University Press.

Gold, T. B. 1986. *State and Society in the Taiwan Miracle*. Armonk, NY: M. E. Sharpe.

Goldstein, J. 1993. *Ideas, Interests, and American Trade Policy*. Ithaca: Cornell University Press.

Goldstein, J. and R. O. Keohane, eds. 1993. *Ideas and Foreign Policy: Beliefs, Institutions, and Political Change*. Ithaca: Cornell University Press.

Gourevitch, P. A. 1986. *Politics in Hard Times: Comparative Responses to International Economic Crises*. Ithaca: Cornell University Press.

Government of India. 1981. *Economic Survey, 1980–1981*. New Delhi: Government of India.

Government of India. 1990a. *Economic Survey, 1989–1990*. New Delhi: Government of India.

Government of India. 1990b. *India 1990, A Reference Annual*. New Delhi: Government of India.

Government of India. 1990c. *Seventh Five Year Plan 1985–1990: Mid Term Appraisal*. New Delhi: Government of India.

Grabowski, R. 1994. "The Successful Developmental State: Where Does It Come From?" *World Development* 22: 413–422.

Graham, O. L., Jr. 1992. *Losing Time: The Industrial Policy Debate*. Cambridge, MA: Harvard University Press.

Greenhalgh, S. 1984. "Networks and Their Nodes: Urban Society in Taiwan." *China Quarterly* 99: 529–552.

Greenhalgh, S. 1988. "Families and Networks in Taiwan's Economic Development." Pp. 224–245 in E. A. Winckler and S. Greenhalgh, eds., *Contending Approaches to the Political Economy of Taiwan*. Armonk, NY: M. E. Sharpe.

Grieco, J. M. 1984. *Between Dependency and Autonomy: India's Experience with the International Computer Industry*. Berkeley: University of California Press.

Griffin, K. 1989. *Alternative Strategies for Economic Development*. London: MacMillan.

Hagen, E. E. 1986. *The Economics of Development*, 4th. ed. Homewood IL: Irwin.

Haggard, S. 1990. *Pathways from the Periphery: The Politics of Growth in the Newly Industrializing Countries*. Ithaca: Cornell University Press.

Haggard, S. and T. J. Cheng. 1987. "State and Foreign Capital in the East Asian NICs." Pp. 84–135 in F. C. Deyo, ed., *The Political Economy of the New Asian Industrialism*. Ithaca: Cornell University Press.

Haggard, S. and C. I. Moon. 1983. "The South Korean State in the International Economy: Liberal, Dependent, or Mercantile?" Pp. 131–189 in J. G. Ruggie, ed., *The Antinomies of Interdependence: National Welfare and the International Division of Labor*. New York: Columbia University Press.

Haggard, S. and C. I. Moon. 1990. "Institutions and Economic Policy: Theory and a Korean Case Study." *World Politics* 42: 210–237.

Hahm, S. D. and L. C. Plein. 1995. "Structural and Rational Foundations for the Decline of Authoritarian Executive-Bureaucratic Politics in Korea." Paper presented at the Conference on the Structure and Organization of Government, International Political Science Association Research Committee, Seoul National University.

Hall, P. A., ed. 1989. *The Political Power of Economic Ideas: Keynsianism Across Nations*. Princeton: Princeton University Press.

Harding, H. 1987. *China's Second Revolution: Reform After Mao*. Washington, DC: The Brookings Institution.

Harrison, B. 1994. *Lean and Mean: The Changing Landscape of Corporate Power in the Age of Flexibility*. New York: Basic Books.

Hart, J. A. 1992. *Rival Capitalists: International Competitiveness in the United States, Japan, and Western Europe*. Ithaca: Cornell University Press.

Hayami, Y. 1975. *A Century of Agricultural Growth in Japan: Its Relevance to Asian Development*. Minneapolis: University of Minnesota Press.

Hayami, Y. 1988. *Japanese Agriculture Under Siege: The Political Economy of Agricultural Policies*. New York: St. Martin's.

Hayami, Y. and S. Yamada. 1970. "Agricultural Productivity at the Beginning of Industrialization." Pp. 105–135 in K. Ohkawa, B. F. Johnston, and H. Kaneda, eds., *Agriculture and Economic Growth: Japan's Experience*. Princeton: Princeton University Press.

Heilman, J. G and G. W. Johnson. 1992. *The Politics and Economics of Privatization: The Case of Wastewater Treatment.* Tuscaloosa: University of Alabama Press.

Herring, R. 1983. *Land to the Tiller: The Political Economy of Agrarian Reform in South Asia.* New Haven: Yale University Press.

Hirashima, S. 1986. "Poverty as a Generation's Problem: A Note on the Japanese Experience." Pp. 149–160 in J. W. Mellor and G. M. Desai, eds., *Agricultural Change and Rural Poverty: Variations on a Theme by Dharm Narain.* Delhi: Oxford University Press.

Ho, S. P. S. 1978. *Economic Development in Taiwan, 1860–1970.* New Haven: Yale University Press.

Hofheinz, R., Jr. and K. E. Calder. 1982. *The Eastasia Edge.* New York: Basic Books.

Hoge, J. F. 1995. "Fulfilling Brazil's Promise: A Conversation with President Cardoso." *Foreign Affairs* 74: 62–75.

Hogendorn, J. 1987. *Economic Development.* New York: Harper-Row.

Hollerman, L. 1988. *Japan, Disincorporated: The Economic Liberalization Process.* Stanford: Hoover Institution Press.

Hong, S. G. 1992. "Paths of Glory: Semiconductor Leapfrogging in Taiwan and South Korea." *Pacific Focus* 7: 59–88.

Huntington, S. P. 1991. *The Third Wave: Democratization in the Late Twentieth Century.* Norman: University of Oklahoma Press.

Inkeles, A. 1983. *Exploring Individual Modernity.* New York: Columbia University Press.

International Monetary Fund (IMF). 1988. *International Financial Statistics Yearbook.* Washington, DC: IMF.

Islam, S. and M. Mandelbaum, eds. 1993. *Making Markets: Economic Transformation in Eastern Europe and the Post-Soviet States.* New York: Council on Foreign Relations Press.

Jannuzi, F. T. 1989. *India in Transition: Issues of Political Economy in a Planned Society.* Boulder, CO: Westview.

Jodha, N. S. 1986. "Common Property Resources and the Rural Poor." *Economic and Political Weekly* 21: 1169–1181.

Johnson, C. A. 1982. *MITI and the Japanese Miracle: The Growth of Industrial Policy, 1925–1975.* Stanford: Stanford University Press.

Johnston, B. F. 1970. "The Japanese 'Model' of Agricultural Development: Its Relevance to Developing Nations." Pp. 58–102 in K. Ohkawa, B. F. Johnston, and H. Kaneda, eds., *Agriculture and Economic Growth: Japan's Experience.* Princeton: Princeton University Press.

Jones, L., ed. 1982. *Public Enterprise in Less-Developed Countries.* New York: Cambridge University Press.

Jones, L. and I. Sakong. 1980. *Government, Business, and Entrepreneurship in Economic Development: The Korean Case.* Cambridge: Harvard University Press.

Joshi, V. and I. M. D. Little. 1994. *India: Macroeconomics and Political Economy, 1964–1991.* Delhi: Oxford University Press.

Kang, T. W. 1989. *Is Korea the Next Japan? Understanding the Structure, Strategy, and Tactics of America's Next Competitor.* New York: Free Press.

Katzenstein, P. 1985. *Small States in World Markets: Industrial Policy in Europe.* Ithaca: Cornell University Press.

Keller, M. 1989. *Rude Awakening: The Rise, Fall, and Struggle for Recovery of General Motors.* New York: Morrow.

Kennedy, P. M. 1987. *The Rise and Fall of Great Powers: Economic Change and Military Conflict from 1500 to 2000.* New York: Random House.

Kikuchi, M. and Y. Hayami. 1985. "Agricultural Growth Against a Land-Resource Constraint: Japan, Taiwan, Korea, and the Philippines." Pp. 67–90 in K. Ohkawa, G. Ranis, and K. S. Kokusai, eds., *Japan and the Developing Countries: A Comparative Analysis.* Oxford: Basil Blackwell.

Kim, B. L. P. 1992. *Two Koreas in Development: A Comparative Study of Principles and Strategies of Capitalist and Communist Third World Development.* New Brunswick, NJ: Transaction.

Kohli, A. 1987. *The State and Poverty in India: The Politics of Reform.* New York: Cambridge University Press.

Kohli, A. 1990. *Democracy and Discontent: India's Growing Crisis of Governability.* New York: Cambridge University Press.

Kohli, A. 1994. "Centralization and Powerlessness: India's Democracy in Comparative Perspective." Pp. 89–107 in J. S. Migdal, A. Kohli, and V. Shue, eds., *State Power and Social Forces: Domination and Transformation in the Third World.* New York: Cambridge University Press.

Kovacs, J. M., ed. 1994. *Transition to Capitalism? The Communist Legacy in Eastern Europe.* New Brunswick, NJ: Transaction Books.

Krause, L. B. 1988. "Hong Kong and Singapore: Twins or Kissing Cousins?" *Economic Development and Cultural Change* 36: S11–S43.

Krueger, A. O. 1978. *Foreign Trade Regimes and Economic Development: Liberalization Attempts and Consequences.* Cambridge, MA: Ballinger.

Kuhn, T. S. 1970. *The Structure of Scientific Revolutions,* 2nd ed. Chicago: University of Chicago Press.

Kuo, C. T. 1994. "Privatization *Within* the Chinese State." *Governance* 7: 387–411.

Kuo, C. T. 1995. *Global Competitiveness: Industrial Growth in Taiwan and the Philippines.* Pittsburgh: University of Pittsburgh Press.

Kuo, C. T. 1997. "Private Governance in Taiwan." in S. Chan, C. Clark, and D. Lam, eds. *The Role of the State in Asian Development: Beyond the Developmental State.* London: Macmillan.

Kurien, C. T. 1991. "Indian Economy in the 1980s and on to the 1990s." Pp. 65–91 in M. V. Nadkarni, A. S. Seetharamu, and A. Aziz, eds., *India: The Emerging Challenges.* New Delhi: Sage.

Kuznets, P. W. 1988. "An East Asian Model of Economic Development: Japan, Taiwan, and South Korea." *Economic Development and Cultural Change* 36: S11–S43.

Lake, D. A. 1988. *Power, Protectionism, and Free Trade: International Sources of U.S. Commercial Strategy, 1887–1939.* Ithaca: Cornell University Press.

Lal, D. 1979. "Indian Export Incentives." *Journal of Development Studies* 6: 103–117.

Lal, D. 1988. *The Hindu Equilibrium: Cultural Stability and Economic Stagnation, India c.1500 B.C.–A.D. 1980.* Oxford: Clarendon.

Lam, D. K. K. 1990a. "The Economic Dimensions of 1997." *Asian Affairs* 17: 131–142.

Lam, D. K. K. 1990b. "Independent Economic Sectors and Economic Growth in Hong Kong and Taiwan." *International Studies Notes* 15: 28–34.

Lam, D. K. K. 1992. *Explaining Economic Development: A Case Study of State Policies Towards the Computer and Electronics Industry in Taiwan (1960–1980).* Ottawa: Ph.D. dissertation, Carleton University.

Lam, D. and C. Clark. 1994. "Beyond the Developmental State: The Cultural Roots of 'Guerrilla Capitalism' in Taiwan." *Governance* 7: 412–430.

Lam, D. K. K., and I. Lee. 1992. "Guerrilla Capitalism and the Limits of Statist Theory." Pp. 107–124 in C. Clark and S. Chan, eds., *The Evolving Pacific Basin in the Global Political Economy: Domestic and International Linkages.* Boulder, CO: Lynne Rienner.

Lardy, N. R. 1978. *Economic Growth and Distribution in China.* New York: Cambridge University Press.

Lardy, N. R. 1992. *Foreign Trade and Economic Reform in China, 1978–1990.* New York: Cambridge University Press.

Lardy, N. R. 1994. *China in the World Economy.* Washington, DC: Institute for International Economics.

Leaf, M. J. 1984. *Song of Hope: The Green Revolution in a Panjab Village.* New Brunswick, NJ: Rutgers University Press.

Lee, C. S. and H. S. Sohn. 1995. "South Korea in 1994: A Year of Trial." *Asian Survey* 35: 28–36.

Lee, T. H. 1971. *Intersectoral Capital Flows in the Economic Development of Taiwan, 1895–1960.* Ithaca: Cornell University Press.

Lehmann, J. 1982. *The Roots of Modern Japan.* London: Macmillan.

Li, K. T. 1988. *The Evolution of Policy Behind Taiwan's Developmental Success.* New Haven: Yale University Press.

Lin, C. Y. 1973. *Industrialization in Taiwan, 1946–1972: Trade and Import Substitution Policies for Developing Countries.* New York: Praeger.

Linder, S. B. 1986. *The Pacific Century: Economic and Political Consequences of Asian Pacific Dynamism.* Stanford: Stanford University Press.

Little, I., T. Scitovsky, and M. Scott. 1970. *Industry and Trade in Some Developing Countries.* London: Oxford University Press.

Liu, P. 1993. "The Power of Plastics." *Free China Review* 43: 44–47.

Lucas, R. E. and G. F. Papanek, eds. 1988. *The Indian Economy: Recent Development and Future Prospects.* Boulder, CO: Westview.

March, J. G. and J. Olsen. 1989. *Rediscovering Institutions: The Organizational Basis of Politics.* New York: Free Press.

Mardon, R. 1990. "The State and Effective Control of Foreign Capital: The Case of South Korea." *World Politics* 43: 111–138.

Mardon, R. and W. K. Paik. 1992. "The State, Foreign Investment, and Sustaining Industrial Growth in South Korea and Thailand." Pp. 147–168 in C. Clark and S. Chan, eds., *The Evolving Pacific Basin in the Global Political Economy: Domestic and International Linkages.* Boulder, CO: Lynne Rienner.

Mellor, J. W. 1976. *The New Economics of Growth: A Strategy for India and the Developing World.* Ithaca: Cornell University Press.

Mellor, J. W. 1988. "The Intertwining of Environmental Problems and Poverty." *Environment* 30: 8–13.

Mellor, J. W. and B. F. Johnston. 1984. "The World Food Equation: Interrelations Among Development, Employment, and Food Consumption." *Journal of Economic Literature* 22: 531–574.

Migdal, J. S. 1988. *Strong Societies and Weak States: State-Society Relations and State Capabilities in the Third World.* Princeton: Princeton University Press.

Migdal, J. S., A. Kohli, and V. Shue, eds. 1994. *State Power and Social Forces: Domination and Transformation in the Third World.* New York: Cambridge University Press.

Milner, C., ed. 1990. *Export Promoting Strategies: Theory and Evidence from Developing Countries.* New York: Harvestor Wheatsheaf.

Mirza, H. 1986. *Multinationals and the Growth of the Singapore Economy*. New York: St. Martin's.

Moon, B. E. 1991. *The Political Economy of Basic Human Needs*. Ithaca: Cornell University Press.

Moon, B. E. and W. J. Dixon. 1992. "Basic Needs and Growth–Welfare Trade-Offs." *International Studies Quarterly* 36: 191–212.

Moon, C. I. 1988. "The Demise of a Developmentalist State? Neoconservative Reforms and Political Consequences in South Korea." *Journal of Developing Societies* 4: 67–84.

Moon, C. I. 1990. "Beyond Statism: Rethinking the Political Economy of Growth in South Korea." *International Studies Notes* 15: 24–27.

Moon, C. I. and R. Prasad. 1994. "Beyond the Developmental State: Networks, Politics, and Institutions." *Governance* 7: 360–386.

Morawetz, D. 1981. *Why the Emperor's New Clothes Are Not Made in Colombia: A Case Study of East Asian and Latin American Manufactured Exports*. London: Oxford University Press.

Morris, M. D. 1979. *Measuring the Condition of the World's Poor: The Physical Quality of Life Index*. New York: Pergamon.

Nafziger, E. W. 1990. *The Economics of Developing Countries*. Englewood Cliffs, NJ: Prentice Hall.

Nam, C. H. 1995. "South Korea's Big Business Clientelism in Democratic Reform." *Asian Survey* 35: 357–366.

Napier, R. 1982. "The Transformation of the Japanese Labor Market, 1894–1937." Pp. 342–365 in T. Najita and J. V. Koschmann, eds., *Conflict in Modern Japanese History: The Neglected Tradition*. Princeton: Princeton University Press.

Nau, H. R. 1990. *The Myth of America's Decline: Leading the World Economy into the 1990s*. New York: Oxford University Press.

Nehru, J. 1954. *Jawaharlal Nehru's Speeches, 1949–1953*. Delhi: Government of India.

Nester, W. R. 1991. *Japanese Industrial Targeting: The Neomercantilist Path to Economic Superpower*. New York: St. Martin's.

Noble, G. 1994. "Japan in 1993: Humpty Dumpty Had a Great Fall." *Asian Survey* 34: 19–29.

North, D. C. 1990. *Institutions, Institutional Change, and Economic Performance*. Cambridge: Cambridge University Press.

Nurkse, R. 1953. *Problems of Capital Formation in Underdeveloped Countries*. New York: Oxford University Press.

Nurkse, R. 1959. *Patterns of Trade and Development*. Stockholm: Almquist and Wicksell.

Oi, J. C. 1989. *State and Peasant in Contemporary China: The Political Economy of Village Government*. Berkeley: University of California Press.

Okimoto, D. I. 1989. *Between MITI and the Market: Japanese Industrial Policy for High Technology*. Stanford: Stanford University Press.

Olson, M., Jr. 1982. *The Rise and Decline of Nations: Economic Growth, Stagflation, and Social Rigidities*. New Haven: Yale University Press.

Onis, Z. 1991. "The Logic of the Developmentalist State." *Comparative Politics* 24: 109–121.

Osborne, D. and T. Gaebler. 1992. *Reinventing Government: How the Entrepreneurial Spirit Is Transforming the Public Sector*. New York: Penguin.

Oshima, H. T. 1987. *Economic Growth in Monsoon Asia: A Comparative Survey*. Tokyo: University of Tokyo Press.

Oshima, H. T. 1993. *Strategic Processes in Monsoon Asia's Economic Development*. Baltimore: Johns Hopkins University Press.

Pearson, M. M. 1991. *Joint Ventures in the People's Republic of China: The Control of Foreign Direct Investment Under Socialism*. Princeton: Princeton University Press.

Pei, M. 1994. *From Reform to Revolution: The Demise of Communism in China and the Soviet Union*. Cambridge: Harvard University Press.

Pendse, D. R., ed. 1988. *Statistical Outline of India, 1988–1989*. Bombay: Tata Services Limited.

Peters, B. G. 1991. *European Politics Reconsidered*. New York: Holmes & Meier.

Piore, M. J. and C. F. Sabel. 1984. *The Second Industrial Divide: Possibilities for Prosperity*. New York: Basic Books.

Porter, M. 1990. *The Competitive Advantage of Nations*. New York: Free Press.

Prebisch, R. 1971. *Change and Development: Latin America's Great Task*. New York: Praeger.

Prestowitz, C. V., Jr. 1988. *Trading Places: How We Allowed Japan to Take the Lead*. New York: Basic Books.

Prybyla, J. S. 1981. *The Chinese Economy: Problems and Policies*. Columbia: University of South Carolina Press.

Prybyla, J. S. 1987. *Market and Plan Under Socialism: The Bird in the Cage*. Stanford: Hoover Institution Press.

Przeworski, A. 1991. *Democracy and the Market: Political and Economic Reforms in Eastern Europe and Latin America*. New York: Cambridge University Press.

Pun, A. 1992. "FPG Retools its Naphtha Cracker Proposal." *Free China Journal*, November 27, p. 3.

Pye, L. W. 1966. *Aspects of Political Development*. Boston: Little, Brown.

Pye, L. W. 1981. *The Dynamics of Chinese Politics*. Cambridge, MA: Oelgeschlager, Gunn & Hain.

Pye, L. W. 1988. *The Mandarin and the Cadre: China's Political Cultures*. Ann Arbor: University of Michigan Press.

Pye, L. W. 1991. *China: An Introduction*, 4th ed. Boston: Little, Brown.

Pye, L. W. with M. W. Pye. 1985. *Asian Power and Politics: The Cultural Dimensions of Authority*. Cambridge: Harvard University Press.

Rabushka, A. 1979. *Hong Kong: A Study in Economic Freedom*. Chicago: University of Chicago Press.

Randall, V. and R. Theobald. 1985. *Political Change and Underdevelopment: A Critical Introduction to Third World Politics*. Durham: Duke University Press.

Ranis, G., ed. 1992. *Taiwan: From Developing to Mature Economy*. Boulder, CO: Westview.

Reich, R. B. 1991. *The Work of Nations: Preparing Ourselves for 21st-Century Capitalism*. New York: Knopf.

Reischauer, E. O. 1988. *The Japanese Today: Change and Continuity*. Cambridge: Harvard University Press.

Reserve Bank of India. 1985/86. *Report on Currency and Finance*, Vol. 1. Bombay: Reserve Bank of India.

Reynolds, L. G. 1985. *Economic Growth in the Third World, 1850–1980*. New Haven: Yale University Press.

Risse-Kappen, T. 1995. "Bringing Transnational Relations Back In: Introduction." Pp. 3–33 in T. Risse-Kappen, ed., *Bringing Transnational Relations Back In: Non-State Actors, Domestic Structures, and International Institutions*. Cambridge: Cambridge University Press.

Rodan, G. 1989. *The Political Economy of Singapore's Industrialization: National, State and International Capital*. New York: St. Martin's.

Rogowski, R. 1989. *Commerce and Coalitions: How Trade Affects Domestic Political Alliances*. Princeton: Princeton University Press.

Rosecrance, R. 1986. *The Rise of the Trading State: Commerce and Conquest in the Modern World*. New York: Basic Books.

Rosen, G. 1992. *Contrasting Styles of Industrial Reform: China and India in the 1980s*. Chicago: University of Chicago Press.

Rosenberg, N. and L. E. Birdzell, Jr. 1986. *How the West Grew Rich: The Economic Transformation of the Industrial World*. New York: Basic Books.

Rostow, W. W. 1960. *The Stages of Economic Growth: A Non-Communist Manifesto*. Cambridge: Cambridge University Press.

Roumasset, J. A. and S. Barr, eds. 1992. *The Economics of Cooperation: East Asian Development and the Case for Pro-Market Intervention*. Boulder, CO: Westview.

Roy, K. C. 1986. *Foreign Aid and Indian Development: A Study from the View Point of Peace and Development*. Ahmedabad: Gujarat Vidyapith.

Roy, K. C. 1988. *The Sub-Continent in the International Economy, 1850–1900*. Hong Kong: International Consortium of Asian Studies.

Roy, K. C. 1991a. "Development, Income Inequality and Poverty in LDCs Revisited." *International Studies Notes* 16: 55–59.

Roy, K. C. 1991b. "Public Sector Performance and Managerial Efficiency Under Planned Development: India's Experience." *Economia Internazionale* 44: 254–268.

Roy, K.C. 1994. "Landless and Land-Poor Women in India Under Technological Change: A Case for Technology Transfer." Pp. 65–79 in K. C. Roy and C. Clark, eds., *Technological Change and Rural Development in Poor Countries: Neglected Issues*. Delhi: Oxford University Press.

Roy, K. C. and C. Clark, eds. 1994. *Technological Change and Rural Development in Poor Countries: Neglected Issues*. Delhi: Oxford University Press.

Roy, K. C. and A. L. Lougheed. 1977. "The Green Revolution in India: Progress and Problems." *World Review* 16: 16–27.

Roy, K. C. and R. K. Sen. 1991 "On the Domestic Debt and Its Effects on LDCs Internal and External Balance." *Rivista Internazionale Di Scienze Economiche E Commerciali* 38: 1003–1013.

Roy, K. C. and C. A. Tisdell. 1992a. "Gandhi's Concept of Development and Nehru's Centralized Planning: Idealism vs Realities." Pp. 1–16 in K. C. Roy, C. A. Tisdell, and R. K. Sen, eds., *Economic Development and Environment: A Case Study of India*. Calcutta: Oxford University Press.

Roy, K. C. and C. A. Tisdell. 1992b. "Technological Change, Environment and Sustainability of Rural Communities." Pp. 71–95 in K. C. Roy, C. A. Tisdell, and R. K. Sen, eds., *Economic Development and Environment: A Case Study of India*. Calcutta: Oxford University Press.

Rudolph, L. I and S. H. Rudolph. 1987. *In Pursuit of Lakshmi: The Political Economy of the Indian State*. Chicago: University of Chicago Press.

Rueschemeyer, D. and P. B. Evans. 1985. "The State and Economic Transformation: Toward an Analysis of the Conditions Underlying Effective Intervention." Pp. 44–77 in P. B. Evans, D. Rueschemeyer, and T. Skocpol, eds., *Bringing the State Back In*. New York: Cambridge University Press.

Russett, B. M., H. R. Alker, Jr., K. W. Deutsch, and H. D. Lasswell. 1964. *World Handbook of Political and Social Indicators*. New Haven: Yale University Press.

Samuels, R. J. 1987. *The Business of the Japanese State: Energy Markets in Comparative and Historical Perspective*. Ithaca: Cornell University Press.

Samuels, R. J. 1994. *"Rich Nation, Strong Army:" National Security and the Technological Transformation of Japan*. Ithaca: Cornell University Press.

Schiffer, J. R. 1991. "State Policy and Economic Growth: A Note on the Hong Kong Model." *International Journal of Urban and Regional Research* 15: 180–196.

Schive, C. 1990. *The Foreign Factor: The Multinational Corporation's Contribution to the Economic Modernization of the Republic of China*. Stanford: Hoover Institution Press.

Schurmann, F. 1966. *Ideology and Organization in Communist China*. Berkeley: University of California Press.

Sender, H. 1995. "Nippon's Choice." *Far Eastern Economic Review*, June 8, pp. 38–45.

Sharma, R. and T. T. Poleman. 1993. *The New Economics of India's Green Revolution: Income and Employment Diffusion in Uttar Pradesh*. Ithaca: Cornell University Press.

Shin, R. W. 1991. "The Role of Industrial Policy Agents: A Study of Korean Intermediate Organization as a Policy Network." *Pacific Focus* 6: 49–64.

Shirk, S. L. 1993. *The Political Logic of Economic Reform in China*. Berkeley: University of California Press.

Silin, R. H. 1976. *Leadership and Values: The Organization of Large-Scale Taiwanese Enterprises*. Cambridge: Harvard University Press.

Simon, D. F. 1992. "Taiwan's Strategy for Creating Competitive Advantage: The Role of the State in Managing Foreign Technology." Pp. 97–122 in N. T. Wang, ed., *Taiwan's Enterprises in Global Perspective*. Armonk, NY: M. E. Sharpe.

Singer, H. W. 1977. *Rich and Poor Countries*. Baltimore: Johns Hopkins University Press.

Smethurst, R. J. 1986. *Agricultural Development and Tenancy Disputes in Japan, 1870–1940*. Princeton: Princeton University Press.

Smith, T. C. 1995. *The Agrarian Origins of Modern Japan*. Stanford: Stanford University Press.

Solinger, D. J. 1993. *China's Transition from Socialism: State Legacies and Market Reforms 1980–1990*. Armonk, NY: M. E. Sharpe.

Steinmo, S., K. Thelen, and F. Longstreth, eds. 1992. *Structuring Politics: Historical Institutionalism in Comparative Analysis*. Cambridge: Cambridge University Press.

Stokes, G. 1993. *The Walls Came Tumbling Down: The Collapse of Communism in Eastern Europe*. New York: Oxford University Press.

Subramaniam, C. 1979. *The New Strategy in Indian Agriculture: The First Decade and After*. New Delhi: Vikas.

Syrquin, M. and H. B. Chenery. 1989. "Patterns of Development: 1950–1983." *World Bank Discussion Papers*. Washington, DC: World Bank.

Tai, H. C. 1989. "The Oriental Alternative: A Hypothesis on East Asian Culture and Economy." *Issues and Studies* 25: 10–36.

Taiwan Statistical Data Book. 1991 & 1995. Taipei: Council for Economic Planning and Development.

Teece, D. J. 1990. "Contributions and Impediments of Economic Analysis to the Study of Strategic Management." Pp. 39–80 in J. W. Fredrickson, ed., *Perspectives on Strategic Management*. New York: Harper & Row.

Thurow, L. 1992. *Head to Head: The Coming Battle Among Japan, Europe, and America*. New York: Warner.

Tinari, F. D. and D. K. K. Lam. 1991. "China's Resistance to Economic Reforms." *Contemporary Policy Issues* 9: 82–92.

Tisdell, C. A. 1990. "Economic Impact of Biological Control of Weeds and Insects." Pp. 301–316 in M. Mackauer, J. Ehler, and J. Roland, eds., *Critical Issues in Biological Control*. Andover, Hants, UK: Intercept Ltd.

Tisdell, C. A. 1991. "Population Growth and Environmental Protection: The Situation of Developing Countries in Global Perspective." Pp. 222–236 in K. C. Roy, C. A. Tisdell, R. K. Sen, and M. Alauddin, eds., *Economic Development of Poor Countries, Experiences, Obstacles, Sustainability in Global Perspective*. Calcutta: World Press.

Trinque, B. M. 1992. *"The New Economics of Growth:* An Assessment After 15 Years." *Contemporary South Asia* 1: 67–91.

Tyson, L. D. 1992. *Who's Bashing Whom? Trade Conflict in High Technology Industries*. Washington, DC: Institute for International Economics.

Upadhya, C. B. 1988. "The Farmer-Capitalists of Coastal Andhra Pradesh." *Economic and Political Weekly* 23: 1376–1382 & 1433–1442.

Vernon, R. 1966. "International Investment and International Trade in the Product Cycle." *Quarterly Journal of Economics* 80: 190–207.

Vogel, E. F. 1979. *Japan as Number One*. Cambridge: Harvard University Press.

Vogel, E. F. 1989. *One Step Ahead in China: Guangdong Under Reform*. Cambridge: Harvard University Press.

Vohra, B. B. 1982. "Land and Water Management Problems." New Delhi: Ministry of Home Affairs.

von Mises, L. 1983. *Nation, State, and Economy: Contributions to the Politics and History of Our Time*. New York: New York University Press.

Wachman, A. M. 1994. *Taiwan: National Identity and Democratization*. Armonk, NY: M. E. Sharpe.

Wade, R. 1985. "East Asian Financial Systems as a Challenge to Economics: Lessons from Taiwan." *California Management Review* 27: 106–127.

Wade. R. 1990. *Governing the Market: Economic Theory and the Role of Government in East Asian Industrialization*. Princeton: Princeton University Press.

Walder, A. G. 1986. *Communist Neo-Traditionalism: Work and Authority in Chinese Industry*. Berkeley: University of California Press.

Wallerstein, I. 1979. *The Capitalist World Economy*. Cambridge: Cambridge University Press.

Wang, N. T., ed. 1992. *Taiwan's Enterprises in Global Perspective*. Armonk, NY: M. E. Sharpe.

Waswo, A. 1982. "In Search of Equity: Japanese Tenant Unions in the 1920s." Pp. 365–411 in T. Najita and J. V. Koschmann, eds., *Conflict in Modern Japanese History: The Neglected Tradition*. Princeton: Princeton University Press.

Weber, M. 1951. *The Religion of China: Confucianism and Taoism*. Glencoe, IL: Free Press.

Weiner, M. 1991. *The Child and the State in India*. Princeton: Princeton University Press.

Wells, L. T. 1972. *Product Life Cycle and International Trade*. Boston: Harvard Business School.

White, G., ed. 1988. *Developmental States in East Asia*. New York: St. Martin's.

White, L. T. 1989. *Policies of Chaos: The Organizational Causes of China's Cultural Revolution*. Princeton: Princeton University Press.

Winckler, E. A. and S. Greenhalgh, eds. 1988. *Contending Approaches to the Political Economy of Taiwan*. Armonk, NY: M. E. Sharpe.

Womack, J. P., D. T. Jones, and D. Roos. 1990. *The Machine that Changed the World: The Story of Lean Production.* New York: MacMillan.

Wong, S. L. 1986. "Modernization and Chinese Culture in Hong Kong." *China Quarterly* 106: 306–325.

Wong, S. L. 1988. *Emigrant Entrepreneurs: Shanghai Industrialists in Hong Kong.* Hong Kong: Oxford University Press.

Woo, J. E. 1991. *Race to Swift: State and Finance in Korean Industrialization.* New York: Columbia University Press.

World Bank. 1979, 1983, 1984, 1991 & 1995. *World Development Report.* New York: Oxford University Press.

World Bank. 1990. *India: An Industrializing Economy in Transition.* Washington, DC: World Bank.

World Bank. 1993. *The East Asian Miracle: Economic Growth and Public Policy.* New York: Oxford University Press.

Wu, Y. L. 1985. *Becoming an Industrialized Nation: ROC's Development on Taiwan.* New York: Praeger.

Wu, Y. S. 1994. *Comparative Economic Transformations: Mainland China, Hungary, the Soviet Union, and Taiwan.* Stanford: Stanford University Press.

Wu, Y. S. 1995. "Economic Reform, Cross-Straits Relations, and the Politics of Issue Linkage." Pp. 111–133 in T. J. Cheng, C. Huang, and S. S. G. Wu, eds., *Inherited Rivalry: Conflict Across the Taiwan Straits.* Boulder, CO: Lynne Rienner.

Yang, M. M. C. 1970. *Socio-Economic Results of Land Reform in Taiwan.* Honolulu: East-West Center Press.

Yoffie, D. B. 1983. *Power and Protectionism: Strategies of the Newly Industrializing Countries.* New York: Columbia University Press.

Zeigler, H. 1988. *Pluralism, Corporatism, and Confucianism: Political Association and Conflict Resolution in the United States, Europe, and Taiwan.* Philadelphia: Temple University Press.

Zysman, J. 1983. *Governments, Markets, and Growth: Financial Systems and the Politics of Industrial Change.* Ithaca: Cornell University Press.

INDEX

ABOUT THE BOOK

For much of the postwar era, industrialized East Asia has been the most economically dynamic region in the world, whereas agrarian South Asia has remained mired in poverty. As of the early 1990s, though, the economic performance of South Asia, led by India, has improved considerably.

Seeking to explain these patterns, this book explores the evolving political economies of East and South Asia in the context of contending theories about development. The authors demonstrate that whereas the Asian experience seemed initially to validate laissez-faire economics, there was in fact massive state intervention in the East Asian capitalist economies. The theory that the successes in East Asia were primarily the result of enlightened policies by strong and autonomous developmental states, however, does not explain the failure of the developmental state in South Asia.

The authors' analysis leads them to argue against an exclusive focus on either state or market and to advocate a strong consideration of the vital contributions of society to development—contributions typically ignored by both neoclassical and developmental state models. Both a strong state and a strong society, they conclude, are necessary conditions for developmental dynamism.

Cal Clark is professor of political science at Auburn University. His publications include *Taiwan's Development, Women in Taiwan Politics* (Rienner, 1990), and *The Evolving Pacific Basin* (Rienner, 1994). **Kartik C. Roy** is a senior lecturer of economics at the University of Queensland. His books include *The Sub-Continent in the International Economy, 1850–1900, Economic Development of Poor Countries*, and *Technological Change and Rural Development in Poor Countries*.